The Edison Gene

Also by Thom Hartmann

ADD Success Stories:
A Guide to Fulfillment for Families
with Attention Deficit Disorder

ADHD Secrets of Success:
Coaching Yourself to Fulfillment in the Business World

Attention Deficit Disorder:
A Different Perception

Beyond ADD:
Hunting for Reasons in the Past and Present

Focus Your Energy:
Hunting for Success in Business
with Attention Deficit Disorder

Healing ADD:
Simple Exercises That Will Change Your Life

Think Fast!: The ADD Experience

Thom Hartmann's Complete Guide to ADHD

The Greatest Spiritual Secret of the Century

The Last Hours of Ancient Sunlight:
Waking Up to Personal and Global Transformation

The Prophet's Way: Touching the Power of Life

Unequal Protection:
The Rise of Corporate Dominance
and the Theft of Human Rights

The Edison Gene

ADHD and the Gift of the Hunter Child

Thom Hartmann

Park Street Press
Rochester, Vermont

Park Street Press
One Park Street
Rochester, Vermont 05767
www.InnerTraditions.com

Park Street Press is a division of Inner Traditions International, Inc.

Library of Congress Cataloging-in-Publication Data
Hartmann, Thom.
  The Edison gene : ADHD and the gift of the hunter child / Thom Hartmann.
      p. cm.
Includes index.
  ISBN 0-89281-128-5 (hardcover)
  1. Attention-deficit hyperactivity disorder—Miscellanea.
2. Attention in children. 3. Divergent thinking. I. Title.
  RJ506.H9H3837 2003
  618.92'8589—dc21

                                                          2003012407

Printed and bound in the United States at Lake Book Manufacturing, Inc.

10 9 8 7 6 5 4 3 2 1

Text design and layout by Rachel Goldenberg
This book was typeset in Sabon

A modified version of the chapter "Edison-gene Girls and Women" first appeared in the anthology *Understanding Women with AD/HD,* edited by Kathleen G. Nadeau (Silver Spring, Md.: Advantage Books, 2002).

This book is dedicated to my father,
Carl Hartmann, who taught my brothers
and me the meanings of integrity, compassion,
and courage through the extraordinary
example of his life.

Contents

Drugs for Edison-Gene Children • Medications Bite Back •
Burning Out Brain Cells? • Do Drugs Help Over the Long
Term? • The Loss of Play • EEG Neurofeedback •
Exercise: The Optimal "Treatment"?

Nurturing the Hunters • Reward/Punishment versus
Inclusion/Interdependence • Separating Person from
Behavior • Break the Pattern with a Positive Message •
Watch for Islands of Success • The Importance of Mastery •
Turn Off the Television

Promote Mutual Respect • Encourage • Foster Security •
Avoid Reward and Punishment • Use Natural and Logical
Consequences • Act Instead of Talk in Conflict Situations •
Use Withdrawal as a Counteraction • Withdraw from the
Provocation, Not from the Child • Don't Interfere in
Children's Fights • Fighting Requires Cooperation • Take
Time to Teach Essential Skills and Habits • Never Do for a
Child What He Can Do for Himself • Don't Overprotect •
Avoid Being Overly Responsible • Distinguish Between
Positive and Negative Attention • Understand the Child's
Goal • A Habit Is Maintained If It Achieves Its Purpose •
Minimize Mistakes • Try a Family Council and Have Fun
Together • The Edison-Gene Family

Learned Helplessness • Reframing Identity = Success in
Learning • Government Studies Pronounce on Medication •
They Ignored the Environment • The Study Proved Ritalin
Doesn't Improve Learning • But It Makes the Teachers
Happy • Lighting a Fire for Learning • Education and
Testing Corporations • How Modern Education Came
About • German Schools Come to America • American
Education and the Catholic Problem • Backlash Against the
Authoritarian Model of Public Education • Maria
Montessori • Rudolf Steiner • Free and Alternative Schools
• Homeschooling and Internet Schooling • But What

Foreword

As Thomas Edison once said, "The most certain way to succeed is always to try just one more time." Often Edison kids with ADHD—an umbrella term that includes attention deficit disorder (ADD)—quit trying. Typically, these kids are weary of not fitting in or are furious at feeling forced to do so. Self-protectively, they invent countless ways to avoid, divert, and procrastinate. Ten years ago, when I first learned of Thom Hartmann's metaphor "hunters in a farmer's world," I started to tell Edison kids in my practice about it. I watched as they grinned with hope at this new mind-set. I've used similar metaphors, such as "photographer's attention." These descriptions help to restore a child's willingness to try again.

Then, in January 2002, the University of California at Irvine issued a press release stating that gene researchers had found a significant positive selection for the genetic variation associated with novelty-seeking behavior and ADHD. How about that? Now we learn Thom's metaphor is a biological reality. The Edison gene has served a unique adaptive purpose for our species. It exists for the sake of genetic diversity, apparently for our own collective well-being. But what is the Edison gene? You are about to read Thom Hartmann's fascinating account of this set of inherited "hunter" characteristics often associated with ADHD.

Thom and I approach the concept of the Edison gene from different directions. I am the author of *Dreamers, Discoverers and Dynamos: How to Help the Child Who Is Bright, Bored and Having Problems In School*. The original title of my book, when it first appeared in hard cover in 1997, was *The Edison Trait: Saving the Spirit of Your Non-conforming*

Child. My approach stems from my interest in cognitive science and the study of divergent and convergent styles of thinking. Divergent thinking is spontaneous, nonlinear brainstorming. Convergent thinking is logical, sequential reasoning. People who have the Edison trait are divergent-thinking dominant. Like Thomas Edison, they are resourceful, inventive, individualistic, in the minority, and at odds with traditional classroom learning.

Is the Edison trait the same as ADHD? I do not equate the two. Like other health care providers, I use the term ADHD technically to describe a specific diagnosis and thereby signal that a problem is serious enough to treat. In this framework, the Edison trait signals a genetic susceptibility to ADHD, but having the Edison trait itself signals not the same as having ADHD.

In my work I've met hundreds of Edison-trait children and adults who also have ADHD. Because their problems with inattention, impulsivity, or hyperactivity are extreme and interfere with their daily lives, they qualify for the technical diagnosis of ADHD. Through the years, I've also have met hundreds of Edison-trait children and adults who don't have ADHD; because their problems with inattention, impulsivity, or hyperactivity do not interfere with their daily lives, they do not qualify for an ADHD diagnosis. In diagnostic terms, *interference with daily living* is the critical line that separates personality and pathology. People with ADHD may move back across that line when they adapt to their environment or their environment adapts to accommodate them.

While I don't like to use the word pathology to refer to ADHD, it does serve a purpose. For practical reasons, we need a defining line in order to decide what calls for professional treatment and what does not. Confusion arises because ordinary words can have special, diagnostic meanings in psychology. If you're having a bad-hair day and you say, "I'm so depressed," you're describing a mood, not a diagnosis. If you habitually cry easily at sad moments, you're describing a personality pattern, probably that of a highly sensitive person. However, if you're losing sleep, can't find joy in life, and every day is a bad-hair day, you may qualify for a diagnosis of clinical depression, a pathology that calls for treatment.

Similarly, if you misplace your checkbook and you say, "I'm so attention deficit," you are describing a behavior, not a diagnosis. If you misplace it frequently, you are describing a personality pattern, probably the Edison trait. However, if you're in trouble chronically at work or school due to lateness or unfinished work, and you're so disorganized that even if you found your checkbook it wouldn't matter because you have not balanced it in years, you may qualify for a formal diagnosis of ADHD, a pathology that calls for treatment. Your problems cross the line and "interfere with daily living." They lie on the "pathology" side of the line.

Some day, we hope, our schools and society will be fully responsive to the needs of Edison-trait children and adults. When this happens, we will see much less pathology. (Genetic susceptibility requires environmental interaction for expression of pathology.) For now, though, we need ways to discuss and make treatment decisions for individuals. The technical use of terms such as *ADHD* and *pathology* are part of a vocabulary we use to communicate the severity and frequency of problem behaviors in order to help those who suffer because of them.

Another reason I don't equate the Edison trait with ADHD is that ADHD is heterogeneous, with multiple causes. While genetic susceptibility appears to account for approximately 50 percent of its occurrences, ADHD is also a known outcome of neurological injury or disease, prenatal exposure to toxic substances, and prenatal variables such as prematurity, low birth weight, and birth anoxia. The connection between ADHD symptoms and depression is not fully understood, nor is the place of ADHD on the autistic spectrum. At two major neuroscientific conferences I attended this year, the consensus was that ADHD is a final "common symptom pathway" for a variety of causes, some acting synergistically. An analogy to this is fever, which can reflect a variety of infections or immune reactions in different organs or body parts. Another is arthritis, which can result from injury, aging, overuse, infection, or inflammation.

How do we treat ADHD? Is medication necessary? Every treatment choice demands that we consider its cost-to-benefit ratio. With ADHD, the cost-to-benefit ratio of prescribing medicine is different for each individual. It's even different for the same individual at different times in life. In *Dreamers, Discoverers and Dynamos,* I named the chapter on medication "A Personal Decision." This is true for adults, and especially true when deciding for children, who cannot weigh the ratio for themselves. What is right for someone else's child may not be right for yours. And what is right for your child today may not be right for your child tomorrow.

Although we have practical reasons to use terms like *pathology* and *ADHD* to communicate diagnoses professionally, we have a responsibility to watch our language in front of our children, who are formative and vulnerable. Thom Hartmann is a champion of children who are at risk of regarding themselves as "damaged goods." Here he goes a step further by providing a positive light for Edison-trait children with ADHD. This is critical because strength-centered approaches motivate, while pathology-centered ones do not. And for children with ADHD, motivation is key.

Most of us in the field are intensely interested in why some children with ADHD grow out of it and some don't. (Keep in mind that I am using ADHD as a diagnostic term here, meaning that symptoms interfere with daily living.) The Edison-trait personality endures. Read the biographies of successful artists, athletes, inventors, entrepreneurs, and pilots and you will recognize their lifelong divergent thinking styles. Like Thomas Edison, however, they developed convergent thinking skills too, and learned to keep their balance. Thomas Edison was the most prolific inventor in the history of America. At the same time, he acquired enough bean-counting skill to found and run our largest utility companies, some of which still bear his name today.

Most neuroscientists agree that ADHD symptoms actually indicate problems in the executive functioning of the brain. Executive functions include working memory, foresight, planning, sense of time, and ability to inhibit impulses. These functions are associated with the prefrontal lobes, the last structures to fully develop as the brain matures, and are still being honed in late adolescence and early adulthood. It's not unusual to see an Edison-trait student blossom rapidly in college.

Keeping in mind this fact, as well as an understanding of the normal *plasticity* of a developing brain (the term used by neuroscientists to describe the fact that the structure of the brain changes and grows, especially in children), it is wrong to assume that a child with ADHD will have ADHD for life. If we do assume this, we risk creating a harmful self-fulfilling prophecy. It's a well-known fact that stimulation is required for brain growth: A child needs to exercise executive functions in order for these functions to develop. Further, a child's confidence determines how much effort he or she makes: If we believe we can do something, we'll try our best; if we don't believe we can do it, we're less likely to try. For a child, a parent's or teacher's belief can be pivotal. In one longitudinal study, the only factor that determined whether a child with ADHD became successful as an adult was whether he or she had at least one adult who believed in him or her as a child. As we believe in our children, our children believe in themselves.

This is what makes Thom Hartmann's work such a treasure. He gives Edison-trait children and their families reason to believe. He provides a non-pathological understanding of the problems Edison kids face. You are about to read ideas that are original, thought provoking, and a gift to our children. They increase the likelihood that Edison-trait kids will succeed by encouraging them to try just one more time.

LUCY JO PALLADINO, PH.D.
AUTHOR OF *DREAMERS, DISCOVERS AND DYNAMOS:*
HOW TO HELP THE CHILD WHO IS BRIGHT,
BORED, AND HAVING PROBLEMS IN SCHOOL

Acknowledgments

If I have seen further [than you and Descartes]
it is by standing upon the shoulders of giants.

SIR ISAAC NEWTON,
FROM A LETTER TO ROBERT HOOKE

Back in 1992, my friend, colleague, and editor Dave deBronkart first coined the phrase "the Edison trait" in a conversation on "The ADD Forum" on CompuServe, which I started and still run. Dave helped me organize and edit my 1993 book *Attention Deficit Disorder: A Different Perception*, and we used "The Edison Trait" as a heading for the chapter that described the lives of famous people having the Edison gene who had changed history in positive ways. A few years later, one of America's best psychologists and a close friend, Lucy Jo Palladino, asked if we would mind if she used the phrase as the title for her book, and we encouraged her to do so. That book, *The Edison Trait*, first published in hardcover and now in print under the title *Dreamers, Discoverers and Dynamos: How to Help the Child Who Is Bright, Bored and Having Problems in School*, does a wonderful job of laying out strategies for working with Edison-gene children—and also manages to avoid altogether referring to ADHD. Bravo to Lucy Jo, and my thanks to her for her enthusiastic encouragement when I called to ask if she would mind if I used Edison in the title and as the theme of this book.

I'm also deeply grateful to Dave deBronkart, who did another brilliant marathon job of editing the first draft of this book. He's helped many of my books gain coherence and focus, and this is no exception. Jon Graham and Ehud Sperling of Inner Traditions • Bear & Company have helped substantially with the editorial process, and gave this book life in the marketplace by publishing it.

I was first introduced by Karen Coshof and Michael Taylor to the work of William H. Calvin and his book *A Brain For All Seasons: Human Evolution and Abrupt Climate Change*. Karen and Michael's guidance, and Calvin's brilliant book (which you should run out now, buy, and read) were pivotal to me in organizing the premise of this book. I also recommend you check out *The Great Warming*, a soon-to-be-released documentary with Leonardo DiCaprio, one of the most enlightened of our Hollywood stars and one of the finest people and best actors I've met in that industry.

My dear friend John Ratey offered particularly valuable help and advice after reading this book's first draft and is a heartfelt champion of this world's Edison-gene children and adults. Robert Moyzis is the genius who cracked the genetic code for the world, and I'm tremendously grateful to him for taking the time from his busy schedule to put up with my interview and persistent questions.

Robert Wolff tolerated my week-long visit to his home on the side of the Kilauea volcano in Hawaii and was so generous in candidly sharing his life and experiences with me. Similarly, Gregory Zielinski, Maine State Climatologist and Research Associate Professor of Quaternary and Climate Studies from the University of Maine generously provided me with much of the data and the graphs in this book and was kind enough to help me in my search for the forty-thousand-year-old volcanic event that may have advanced the Edison gene.

I'm deeply indebted to James Swanson for information on the genetics and studies of ADHD; to my agent, friend, and advisor Bill Gladstone; my best friend and partner in life, Louise Hartmann; and the extraordinary Edison-gene entrepreneur and writer Rob Kall for his quotes, friendship, and inspiration. Special thanks go to Canada's Vaudree LaVallee for her research, help with our online message board, and encouragement; and to Australia's Sandy Moran for her incredibly brilliant insights into the varieties of neurological adaptability among both Europeans and Australian Aboriginal peoples.

And I offer a particular thanks to Elaine Sanborn, a brilliant, careful, methodical former teacher and now my editor for this book, who, while reading my attacks on our school system, gritted her teeth and bit her tongue (well, sometimes), finding—as a good teacher would—the many typos, grammatical errors, and too-short-for-farmers paragraphs in the original manuscript and offering many helpful suggestions on ways to make the book more consistent and readable. I'm sure she'd want you to know that she is neither responsible for, nor agrees 100 percent with, my opinion of our educational system. (But I'm assuming that you wouldn't be reading my book if you didn't want to know my opinions, so my opinions remain intact—even if I did surrender many of my short, punchy paragraphs.)

Introduction

A New View for Our Children

In the space of less than 40,000 years, ever more closely
packed cultural "revolutions" have taken humanity from
the status of a relatively rare large mammal to something
more like a geologic force.
RICHARD G. KLEIN AND BLAKE EDGAR

I was in India in 1993 to help manage a community for orphans and blind children on behalf of a German charity. During the monsoon season, the week of the big Hyderabad earthquake, I took an all-day train ride almost all the way across the subcontinent (from Bombay through Hyderabad to Rajamundri) to visit an obscure town near the Bay of Bengal. In the train compartment with me were several Indian businessmen and a physician, and we had plenty of time to talk as the countryside flew by from sunrise to sunset.

Curious about how they viewed our children diagnosed as having Attention Deficit Hyperactivity Disorder (ADHD), I asked, "Are you familiar with those types of people who seem to crave stimulation, yet have a hard time staying with any one focus for a period of time? They may hop from career to career and sometimes even from relationship to relationship, never seeming to settle into one job or into a life with one person—but the whole time they remain incredibly creative and inventive."

"Ah, we know this type well," one of the men said, the other three nodding in agreement.

"What do you call this personality type?" I asked.

"Very holy," he said. "These are old souls, near the end of their karmic cycle." Again, the other three nodded agreement, perhaps a bit more vigorously in response to my startled look.

"Old souls?" I questioned, thinking that a very odd description for those whom American psychiatrists have diagnosed as having a particular disorder.

"Yes," the physician said. "In our religion, we believe that the purpose of reincarnation is to eventually free oneself from worldly entanglement and desire. In each lifetime we experience certain lessons, until finally we are free of this earth and can merge into the oneness of God. When a soul is very close to the end of those thousands of incarnations, he must take a few lifetimes to do many, many things—to clean up the little threads left over from his previous lives."

"This is a man very close to becoming enlightened," a businessman added. "We have great respect for such individuals, although their lives may be difficult."

Another businessman raised a finger and interjected. "But it is through the difficulties of such lives that the soul is purified." The others nodded agreement.

"In America they consider this behavior indicative of a psychiatric disorder," I said. All three looked startled, then laughed.

"In America you consider our most holy men, our yogis and swamis, to be crazy people as well," said the physician with a touch of sadness in his voice. "So it is with different cultures. We live in different worlds."

We in our Western world have such "holy" and nearly enlightened people among us and we say they must be mad. But as we're about to see, they may instead be our most creative individuals, our most extraordinary thinkers, our most brilliant inventors and pioneers. The children among us whom our teachers and psychiatrists say are "disordered" may, in fact, carry a set of abilities—a skill set—that was necessary for the survival of humanity in the past, that has created much of what we treasure in our present "quality of life," and that will be critical to the survival of the human race in the future.

There is immense power in how we choose to view what's happening around us, and this is terrifically important when we consider how we can best know our children and provide them with the upbringing they need—an upbringing that will lead them to become healthy, happy, functioning adults. The premise of this book is that children who have what we have come to know as ADHD are important and vital gifts to our society and culture, and, in the largest sense, can be an extraordinary gift to the world. In addition, for those adults who have been similarly diagnosed or defined, this book offers a new way of understanding themselves and their relationship to the world—a way that brings insight, empowerment, and success.

GENETICS AND DIFFERENCES

The long history of the human race, as we'll see in this book, has conferred on us—some of us more than others—a set of predilections, temperaments, and abilities carried through the medium of our genetic makeup. These skills were ideally suited to life in the ever-changing world of our ancient ancestors and, we have now discovered, are also ideally suited to the quickly-changing modern world of cyberspace and widespread ecological and political crises that require rapid response. I will call this genetic gift the Edison gene,* after Thomas Edison, who brought us electric lights and phonographs and movies and—literally—ten thousand other inventions. He is the model for the sort of impact a well-nurtured child carrying this gene can have on the world.

While I'm principally referring to the DRD4 gene (see chapter 5), the science of genetics is embryonic, with new discoveries being made every day. No doubt, some time soon we'll have a better, more complete list of specific genes that make up what Dave deBronkart first called the "Edison trait" back in 1992 and Lucy Jo Palladino expanded on considerably in 1997 in her wonderful book *The Edison Trait*. For the moment, however, I'll use the useful shorthand of the "Edison gene."

---

* The Edison gene, of course, is not just a single gene. As is true for all characteristics, particularly those having to do with personality, those related to the Edison gene are actually the result of a complex interaction of many genes. While there is one gene that's been most often associated with what psychiatrists call ADHD—and this one is my best candidate for the Edison gene—there are many others that work with it in different configurations, shading its nuance and power to create the personality of an inventor, explorer, or entrepreneur.

When Edison's schoolteacher threw him out of school in the third grade for being inattentive, fidgety, and "slow," his mother, Nancy Edison, the well-educated daughter of a Presbyterian minister, was deeply offended by the schoolmaster's characterization of her son. As a result, she pulled him out of the school. She became his teacher from then until the day he went off on his own to work for the railroads (inventing, in his first months of employment, a railroad timing and signaling device that was used for nearly a century). She believed in him and wasn't going to let the school thrash out of him his own belief in himself. As a result of that one mother's efforts, the world is a very different place.

"Ah, but we musn't coddle these children!" some say. Consider this: Edison invented, at age sixteen, that device that revolutionized telegraph communication. It started him on a lifelong career of invention that led to the light bulb, the microphone, the motion picture, and the electrification of our cities. Would the world have been better off if he'd been disciplined into "behaving himself"?

The children and adults who carry this gene have and offer multiple gifts, both individually and as members of our society. Sometimes these gifts are unrecognized, misinterpreted, or even punished, and as a result, these exceptional children end up vilified, drugged, or shunted into Special Education. The result is that they often become reactive: sullen, angry, defiant, oppositional, and, in extreme cases, suicidal. Some Edison-gene adults face the same issues, carrying the wounds of school with them into adulthood, often finding themselves in jobs better adapted to stability than creativity.

What exactly defines those bearing this genetic makeup? Edison-gene children and adults are by nature:

Enthusiastic
Creative
Disorganized
Non-linear in their thinking (they leap to new conclusions or
    observations)
Innovative
Easily distracted (or, to put it differently, easily attracted to
    new stimuli)

Capable of extraordinary hyperfocus
Understanding of what it means to be an "outsider"
Determined
Eccentric
Easily bored
Impulsive
Entrepreneurial
Energetic

All of these qualities lead them to be natural:

Explorers
Inventors
Discoverers
Leaders

Those carrying this gene, however, often find themselves in environments where they're coerced, threatened, or shoehorned into a classroom or job that doesn't fit. When Edison-gene children aren't recognized for their gifts but instead are told that they're disordered, broken, or failures, a great emotional and spiritual wounding occurs. This wounding can bring about all sorts of problems for children, for the adults they grow into, and for our society.

I and many scientists, educators, physicians, and therapists believe that when these unique children don't succeed in public schools, it's often because of a disconnect between them—their brains are wired to make them brilliant inventors and entrepreneurs—and our schools, which are set up for children whose brains are wired to make them good workers in the structured environments of a factory or office cubicle.

Those children whom we call "normal" are more methodical, careful, and detail-oriented and are less likely to take risks. They often find it hard to keep it together and perform in the rapid-fire world of the Edison-gene child: They don't do as well with video games, couldn't handle working in an emergency room or on an ambulance crew, and seldom find themselves among the ranks of entrepreneurs, explorers, and salespeople.

Similarly, Edison-gene children have their own strengths and limitations: They don't do well in the school environment of repetition, auditory learning, and rote memorization that has been set up for "normal" kids, and they don't make very good bookkeepers or managers. Genetically these kids are pioneers, explorers, and adventurers. They make great innovators, and they find high levels of success in any field where there's a lot of change, constant challenge, and lots of activity. Such personalities are common among emergency room physicians, surgeons, fighter pilots, and salespeople.

There are many areas in which such people can excel—especially when they make it through childhood with their belief in themselves intact.

1993: THE HUNTER GENE

Dozens of studies over the years have demonstrated that ADHD is genetically transmitted to children from their parents or grandparents. From the 1970s, when this link was first discovered, until 1993, when my first book on the topic was published, conventional wisdom held that ADHD, hyperactivity, and the restive need for high stimulation were all indications of a psychiatric illness that should be treated with powerful, mind-altering, stimulant drugs.

But could it be that ADHD, this psychiatric "illness," has a positive side? I proposed in 1993 that these behaviors and temperaments—often misunderstood in schools—were once, in fact, useful skills for hunter-gatherer people (which, throughout the book, I'll refer to simply as *hunters*), and also have a place in the modern world of emergency rooms, police departments, entrepreneurial businesses, and sales, to which the skills of the hunter can been transferred.

A year later the metaphor entered the popular culture with a *Time* magazine cover story on ADD and a sidebar article about my hypothesis, titled "Hail The Hyperactive Hunter."[1] Here's a chart from my first book, *Attention Deficit Disorder: A Different Perception*, that broadly summarized my 1992 view of Attention Deficit Disorder (ADD) and that contrasts the hunter skill set with the skills of the very first farmers, or agriculturalists, which have become those most favored in our schools and most workplaces:

THE "HUNTER VERSUS FARMER" VIEW OF ADHD

Trait As It Appears in the "Disorder" View	Trait As It Appears in the "Hunter" View	Opposite "Farmer" Trait
Short attention span, which can become intensely focused for long periods of time.	Constant monitoring of the environment	Attention is not easily distracted from the task at hand
Poor planning, disorganization, and impulsivity (tendency to make snap decisions)	Ability to enter the chase on a moment's notice	Ability to sustain a steady, dependable effort
Distorted sense of time; lack of awareness of how long it will take to do something	Flexibility; a readiness to quickly change strategy	Purposeful organization; long-term strategy that's adhered to
Impatience	Tirelessness; the ability to sustain drive, but only when "hot on the trail" of some goal	Awareness of time and timing; tasks are completed "in time," on pace, and with good "staying power"
Inability to convert words into concepts and vice versa; a learning disability may or may not be present	Visual/concrete thinking; clear sight of a tangible goal even if there are no words for it	Patience; an awareness that good things take time; a willingness to wait
Difficulty following directions	Independence	Playing on a team
Daydreaming	Becoming bored by mundane tasks; enjoying new ideas, excitement, the "hunt," or being "hot on the trail"	Focusing on follow-through; tending to details and "taking care of business"
Acting without considering consequences	Willingness and ability to take risks and face danger	Taking care to "look before you leap"
Lacking in social graces	"No time for niceties when there are decisions to be made!"	Nurturing; creating and supporting community values; attuning to whether something will last

Of course, when I referred to farmers in my comparison, I wasn't talking about modern agriculturists who contend with all the equipment and challenges of agriculture today. Instead, I was considering the skill set of the first settled people who engaged in agriculture, those who had to spend hour after hour planting, cultivating, and harvesting crops by hand.

To engage in such early farming activity, three basic behaviors—which we now know are genetically determined and are related to brain dopamine levels—would have to be minimized: *distractibility, impulsivity,* and *risk-taking.* These three behaviors, however, would have been assets to hunters.

Because they are at the core of the ADHD diagnosis—and relate to those with the Edison gene—these behaviors are worth briefly exploring, along with their history in human societies. Here's a summary adapted from the one I included in my book *ADD Success Stories* that's still quite apt:

DISTRACTIBILITY

Distractibility is often incorrectly characterized as the inability of a child or adult to pay attention to a specific task or topic. Yet people with ADHD can pay attention, even for long periods of time (it's called *hyperfocusing*) but only to something that excites or interests them. It's a cliché—but true—that "there is no ADHD in front of a good video game."

ADHD experts often noted that it's not that those with ADHD *can't* pay attention to anything; it's that they pay attention to everything. A better way to characterize the distractibility of ADHD is to describe it as *scanning.* In a classroom, the child with ADHD is the one who notices the janitor mowing the lawn outside the window instead of focusing on the teacher's lecture on long division. Likewise, the bug crawling across the ceiling or the class bully preparing to throw a spitball is infinitely more fascinating than the teacher's analysis of Columbus's place in history.

But while this constant scanning of the environment is a liability in a classroom setting, it may have been a survival skill for our prehistoric ancestors. A primitive hunter who couldn't easily fall into a mental state of constant scanning would be at a huge disadvantage. That flash of motion on the periphery of his vision might be either the rabbit that he needed for lunch, or the tiger or bear hoping to make lunch of him. If he were to focus too heavily on the trail, for example, and therefore miss the other details of his environment, he would either starve or be eaten.

When the agricultural revolution began twelve thousand years ago, however, this scanning turned into a liability for those people whose societies changed from hunting to farming. If the moon was right, the soil held the perfect moisture, and the crops were due to be planted, a farmer couldn't waste his time wandering off into the forest to check out an unusual movement he noticed. He had to keep his attention focused on the task at hand and not be distracted from it.

IMPULSIVITY

Impulsivity has two core manifestations among modern people with ADHD. The first is impulsive behavior: acting without thinking things through or the proverbial "leap before you look." Often this takes the form of interrupting others or blurting things out in conversation. Other times it's reflected in snap judgments or quick decisions.

To the prehistoric hunter impulsivity was an asset because it provided the ability to act on instant decisions, as well as the willingness to explore new, untested areas. If the hunter were chasing a rabbit through the forest with his spear, and a deer ran by, he wouldn't have time to stop and calculate a risk/benefit analysis. He would have to make an instant decision about which animal to pursue, than act on that decision without a second thought.

Thomas Edison eloquently described how his combined distractibility and impulsiveness helped him in his "hunt" for world transforming inventions. He said, "Look, I start here with the intention of going there (drawing an imaginary line) in an experiment, say, to increase the speed of the Atlantic cable; but when I have arrived part way in my straight line, I meet with a phenomenon and it leads me off in another direction, to something totally unexpected."

The second aspect of impulsivity is impatience. For a primitive farmer, however, impatience and impulsivity would spell disaster. If he were to go out into the field and dig up the seeds every day to see if they were growing, the crops would die. (A contemporary manifestation of this is the person who can't leave the oven door shut, but has to keep opening it to check how the food's doing, to the detriment of many a soufflé.)

A very patient approach, all the way down to the process of picking bugs off plants for hours each day, day after day, would have to be hard-wired into the brain of a farmer. The word "boring" couldn't be in his vocabulary. His brain would have to be built in such a way that it tolerated, or even enjoyed, sticking with something until it was finished.

RISK-TAKING

Risk-taking, or, as Dr. Edward Hallowell and Dr. John Ratey describe it in their book *Driven to Distraction,* "a restive search for high stimulation," is perhaps the most destructive of the behaviors associated with ADHD in contemporary society. It probably accounts for the high percentage of people with ADHD among prison populations and plays a role in a wide variety of social problems, from the risky driving of a teenager to the infidelity or job-hopping of an adult.

Yet for a primitive hunter, risk and high-stimulation were a necessary part of daily life. If a hunter were risk- or adrenaline-adverse, he'd never go into the wilds to hunt. For a hunter, the idea of daily risking his life would have felt "normal." In fact, the urge to experience risk, the desire for that adrenaline high, would have been necessary among the members of a hunting society, because it would have propelled their members out into the forest or jungle in search of stimulation and dinner.

If a farmer were a risk-taker, however, the results could lead to starvation. Because decisions made by farmers had such long-ranging consequences, their brains would have to have been wired to avoid risks and to carefully determine the most risk-free way of going about his work. If a farmer were to decide to take a chance and plant a new and different crop—ragweed, for example, instead of the wheat that grew so well the previous year—the result might have led to tragic dietary problems for the tribe or family.

That genetic predispositions to behavior can be leftover survival strategies from prehistoric times is a theme most recently echoed in a *Time* magazine cover story on the brain. The article pointed out that the craving for fat among some people in parts of the world that experienced famine ensured the survival of those who were able to store large quantities of this nutrient under their skin. "But the same tendencies cause mass heart failure when expressed in a fast-food world," the authors point out.

Even the genetic inclination to alcoholism may have positive prehistoric roots, according to evolutionists Randolph Nesse and George Williams in their book *Why We Get Sick*. The persistence of an alcoholic in the face of social, familial, and biological resistance and disaster, they say, reflects an evolutionary tenacity to go after neurochemical rewards despite obstacles. This tenacity may in some way be responsible for the continued growth, survival, and evolution of our species.

So the agricultural revolution highlighted two very different types of human societies: farmers and hunters. Each group lived different lives, in different places. Those with the ADHD gene in farming societies were probably culled from the gene pool by natural selection, or they became warriors for their societies, "hunting" other humans as various tribes came into conflict. In some societies—evolving into the countries of Japan and India, for instance—this role was even institutionalized into a caste system. History is replete with anecdotes about the unique personalities of the warrior castes such as the Kshatriya in India and the Samurai in Japan.

WHERE HAVE ALL THE HUNTERS GONE?

If we accept for a moment the possibility that the gene that causes ADHD was useful in another time and place but has become a liability in our modern, society based on the systems of agriculture and industry, then these question arise: How did we reach a point in human evolution where the farmers so massively outnumber the hunters? If the hunter gene was useful for the survival of people, why have hunting societies largely died out around the world, and why is ADHD seen in only 3 to 20 percent of the population (depending on how you measure it and whose numbers you use), instead of 50 percent or more?

Recent research from several sources shows that hunting societies are always wiped out by farming societies over time. Fewer than 10 percent of the members of a hunting society normally survive when their culture collides with an agricultural society—and it has nothing to do with the hunter's "attention deficits" or with any inherent superiority of the farmers.

In one study reported in *Discover* magazine, the authors traced the root languages of the peoples living throughout central Africa and found that at one time the area was dominated by hunters: the Khoisans and the Pygmies. But over a period of several thousand years, virtually all of the Khoisans and Pygmies (the Hottentots and the Bushmen, as they've been referred to in Western literature) were wiped out and replaced by Bantu-speaking farmers. Two entire groups of people were rendered nearly extinct, while the Bantu-speaking farmers flooded across the continent, dominating central Africa.

There are several reasons for this startling transformation. First, agriculture is more efficient at generating calories than hunting. Because the same amount of land can support up to ten times more people when used for farming rather than hunting, farming societies generally have roughly ten times the population density of hunting societies. In war, numbers are always an advantage, particularly in these ratios. Few armies in history have survived an onslaught by another army ten times larger.

Second, diseases such as chicken pox, influenza, and measles, which virtually wiped out vulnerable populations such as native North and South Americans, who died by the thousands when exposed to the illnesses of the invading Europeans, began as diseases of domesticated animals. The farmers who were regularly exposed to such diseases developed relative immunities; though they would become ill, these germs usually wouldn't kill them. However, those with no prior exposure and thus no immunity, however, would often die. So when farmers encountered hunters, the latter were often killed off simply through exposure to the farmers' disease.

Finally, agriculture provides physical stability to a culture. The tribe stays in one spot while their population grows, which allows its members to specialize in individual jobs. Some people become tool and weapon makers, some build devices that can be used in war, and some create governments, armies, and kingdoms—all of which give farming societies a huge technological advantage over hunting societies, which are generally more focused on day-to-day survival issues.

So now we have an answer to the question: Where have all the hunters gone?

Most were killed off, from Europe to Asia, from Africa to the Americas. Those who survived were brought into farming cultures either through assimilation, kidnapping, or cultural change—and provided the genetic material that appears in the small percentage of people with ADHD today.

Further evidence of the anthropological basis of ADHD is seen among the modern survivors of ancient hunting societies.

INDIGENOUS HUNTERS TODAY

Cultural anthropologist Jay Fikes, Ph.D., points out that members of traditional Native American hunting tribes normally behave differently from those who have traditionally been farmers. The farmers such as the Hopi and other Pueblo Indian tribes are relatively sedate and risk-averse, he says, whereas the hunters, such as the Navajo, are "constantly scanning their environment and are more immediately sensitive to nuances. They're also the ultimate risk-takers. They and the Apaches were great raiders and warriors."

A physician who recently read my first book and concluded that he saw proof of the "hunter versus farmer" concept in his work with some of the Native Americans in Southwest Arizona, dropped me the following unsolicited note over the Internet:

Many of these descendants of the Athabaskan Indians of Western Canada have never chosen to adapt to farming. They had no written language until an Anglo minister, fairly recently, wrote down their language for the first time. They talk "heart to heart," and there is little "clutter" between you and them when you are communicating. They hear and consider everything you say. They are scanning all the time, both visually and auditorily. Time has no special meaning unless it is absolutely necessary (that's something we Anglos have imposed on them). They don't use small talk, but get right to the point, and have a deep understanding of people and the spiritual. And their history shows that they have a love of risk-taking.

Will Krynen, M.D., noted the same differences when he worked for the Canadian government as the physician for several native North American tribes, and during the years he worked as a physician for the Red Cross in Southeast Asia. After reading my first book, he wrote:

> I've worked among indigenous hunting societies in many parts of the world, from Asia to the Americas. Over and over again I see among their adults and children that constellation of behaviors we call ADD. In those societies, however, these behaviors are highly adaptive and actually contribute to the societies' success.

Among the member of the tribes of northern Canada, such as the caribou hunters of the McKenzie Basin, these adaptive characteristics—constantly scanning their environment, quick decision-making (impulsivity), and a willingness to take risks—contribute every year to the tribe's survival.

These same behaviors, however, often make it difficult for tribal children to succeed in Western schools when we try to impose our Western curriculum on them.

But what sent humankind onto the radical social departure from hunting to farming? Few other animals, with the exception of highly organized insects such as ants, have developed a society that is based on anything that approaches agriculture.

In *The Ascent of Man,* Jacob Bronowski points out that twenty thousand years ago every human on Earth was a hunter and forager. The most advanced hunting societies had started following wild herd animals, as is still done by modern Laplanders. This had been the basis of human and pre-human society and lifestyle for several million years.

Until 1995, the earliest hard evidence of human activity (and hunting activity, at that) came from the Olduvai Gorge in Tanzania, Africa, with fragments of stone tools and weapons that dated back 2.5 million years. More recently, University of Southern California anthropologist Craig Stanford is quoted in the *Chicago Tribune* as saying that recent research he conducted in Africa indicates that early hominids may have been tribally hunting as early as six million years ago.

So for six million years our ancestors were hunters, and then, suddenly, in a tiny moment of time (ten thousand years is to six million years what less than three minutes is to a twenty-four-hour day) the entire human race veered in a totally new direction.

THE AGRICULTURAL REVOLUTION

The reason for the change, according to Bronowski and many anthropologists, probably has to do with the end of the last ice age, which roughly corresponds to the beginning of the agricultural revolution. (Bronowski and most authorities place the agricultural revolution as occurring roughly twelve thousand years ago.) At that time, mutated grasses appeared simultaneously on several continents, probably in response to the sudden and radical change in climate. These grasses were the first high-yield, edible ancestors of modern rice and wheat and provided the humans who lived near them an opportunity to nurture and grow these staple foods.

Those people with the farmer-like patience to grow crops evolved into farming societies that emptied their ranks of the impulsive, sensation-seeking hunters among them. Those persons who were not patient enough to wait for rice to grow maintained their hunting tribes, the last remnants of which we see today in a few remaining indigenous peoples on the earth. The Old Testament, for example, is in large part the story of a nomadic hunting tribe moving through the wrenching process, over several generations, of becoming a settled farming tribe.

OUR SOCIETY'S HUNTERS

A year after the *Time* magazine article, the idea of ADHD as a positive condition hit the business press when former *Inc. Magazine* publisher, entrepreneur, and author Wilson L. Harrell wrote in his book *For Entrepreneurs Only*[2] and in his column for *Success Magazine:*[3]

> For two decades I have wrestled with a provocative question: Are entrepreneurs born or made? I've always contended that they are made—anyone can become one. But I've never been entirely satisfied with that answer. There's the nagging fact that entrepreneurial parents tend to have entrepreneurial children. There's the unexplained truth that entrepreneurs' personalities are different from other people's.

Harrell describes reading about my "hunter versus farmer" hypothesis and says:

> There's still a lot of hunter left in our genes and in our hearts. In a world dominated by farmers and corporate types, there are plenty of full-blooded hunters trying to hunt for a living. Those, my friend, are entrepreneurs. . . . Hunters and those with ADD are astoundingly similar. I suspect most entrepreneurs, if they sat still long enough, could be diagnosed as having ADD. . . . And I've passed my ADD (or hunter) genes to my children.

In 1996, the *Journal of Genetic Psychology* published an article titled "Attention Deficit Hyperactivity Disorder: An Evolutionary Perspective," in which they suggested that, "Although no theory entirely explains the occurrence of ADHD, it is worthwhile to note that, at least historically, ADHD may have served an adaptive function and may have been selected by the environment for survival."[4]

In 1997, Peter Jensen, M.D., the head of the Child and Adolescent Psychiatry division of the National Institutes of Mental Health (NIMH), was the lead author of a paper published in the peer-reviewed *Journal of the American Academy of Child and Adolescent Psychiatry*. In that paper, titled "Revolution in Evolution: ADHD as a Disorder of Adaptation,"[5] he and his coauthors strongly argued that ADHD children shouldn't be told they have an illness but that instead parents and teachers should emphasize their positive characteristics. "In reframing the child who has ADHD as 'response ready,' experience-seeking, or alert," they wrote, "the clinician can counsel the child and family to recognize situations in modern society that might favor such an individual, both in terms of school environments, as well as future career opportunities, e.g., athlete, air-traffic-controller, salesperson, soldier, or entrepreneur."[6]

But it was all just speculation until 2000, when the article "Dopamine Genes and ADHD" appeared in *Neuroscience and Biobehavioral Reviews*. This paper, by lead author Dr. James M. Swanson and ten other scientists, noted that, "The literature on these candidate genes and ADHD is increasing. Eight molecular genetic studies have been published, so far, about investigations of a hypothesized association of ADHD with the DAT1 and the DRD4 gene."[7]

Soon other scientists were saying the "hunter gene" may be a good thing. For example, Dr. Robert Moyzis said of an NIMH-funded study of the gene, which he helped conduct, "We found a significant positive selection for the genetic variation associated with ADHD and novelty-seeking behavior in the human genome. This study strengthens significantly the connection between genetic variations and ADHD. It also provides a clue as to why ADHD is so pervasive."[8]

Numerous other scientific journals over the years have published similar reports or studies. There's a growing consensus that such children are carrying a gene for a behavior set that's really a skill set, a collection of *useful adaptations*. And a growing number of voices, such as Howard Gardner *(Frames of Mind: The Theory of Multiple Intelligences)* and Daniel Goleman *(Emotional Intelligence: Why It Can Matter More Than IQ)*, are calling for a wider definition of the kinds of "intelligence" and talent our schools accept and teach to.

Scientists who have studied human DNA have found that the appearance of this gene variation coincided with many of the larger migrations of humans around the world. Researchers have tracked this gene, which they had previously thought of as causing a "disorder," back to a time when it was a gene that caused behaviors necessary for human survival. It may even have been the gene responsible for both the spread of humanity across the globe and the flowering of civilization and modern culture. For all we know, without this "curiosity gene" driving exploration and invention, humans might still be splitting flints and warming themselves around open fires.

THE EDISON GENE

All these discoveries have led me to a new hypothesis built upon my earlier work with the hunter/farmer model.

The early development of this came, in part, from Michael Garnatz, who, with his wife Heidi, has founded and runs the Web site www.hypies.com in Berlin, Germany, one of the largest and most well-known ADHD sites in Germany. Michael confronted me one day with the essential inconsistency of a theory that suggests the Edison gene, which emerged in full form only about forty thousand years ago, was useful for hunters when humans had been hunters for a hundred thousand years before that. Although I'd never called it the farmer gene, Michael pointed out that its emergence in the human genome seemed to coincide with some of the earliest documented examples of ancient peoples experimenting with agriculture. So how could I continue to call it the hunter gene?

I thought about this for some time, trying to figure out how to put together all the pieces in a way that was scientifically consistent and not merely some glib renaming of an older theory. Nothing seemed to work.

And then I read William Calvin's new book, *A Brain For All Seasons*. Calvin had synthesized some of the most remarkable science of the last decade of the twentieth century and had done so in a way that gave sudden and clear meaning to the appearance and persistence of the Edison gene.

THE CRISIS-SURVIVAL GENE

It's amazing what science can learn in a decade. In the early 1990s, most paleoclimatologists believed that climate change was a gradual phenomena, and that ice ages lasting ten thousand or more years were gradually alternated with periods of warmth. Nobody understood what caused the ice ages or even our current warmth, although variations in solar radiation were suspected.

Similarly, paleoanthropologists had known for decades that fully modern humans emerged from Africa about two hundred thousand years ago and, about forty thousand years ago, began behaving in highly organized and cooperative ways. Scientists had figured out that if they could take a child from the world of thirty-eight thousand years ago and raise him in today's world, he would be indistinguishable from the rest of us.

The problem was that nobody could understand why it took these "modern" people so long—up until about ten thousand years ago—to begin building city-states and engaging in intensive agriculture. Of course, people pointed to the ice age that had North America, northern Asia, and Europe in its grip up until ten thousand years ago, but this didn't explain why civilizations weren't being built in still-warm Africa or other equatorial areas of the world.

In part, this confusion was due to the common assumption that ice ages were a relatively constant phenomenon that had come on slowly throughout ancient history, with the glaciers of the most recent one gradually melting about ten thousand years ago, leading to today's weather.

A decade later, however, scientists discovered that what they thought to be true was actually wrong. As William Calvin documents so brilliantly in *A Brain For All Seasons,* it turns out that each and every one of the transitions between the cold, dry, windy ice ages and today's wet, warm weather happened not gradually, over hundreds or thousands of years, but suddenly—in fewer than a dozen years.

The weather might have become strange one year, with a cold summer and hard winter, and then the next year, or the one after that, the summer simply never returned. The winters then became so harsh that very few humans could survive them (with the exception, it seems, of the Neanderthals, who could—and did—more easily, because their bodies were better adapted to cold).

Although ice gripped the north during these times, the weather changes also hit Africa and southern Asia: When it became cold in the north, drought struck the equatorial regions. Water holes dried up, rivers stopped flowing, jungles and rainforests turned to tinder and then blazed in massive, continent-consuming wildfires.

When, a thousand or so years later, the worldwide weather switched to being wet and warm, ice in the north thawed and monsoonlike floods swept Africa, tearing away what life had managed to hang onto survival during the cool, dry, windy period.

This is the cauldron in which humans evolved. When we look at a graph of worldwide temperatures, we discover that in the past one hundred fifty thousand years—virtually the whole of human history—there has rarely been a period of ten thousand years (or even as much as two thousand years) of steady, warm, comfortable weather. The single exception is the past ten thousand years, which is referred to as the Holocene period.

HUNTERS BEFORE THE HOLOCENE

When the climate is stable, farmers are at an advantage. During the summer they can plant and harvest crops, which they can eat during the winter. Life is good, and they're able to extract at least ten times the calories from a given area of land that hunter people can. However, when the climate is constantly changing, farming becomes impossible. Hunters rarely suffer from the affliction of farmers—famine—because when a hunting area is hit by drought or flood, heat or cold, such people simply move to another place. When one primary food plant or animal dies off, they switch to others. When the pickings get slim, hunters expand their range.

The diet of hunters is incredibly diverse because of their ranging and nomadic existence. This is why, until the development of antibiotics around the time of World War II, no agricultural peoples in the eight thousand–year history of agriculture had achieved the health of hunters. Both modern *and* ancient hunters consistently have had stronger bones and taller bodies, have lost fewer teeth, and have lived longer than typical Europeans from the earliest cities as recently as fifty years ago.

While popular culture portrays the lives of hunter people as harsh and miserable, the ones I've met and known on four continents enjoy high-quality lives. Indeed, according to anthropologists, hunters represent the original leisure society, typically working only two to four hours a day to secure all their food and shelter needs, and spending the rest of the time playing with their families, talking, singing, and building community. (Dr. Robert Wolff wrote one of the best books on this, titled *Original Wisdom,* about his time with the Sng'oi hunter people of Malaysia.)

ADAPTED TO ADVERSITY AND CHANGE

Thus, we find that hunters were ideally suited to the climate of the world for most of its history, just as agricultural peoples are well suited to it as it is today. In both of these cultures, there is and has always been a place and a need for those nonconformist, creative individuals who are best adapted to change. Especially when the climate undergoes one of its regular flip-flops (to use Calvin's term).

During ancient hunter times, it was the creative nonconformists who broke with one hundred thousand years of tradition and invented ostrich shell beads to exchange with other tribes as a way of sealing mutual deals for hunting rights. During more recent agricultural and industrial times, it was the creative nonconformist Thomas Edison who brought us electric lights, movies, and a thousand other inventions.

The gene for wanderlust, adventure, and innovation is relatively rare, carried by fewer than 10 percent of our population. But it's incredibly valuable, and it's even possible that one day the survival of the human race will depend on it.

It certainly has in the past.

Part 1

The Past

Remember, remember always,
that all of us, and you and I especially,
are descended from immigrants and revolutionists.

FRANKLIN D. ROOSEVELT

F orty thousand years ago, the world was a very different place, although all available science indicates that the humans in it were identical to you and me in both physical and mental abilities. Why, then, did they live in caves instead of building cities and civilizations?

When you and I were in school, we learned about the recent part of the Paleolithic Ice Age, which ended a bit over ten thousand years ago, when the current Holocene era began. We learned that the glaciers gradually melted as much of the world thawed out, leading to the climate we've enjoyed for the past ten millennia and paving the way for agriculture and modern civilization.

We learned that the glaciers started to advance gradually three million years ago (more or less, depending on the textbook you read and the decade in which you read it), advanced in long-term cycles, the last one reaching a peak about eighteen thousand years ago (the LGM or Last Glacial Maximum), and gradually began to recede around ten thousand to twelve thousand years ago, leading to the climate we have today.

This, through most of the twentieth century, was what was written in every textbook. It's what is still in most textbooks used in schools today. We thought we understood how the weather changed historically, and why, and how that affected human evolution.

We were wrong.

1

The World of the Edison-Gene Child

The human race built most nobly when limitations were
greatest and therefore when most was required
of imagination to build at all.
FRANK LLOYD WRIGHT

In the North Atlantic Ocean, a few hundred miles off the coast of Greenland, there swirl and gurgle giant whirlpools big enough to slightly tilt an ocean liner. Ancient seafarers included them on their maps and marked them "the Edge of the World." Usually seen only as indentations on the surface of the sea, in the late winter they can grow to more than five miles in width, giant sucking vortexes visible from a boat or plane. When they stop their swirling, civilization as we know it will cease to exist. It's happened before and will certainly happen again.

The Edison gene emerged forty thousand years ago, during one such calming of those waters and will likely prove necessary when the next one occurs, which may be in our lifetime and will almost certainly be seen by our grandchildren or their grandchildren.

But we're getting ahead of ourselves. First a little background.

THE ANCIENT WORLD

The transition from the previous incarnation of the *Homo* species to the fully modern *Homo sapiens* was dramatic and abrupt, happening over the biologically brief period of just the past forty thousand to seventy thousand years. The rapidity of this event—and the shortage of fossils to document it—have given creationists and those believing our origins lie with aliens what they consider ammunition for their arguments. Science has proved beyond any reasonable doubt that modern humans appeared on the scene in a geological and evolutionary blink of the eye, but, until the 1990s, nobody knew why.

Then a group of scientists went to Greenland to drill into the largest glaciers and ice layers there with newly developed equipment so sophisticated it could distinguish between individual years of snowfall in the ice core samples they extracted. What they found has flipped the worlds of climatology, biology, and paleontology on their heads.

It turns out that the ice-age period of the last evolutionary leap of humanity wasn't a smooth and continuous era that gradually came to an end. Instead, for the better part of the past sixty thousand years the climate of this planet has whipsawed back and forth between two extremes—the current warm, wet period and ice-age-like periods that were cold, dry, and windy—most often on 750- or 1500-year cycles.

What's more, it seems the transition times into and out of these violent extremes of climate were neither long nor easy. Instead, the planet gradually warmed up until a certain threshold was reached—like the slow lifting of a light switch until it clicks—and when that threshold was reached, the planet was suddenly plunged into an ice age. Once the switch was thrown, the typical transition time from warmth to ice was between three and twelve years. An ice age lasted 750 to 1500 hundred years, and then the world inexplicably became warm again.

Europe was covered by an unrelenting winter for a few hundred years, while drought and wildfires stalked the peoples of Africa and the Middle East. Then, transition: Summer would come to Europe, accompanied by monsoonlike floods as billions of tons of snow and ice melted, evaporated, saturated the atmosphere, and came back down as rain. As Europe warmed, the rains returned to Africa and the Middle East, and jungles and forests came to life there. Within a couple of years the world's weather would moderate to a state similar to what we have today. But only for another 750 to 1500 years. (See fig. 1.1.) For the people alive at the times of transition, it must have been totally disorienting.

From about seventy thousand years ago until about ten thousand

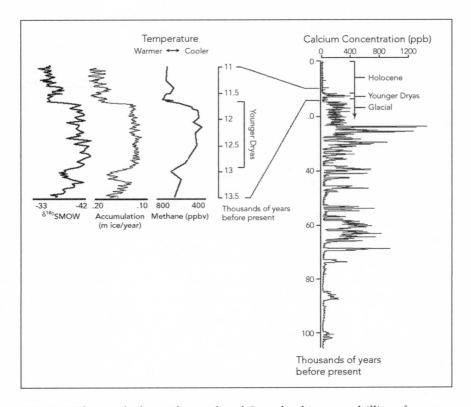

Fig. 1.1. The graph shows the results of Greenland ice core drillings from as far back as 110,000 years ago. On the right-hand scale, the higher calcium levels indicate times of planetary low temperatures (cold, dry, windy periods). The breakout on the left of a small part of the range shows the years just before and during the start of our current prolonged period of warming.

years ago, the entire planet, every few hundred years, regularly swung from extremes of wet warmth to extremes of dry, windy cold. These oscillations allowed people, in warm and wet times, to grow crops, build cities, and start civilizations for only a few dozen or a few hundred years, perhaps as much as a thousand or 1500 years, but then—in a period typically as short as three to twelve years—the weather swung to such severe cold that most of the northern American, European, and Asian land masses were covered by sheets of ice or ripped bare by frigid, dry, gale-force winds that never relented. The cold remained for several hundred to a thousand years, and then—again in a period as short as three to twelve years—the climate swung again to the wet warmth we're familiar with today.

These sudden weather changes happened so fast that most people of the time couldn't flee. Families, tribes, clans, entire nations of people were wiped out within a few seasons, killed by cold or floods, starvation or drowning, fire or typhoons.

THE SALT PUMP

The reason London and Amsterdam, at similar latitudes to Calgary and Edmonton, have weather like that of Europe rather than of Canada is an Atlantic Ocean current driven by salt.

The North Atlantic Ocean is saltier than the North Pacific Ocean because it is warmer than the Pacific, causing water to evaporate faster (which provides rainfall for Europe) and leaving behind salt. And the reason the North Atlantic is warmer is because it's saltier.

Yes, it's circular, and that's the beauty—and the danger—of it.

In 1855, oceanographer Matthew Maury wrote:

> There is a river in the ocean. In the severest droughts it never fails, and in the mightiest floods it never overflows; its banks and its bottom are of cold water, while its current is of warm; the Gulf of Mexico is its fountain, and its mouth is the Arctic Sea. It is the Gulf Stream. There is in the world no other such majestic flow of waters.

And, indeed, there is a huge river—hundreds of times larger than the largest on-land river—that runs through the Atlantic Ocean.

Imagine you're looking at a globe, with North and South America on the left, the Atlantic in the middle, and Africa and Europe on the right. The Great Conveyor Belt (see fig 1.2), as the river is sometimes called, begins out of sight on your right, in the Pacific, where fresher, less salty water flows under the southern tip of Africa into the Atlantic, propelled in part by the rotation of the earth.

The water then flows northward, drifting over to the northern coast of South America, into the concave area of Central America and

Mexico, up past Texas and around Florida, up the eastern coast of the United States, and then across the Atlantic Ocean toward Europe. By now this river of fresher water has picked up tremendous amounts of heat from the equatorial regions. Now called the Gulf Stream, it continues flowing on this part of its journey, glancing off the edge of the British Isles, heading up along the coast of Norway, then curving toward Greenland.

As it passes along the surface of the colder Atlantic, the Gulf Stream releases huge amounts of heat and evaporative moisture that blow westerly across Europe, warming and moistening that continent. When it reaches the northernmost parts of the North Atlantic, having spent its heat and much of its moisture, it cools suddenly and sinks thousands of feet to the floor of the ocean. This is where and why the whirlpools mentioned earlier are formed.

The water, now cool and dense with salt, flows south deep in the ocean along the coast of North America, taking an almost straight shot down to the east coast of South America, and finally down to the southernmost part of the Atlantic, where it flows around the deepest waters at the southern tip of Africa to replenish the salt and water the Pacific is losing as it feeds the Atlantic at the surface.

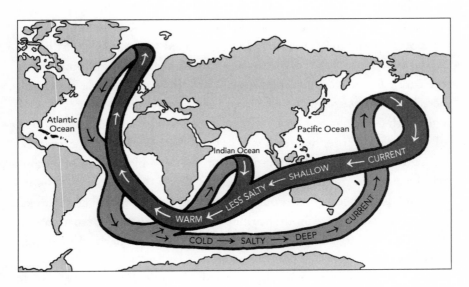

Fig. 1.2. The movement of the Great Conveyor Belt as it exists today

As long as the giant whirlpools are spinning, we know the Great Conveyer Belt is running, bringing heat up from the Equator to warm Europe, spinning and sinking to the sea floor, and taking salt and cold back to the Pacific.

THE GREAT ICE AGE

Our seasons change here in Vermont four times a year, from spring through summer to autumn and into winter. As I write these words in mid-January, the temperature outside my window is 14 degrees Fahrenheit, and it's predicted to get to 20 degrees below zero tonight. Almost two feet of snow have fallen, and it's been so cold since it fell that several tons of it are still stuck to the roof of my house. We walked into town today, wrapped warm with sweaters and scarves and two-layer wool-and-leather gloves, and wearing on our feet L.L. Bean "snow tennis shoes" that latch with Velcro well above the ankle and have a quarter-inch of tread to bite into the snow. The air was so cold it felt at times as though something was nipping at the skin of my cheeks, and the edges of my ears lost their feeling for a while.

Most people think this cold we're experiencing is a result of the earth being farther from the sun than it is in the summer, but the truth is we're now closer to the sun than we'll be in June. Neither is it this cold because the tilt of the earth has positioned the southern part of the planet on a more direct plane to the sun than the north (although that's the case). Rome, for example, is at about the same latitude as we are here in Vermont and will have about the same number of hours of sunlight with the same intensity. But people there experienced a high today of 60 degrees Fahrenheit, and will have a low tonight of 47. Similarly, the town of Eureka in Northern California had a high today of 64 and will have a low tonight of 44.

The difference between our weather and that of Rome and Eureka exists because they're both warmed by north-flowing ocean currents and, perhaps most important, we're cooled by southerly flowing air currents off the arctic region of Canada.

We think the last ice age ended ten thousand years ago, but in reality, it's just moderated by a few degrees, giving us our current summer and winter seasons and the permafrost and tundra of the arctic. We're still in the Great Ice Age that started three million years ago and will remain in it as long as the isthmus of Panama is above water.

HEATED BY THE GREAT CONVEYOR BELT

A bit more than three million years ago—before the Great Ice Age started—the winters here in Vermont were pretty much like the current winters in Rome and Eureka, and, as in Eureka, our summers were much cooler. The total amount of heat in the Northern Hemisphere hadn't increased or decreased; it was just distributed differently. Winter temperatures never went below freezing, and permanent ice didn't exist all the way up to the arctic. Summers never grew particularly hot here; the oceans cooled the continents in the summer just as they warmed them in the winter, much as they do for England today.

The extremes between the seasons had evened out because the isthmus that connects North and South America—Panama—was open, allowing the Pacific Ocean's fresher water to flow directly into the Atlantic at its mid-point. From there, the water from the Pacific split, with one branch flowing across the Atlantic south to Africa and the other running north over Europe, into the Arctic Ocean (which wasn't frozen then), over Siberia, and back into the Pacific between Siberia and Alaska.

This flow of water kept the temperature comfortable in the entire Northern Hemisphere, supporting animals such as the llamas that traveled to South America when the land bridge between the continents filled in and thus escaped the ice age in North America. It provided for a long period of growth of flora and fauna.

But then the plates of North and South America moved closer together, or the land between them rose up (or both), and the area between the two continents was filled in where Panama exists today, cutting off the flow of warm water from the Pacific into the Atlantic. Now, to stabilize the relative salt levels of the two oceans, water had to flow down around the southern tip of Africa, altering totally the weather patterns of both the Northern and the Southern Hemispheres.

The Great Ice Age had begun.

2

The Dawn of Civilization

[T]he only people for me are the mad ones, the ones who
are mad to live, mad to talk, mad to be saved, desirous
of everything at the same time, the ones who never yawn
or say a commonplace thing, but burn, burn, burn, like
fabulous yellow roman candles exploding like spiders
across the stars and in the middle you see the blue cen-
terlight pop and everybody goes, "Awww!"

JACK KEROUAC, *ON THE ROAD*

Dr. Stanley Ambrose, an anthropologist with the University of Illinois, recently made a startling discovery in Africa. "We excavated a rock shelter with a very deep archaeological sequence," he told me in a 2002 interview:

> The [place] is Enkapune Ya Muto and it overlooks Lake Naivasha in the Central Rift Valley of Kenya. Down around three and a half meters below the surface, below a volcanic ash layer, we found fragments of ostrich egg shell, about six or seven hundred of them, and a couple of dozen pieces that had been drilled and partially ground and shaken and broken while drilling, and some whole beads as well, about a dozen. This was an activity area where they were making beads and maybe restringing old ones, finishing old ones and making new ones.

And they were ancient. He said, "We got radiocarbon dates right off the shell and they came out to thirty-seven thousand to forty thousand years old. They're the oldest directly dated beads in the world."

Ambrose's discovery has re-opened a longstanding debate within the anthropology world about when our ancestors became fully modern humans. His discovery points to a time around forty thousand years ago. "This was the product of modern humans," he said, "possibly the earliest in the world."

What's significant about the beads is that they were not utilitarian. Our ancestors were making stone tools several million years ago. A quarter million years ago, according to Ambrose, they were communicating with complex language and had developed elaborate tribal and clan rituals of exchange and gift-giving, although the gifts were utilitarian—obsidian knives and similar tools.

Such activity, however, was generally local and occurred within tribes. It appears that prior to forty thousand years ago, humans behaved in one respect much like our chimp cousins: They were intensely territorial. If two tribes of the earliest hunters had staked out two territories, and someone from one territory strayed into the other, the evidence implies that he would have been killed, the same as happens when chimps from one troupe wander into the territory of another troupe. Raiding neighbors to steal their young (particularly females) contributed more to genetic diversity than did neighborly relations.

But neither the means of trade nor the take in raids was the purpose or source of Ambrose's ostrich shell beads. "I believe the beads were given among individuals as gifts, and they symbolized the bonds of mutual reliance," he said. Through this early system of nonutilitarian gift giving, tribes gained permission to access other tribes' areas during times of crisis.

"Gift giving is most intense between hunter-gathering groups who live in the most severe environments," Ambrose said, pointing to research conducted across the world on hunter people.

The Bushmen of the Kalahari desert give gifts over long distances and have many gift-giving partners. This allows them reciprocal access to each other's territories in case there's a drought or something like that that makes them run out of food. The Australian Aborigines—especially in the desert—do this. The more reliable the environment, the less likely they are to have these reciprocal, long-distance-exchange relationships.

But it wasn't until forty thousand years ago that somebody came up with the idea of investing tremendous amounts of time and energy to manufacture something that had no practical or utilitarian value, but only symbolic meaning within a cultural context: "The beads are a nice, tangible kind of gift and they have no utilitarian value like eating it or making a tool out of it," Ambrose said. "All you can do is give it to somebody and have them obligated to you."

Interestingly, the word for "gift" used today by the hunter tribe of Kenya's Kalahari Desert—the Bushmen or !Kung people—is the same as the word for sewn ostrich beads. "We're talking about a tradition that's gone on for a long time and has deep origins," Ambrose said. "It's sort of like a social security system."

Which raises the question: What happened in the world—or what happened in humans' brains—that brought about this dramatic change in behavior?

WHAT MADE US HUMAN?

In 1977, scientists Stephen Jay Gould and Niles Eldredge published a groundbreaking paper in the journal *Paleobiology*.[1] Pointing out that the fossil record shows long periods of little evolutionary change punctuated by abrupt shifts—the end of the dinosaurs being the one most familiar to us—they suggested that Darwin's theory of gradual evolution needed revision.

Instead of species changing slowly over long periods of time, they said, the archaeological, paleontological, and anthropological records show that evolution happens instead in fits and starts, most likely in response to sudden changes in the environment that kill off most of a species. Long periods of relative equilibrium abruptly crash, and out of the ensuing chaos climb new forms that have been carrying previously ignored genetic mutations or variations that allow survival because they're better adapted to the new conditions.

Gould and Eldredge named this new concept *punctuated equilibrium*, and in the past twenty years it's come to be widely accepted in scientific circles. Punctuated equilibrium explains, among other things, why there are so few fossils of "missing link" species.

The theory proposes "bottlenecks" that occur at evolutionary transition points, when conditions are so severe that most living members of a species die out. The small number of survivors—the bottleneck— live on because they carry some genetic variation that has made them uniquely capable of surviving the crisis that killed off most of their peers.

THE BACTERIA THAT TOOK OVER THE WORLD

To understand how this works, consider a modern example. Fifty years ago, it was unusual for people ever to become ill from eating rare or uncooked meat. Indeed, many tribes around the world have existed for thousands of years on raw meat, and *steak tartare*—raw beef—was long considered a delicacy and was served in restaurants all across the United States and Europe. Even though raw meat is almost always contaminated with a cow intestinal bacterium known as *Escherichia coli (E. coli),* this didn't present a problem because *E. coli* is also a common and normal resident of the human gut, helping with the decomposition and absorption of foods.

But about fifty years ago, pharmaceutical companies began promoting the routine use of antibiotics in animal feed as a way of staving off infections and helping feed animals to fatten more quickly. This enormously profitable practice became so widespread that today half of all the antibiotics manufactured in the United States are fed to livestock.

The antibiotics in the cow feed wiped out the normal *E. coli* in the guts of cows across the United States, but somewhere, in some now-forgotten cow's stomach, there was an *E. coli* bacterium carrying a gene mutation that allowed it to survive the antibiotics. As all the other benign, competing *E. coli* around it died off, this one antibiotic-resistant *E. coli* variation—now called *E. coli* 0157:H—emerged to fill the ecological vacuum created by the mass deaths of its cousins. It grew and proliferated, spreading from cow to cow, herd to herd, city to city.

The summer of 1987 saw the first outbreak of bloody diarrhea in humans, and the Centers For Disease Control (CDC) tracked it to the new and previously unknown germ: *E. coli* 0157:H7. Over the next few years, it was discovered that this new antibiotic-resistant bacteria not only causes diarrhea in the person who ate the infected meat, but also brings on a rare condition called *hemolytic uremic syndrome*, in which the red blood cells break down and the kidneys fail, leading to death.

As the CDC notes on its Web site: "In the United States, hemolytic uremic syndrome is the principal cause of acute kidney failure in children, and most cases of hemolytic uremic syndrome are caused by *E. coli* 0157:H7." And it's now a large problem in the United States. The CDC notes that "About 2–7percent of [all *E. coli* 0157:H7] infections lead to this complication."[2] The bacterium has now become so ubiquitous that it infects meat, dairy products, and even fruits, vegetables, and sprouts.

Having survived the bottleneck, it's now taking over the world of colon-living bacteria in farm animals.

THE HUMAN BOTTLENECK

But is it possible that humans have faced the same sort of massive die-offs that the original *E. coli* bacteria faced when they were wiped out by antibiotics? Could something at one time have killed the vast majority of all living humans, creating a bottleneck out of which survived a small band of humans carrying a few useful mutations? And is it possible it's happened more than once?

During Darwin's time, scientists believed the earth's climate and geography had been relatively stable for millions of years; this belief was pervasive even up to the middle of the twentieth century. But as sophisticated techniques have emerged to date carbon and oxygen trapped in glacial ice layers, a new picture has come into view. Not only do scientists now agree that rather than having a relatively calm and steady climate throughout human history, the planet has careened wildly from one environmental extreme to another; they've also found that Gould and Eldredge's punctuated equilibrium applies to humans just as it does to *E. coli*, and that the most powerful variable that has swung our populations has been climate.

The past eight to ten thousand years, it turns out, have been a period of relatively unusual stability, although even during this period there occurred a series of smaller climate changes that led to the rise and fall of civilizations in the Middle East, Asia, and North and South America. (The largest was probably that instigated by the eruption 535 C.E. of Krakatoa, off the coast of Sumatra, which so altered the world's weather that droughts resulting from it ultimately brought about the end of the Roman Empire; drove rodents out of their normal habitats into human communities and thus caused the first eruptions of the Bubonic Plague; and brought out of this chaos the rise of Islam.)[3]

These climate changes over the past eight thousand years, however, haven't been large enough to kill off *most* humans, and thus haven't created the extreme bottleneck necessary for a true evolutionary punctuation in the timeline of modern humans. The available genetic and anthropological evidence shows that we're pretty much the same today as we were forty thousand years ago—but mentally and culturally quite different from our ancestors who lived more before then.

In fact, a group of scientists did a study of the Y (male) chromosome in European men and found, as published in the journal *Science*, that, "Eighty percent of modern European men's Y chromosomes stem from two ancient haplotypes [ancestors]."[4] They add that those two ancient ancestors separated from the rest of the human race about forty thousand years ago.[5] It's also interesting to note that the oldest artwork indicative of a fully modern mind-set—cave paintings in Lascaux and Chauvet, and artwork and ornaments in Africa—is dated to about thirty five thousand to forty thousand years ago.

While fossils show that the skeletons of humans from one hundred thousand years ago are indistinguishable from those of you or me something set us apart from them mentally and culturally, and all the available evidence points to that something having emerged forty millennia ago.

BEFORE THE BOTTLENECK

Prior to forty thousand years ago, humans lived across much of Africa, the Middle East, Europe, and Asia. They looked like modern people and had brains of the same size and complexity as ours. In their appearance they were what anthropologists would call "fully modern humans," the species *Homo sapiens*. They made tools, hunted in groups with spears and axes, had death rituals, and used fire. The oldest fossils of their type date back one hundred ninety six thousand years. In Africa, they lived alongside numerous other primates and perhaps with other *Homo* species; in Europe and western Asia they coexisted with more ancient groups of hominids known today as Neanderthals and various other more ancient Asian members of the genus *Homo*.

These early humans were accomplished hunters, gatherers, and scavengers. Like their ape cousins, they had complex social orders and sophisticated forms of communication, and they spread across much of the ancient world. But they were somehow different from the humans who would soon come and replace them (either through interbreeding or warfare or both) and who would also wipe out their European *Homo neanderthalis* and early Asian *Homo sapiens* neighbors.

When the "new" humans arrived in Europe between thirty thousand and forty thousand years ago, they brought with them from Africa the ability to produce sophisticated art, much of which survives today in cave paintings in France, Spain, and Germany that are similar in kind and are of equal antiquity to art that exists in the Southern Hemisphere from Africa to Australia. These new people had invented spear-throwing tools and arrows that made their hunting so effective they managed to wipe out the largest land mammals on every continent they visited, from the wooly mammoths of Europe, Asia, and North America to the giant Mao birds of New Zealand.

And the "new" humans traded and cooperated with each other in ways the "old" humans didn't. Stone, flint, and obsidian tools and weapons made more than forty thousand years ago are almost always found near the places where the material for them was quarried; those made after this point are often found hundreds or even thousands of miles from the site of the materials from which they're made.

For these reasons, this particular point in time—about forty thousand years ago—is referred to as "the dawn of human civilization."

3

Three Ways Humans Were Killed Off by Weather

Nature is most dangerous and
most beautiful at its extremes.

ROB KALL

The question paleoanthropologists around the world confront today is this: What happened forty thousand years ago that may have caused a "bottleneck" in the human population and thus punctuated the equilibrium of human evolution? What caused a change in the human genome, influencing our behavior forty thousand years ago and still influencing us today?

Once the isthmus of Panama was filled in three million years ago, the current that carried warmth in and salt out of the North Atlantic was forced to flow all the way around the frigid southern tip of Africa (where it mixed with waters from the Antarctic Circumpolar Stream) then up to Europe, Greenland, and the Arctic Ocean. Thus began the Great Conveyor Belt of the Gulf Stream, and winter settled over North America and Europe for a few months each year.

The Great Conveyor Belt wasn't particularly stable, however. All it took was a relatively small change in temperature in the North Atlantic—just a few degrees—to shut it down. Throughout the three million years of the Great Ice Age, including the time up to the present, this temperature change has usually been caused by one of three agents: the sun, active volcanoes, or the release of large amounts of CO_2 into the atmosphere, as in the current manmade global warming phenomenon. (At the end of this book we'll visit more in depth this third cause of the Gulf Stream's shut down.)

WARMING BY THE SUN

Interestingly, warming by the sun has apparently been the most common reason for the climate's flip-flops from temperate to ice age. The sun has a normal cycle of about 1500 years during which its solar radiation gradually increases and then decreases, pulsing like a heartbeat. The systolic, "pushing" beat increases the warmth of the Earth. About 750 years later, the diastolic, "reducing" beat cools the Earth. After another 750 years (more or less) the pushing beat is again ascendant and the Earth warms again.

Because the Great Conveyor Belt is relatively unstable, and was particularly unstable more than ten thousand years ago, not much change was required—just a single degree or two—to shut it down and thereby alter global temperatures. All it took was a small nudge of extra heat, too much fresh water, or not enough cold water to cause surface water to sink, to shut down the Gulf Stream and plunge Europe into an ice age. Throughout the three million years of the current ice age, since the closure of the isthmus of Panama, it has often shut down simply as a result of solar variations.

At such times, when the sun warmed the north enough to melt arctic and Greenland ice, rivers full of cold, fresh water pour into the North Atlantic. This diluted the saltiness of the North Atlantic, changing the density of the cold, falling water and shutting down the southerly return flow of the Great Conveyor Belt. Because warm water was no longer being drawn up in the Gulf Stream, the Atlantic cooled and no longer released heat to Europe.

When the Great Conveyor Belt stopped running, it took only a few years—again, between three and a dozen—for the Atlantic to cool, which then caused Europe's weather to shift to Alaska-like weather (Northern England and Scotland are about the same latitude as Juneau, Alaska). At such times, forests died off, replaced by tundra and permafrost, and all the humans who depended on agriculture for their food were wiped out. Only the nomads, who could quickly change their food supply and easily move from place to place, survived.

South of Europe, in Africa, the shutting down of the Great Conveyor Belt and the resultant cooling of the Atlantic meant that evaporation dropped off from the ocean's now not-so-warm surface. The result wasn't ice, but equally dangerous drought, famine, and wildfires across the continent that were just as deadly to the evolving humans as were the sheets of ice covering the European and Asian continents to the north.

So we see that for much of what we used to think of as a continuous ice age, there were instead 750- to 1500-year cycles of ice age–type weather interspersed with similarly timed periods of weather akin to what we have today. As mentioned, the ice ages came on so suddenly that they killed off most of the humans who were either tied to the land (farmers) or were unwilling or unable to move quickly or innovate.

To make matters even worse, in the midst of all this climactic upheaval, periodically there were huge volcanic events that threw the entire planet into "volcanic winters" that could last years—the sun turned dull red, the rains and snows ceased altogether, and the world was plunged even further into a deep freeze. These volcanic punctuations in the solar-driven cycles of climate change created the truly horrific bottleneck conditions necessary to drive the pump of evolution.

VULCAN'S HAMMER

On June 15, 1991, the volcano Mt. Pinatubo in the Philippines erupted, blasting a cubic mile of rock, gases, and ash as deep as twenty-two miles into the atmosphere. The twenty million tons of sulfur dioxide Pinatubo injected into the stratosphere caused the following year to be cooler than normal by a half degree Celsius, leading Americas' El Niño phenomenon.

And, although the eruption of Mt. Pinatubo was a big event for the twentieth century, on time's large scale, it was a small volcano. Consider the Bulsan Volcano, which rises about a mile into the air above Sorsogon province in the Philippines, with four distinct craters and a base area covering over four hundred square kilometers.

Although it's erupted eighteen times since 1852, the gigantic event that formed it—and perhaps many of the other volcanoes in the long chain that stretches through the Philippines—occurred forty thousand years ago, according to the Philippine government.[1] The explosion alone would have darkened much of southeast Asia for days, raining deadly ash, rock, and gases for thousands of square miles. It would have cooled the planet so significantly that for as many as thirty years afterward rainforests would have become deserts, deserts would have become floodplains, and virtually every region of the earth would have experienced devastating consequences.

And then there is Elbrus, rising more than three and a half miles into the air, the highest peak of the Caucuses in Eastern Europe. The volcanic eruption that formed this mountain and the others in its chain, including Mt. Bolshoi, Mt. Malye, and Mt. Shatshamaz, would have been so devastating as to cause worldwide conditions like those of a nuclear winter, creating a vast die-off of plant and animals. Like so many such occurrences, it happened approximately forty thousand years ago.[2]

And there is Nisyros, an ancient volcano that forms one of the Greek islands and is home to the town of Mandraki. The last major eruption in the Mediterranean region was recorded by Pliny the Younger. When Vesuvius, in southern Italy, erupted in 79 c.e., Pliny wrote that the blackness that enclosed the day was more like a closed room than a dark night; people couldn't see those just feet away from them. Thousands died, but that was the small eruption of a single volcano. The entire chain was ablaze during a time estimated to be about forty thousand years ago.[3]

Also in Italy is the 924-meter-high volcano Stromboli that's in constant activity to this day, with its last "big" eruption occurring in 1930. The island is, according to some sources, forty thousand years old.[4]

And perhaps most significant for us in the United States, the mountains of America's Pacific Northwest have a long history. According to the U.S. Park Service, "Many of the lavas that make up upper Mount Rainier overlie, and are thus younger than, a lava that erupted forty thousand years ago (as measured by radiometric techniques)."[5]

Looking at volcanic activity around the world, it seems that the time of forty thousand years ago wasn't just a period of significant change in the human genome; it was also a period of massive pyrotechnic display on at least three continents, all dramatically altering the world's weather. Volcanoes are hot, but their climatic consequence worldwide is cold weather because the gases and ash they project into the atmosphere keep sunlight from the earth. The amount of climate change produced by a volcanic eruption is a function of the amount of sulfuric acid the volcano throws up into the stratosphere, where it reflects sunlight and cools the earth below.

When scientists bored into the Greenland ice sheet in 1996, they discovered that the layers could be measured to 110,000 years ago. According to data from Gregory Zielinski of the University of Maine, a member of the team that pulled the data from the Greenland ice, the sixteenth largest period for atmospheric sulfuric acid produced by volcanoes in the past 110,000 years was 40,062 years ago, when the concentration was 374 parts per billion. (By contrast, the average annual value during the past five thousand years was 5 ppb.) The following graph (fig. 3.1) depicts the values from about that time, dated in "years before 2000."

While the events of this time weren't as huge as the interstellar impact that ended the reign of the dinosaurs sixty-five million years ago, and thus wouldn't have left such conspicuous "boundary layer" sediments all over the world, they could easily have been serious enough to disrupt the food supply for humans, particularly if they were experimenting with agriculture (and there is evidence of agricultural experiments going back more than one hundred thousand years).

Perhaps most important, at a time when the North Atlantic current (the Great Conveyor Belt of the Gulf Stream) was so unstable that it could cease as the result of a small change in global temperature caused by solar variations, such volcanic events could easily have altered the planet's temperature enough to flip-flop that current and suddenly change the world's climate for the next thousand or more years.

The result would be that the only humans to survive were those with a small genetic difference, a tiny mutation—perhaps carried by a single tribe or family (remember that the Y chromosome tests done in 2000 indicated that all men in Europe may be descended from two individuals)—and these people reproduced and repopulated the world.

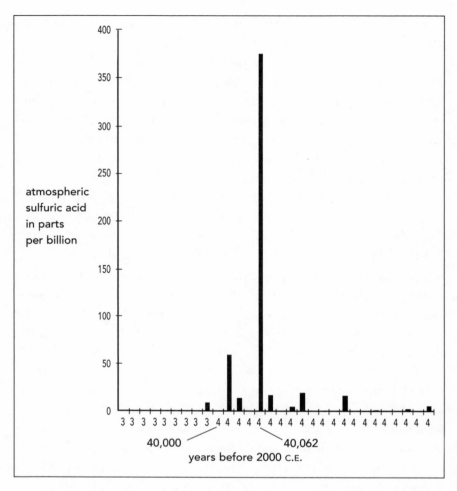

Fig. 3.1. Atmospheric Evidence Of Volcano-Induced Weather Changes

In 1998, volcanologists Michael Rampino, Stephen Self, and Greg Zielinski determined that seventy-one thousand years ago there was a severe volcanic explosion in the Toba volcano in Sumatra. According to *Science Daily* magazine,[6] the eruption produced six consecutive years of "a horrific volcanic winter" that was "followed by the coldest 1000 years of the last Ice Age, [which] brought widespread famine and death to modern human populations around the world."

Dr. Stanley Ambrose proposed a "Weak Garden Of Eden/Volcanic

Winter" hypothesis based on this information, suggesting that of the entire planet's human population "no more than fifteen thousand to forty thousand people survived." The result was that the genetic variations or mutations among that small number became amplified as they reproduced and repopulated the earth, transforming the nature of *Homo sapiens*. It was a bottleneck event in the classic model of evolutionary punctuated equilibrium.

A less severe event thirty thousand years later apparently led to the emergence of the novelty-seeking and distractibility/scanning genes that we're finding so common today.

SURVIVORS: AIDS CHIMPS AND THE BLACK PLAGUE

Weather changes aren't the only thing that can crash a population and produce a bottleneck that causes an evolutionary jump. Historically, mutations or changes in the habitats of viruses or bacteria have probably prompted as many species crashes and resulting bottlenecks— leading to evolutionary leaps—as have weather. And, of course, it doesn't just happen in humans.

For example, in the past five years, scientists specializing in HIV have found two interesting bits of data. The first came when it was learned that chimpanzees across Africa are nearly all infected with a simian form of HIV. "Dutch researchers theorize that an AIDS-like epidemic wiped out huge numbers of chimpanzees 2 million years ago," the Associated Press reported on August 20, 2002, "leaving modern chimps with resistance to the AIDS virus and its variants. If true, the hypothesis would explain why chimps, which share more than 98 percent of their DNA with humans, don't develop AIDS."

Similarly, in the 1990s, scientists discovered that some humans are immune to AIDS, and they tracked this immunity to a rare gene variation known as CCR5-delta32. A very few people of European ancestry carry one copy of this gene, and a much smaller number of people inherit two copies of it, one from each parent. Those people with two CCR5-delta32 genes are immune to AIDS, even though they can carry HIV.

Perhaps most interesting is the revelation that the gene that gives immunity to AIDS also confers immunity to the bacterium *Yersinia pestis*, cause of the black plague, which wiped out as much as a third of all Europeans in its first wave across the continent in 1347. Somebody carrying the CCR5-delta32 gene mutation survived and passed the gene along to his or her offspring. Survivors married survivors and produced children carrying the gene variation, amplifying the gene in the European gene pool over the three centuries of plague epidemics to the point where 10 percent of Europeans carry one copy of it—but virtually no other humans from other parts of the world carry the gene, including Caucasians of European ancestry, unless their ancestors were in Europe in the fourteenth century. (In order to be immune to AIDS, a person must carry two copies of the gene, one from each parent, which is a rare occurrence.)

Thus, another possibility for the event that caused the crash and bottleneck of human populations forty thousand years ago is that some disease ran through the world's people, wiping out some but not others. The dopamine genes—those associated with both ADHD and obsessive-compulsive disorder (OCD)—may have been an advantage if, for instance, the disease were transmissible through poor hygiene: People who were fastidiously clean (such as those who washed their hands compulsively, an OCD behavior) would have avoided getting sick.

CREATIVITY SAVES THE DAY

But the most likely way humans made it through one or more of these crises is through the same evolutionary means that drove the increase in the brain's size and complexity: creativity.

When weather changed or people started dropping dead from an unknown disease, those who slavishly continued to do things the way they'd always been done were the most likely to be wiped out. Farmers who believed they could weather a few bad winters would have starved to death within a year or two, depending on how good their stores were.

The crumbling remains of now-lost civilizations tell a similar story: When circumstances changed, leaders continued to insist that business be carried out as it had been before, using the same methods of producing food and the same forms of governance, and propitiating the same gods, until everything around them was a shambles.

For example, the introduction of smallpox to Mexico by Spaniards looking for gold in 1520 led to a raging epidemic that wiped out between 65 and 95 percent of all humans living in Central and South America. Europeans carried the disease but also carried the gene for relative immunity to it; only 5 to 20 percent of infected Europeans died from smallpox. Most, like the pock-marked George Washington, merely carried the scars of the infection. The native residents of the Americas, however, had never before been exposed to smallpox, so they died in such huge numbers that Pizarro was able to conquer the entire Incan civilization—most of South America—with fewer than three hundred men.

The native South Americans who survived, however, were peoples like the Kogi of Colombia, who separated themselves from the larger culture, retreating to a remote mountain community fed by glacier water, and invented for themselves a new way to live. They survive to this day (although their glacier is now melting so fast from global warming that their water supply may be gone within fifty years).

When the 535 C.E. eruption of Krakatoa threw the world into several years of volcanic winter, a similar scenario of upended civilization was set into motion. Crops failed across the Middle East, Asia, and Europe. The drought in Africa was so severe that plague-carrying gerbils left their remote habitat and tried to compete with rats for the scraps from human tables in the cities along the coast of the Indian Ocean. Traders sailing north from the plague-infested cities of eastern Africa carried the disease to the Middle East and Europe in waves over the successive centuries, altering the political and social landscape every time they passed through. The political dislocation caused by the famines that followed the crop failures badly cracked the Roman Empire, setting the stage for its overthrow in the Middle East by the upstart religion of Islam.

The lessons of history show that the creative individuals—Mohammed and his followers in the Middle East, members of the Kogi and other tribes of South America who split away from the Inca, the British settlers who were offended by King George II and were so enraged by King George III that they declared independence from him and created the United States of America—are the ones who survived and prospered.

It's not much of a stretch to think that those people who, forty thousand years ago, carried the Edison gene and were willing to try new things, live in new ways, and move to new lands were the ones who not only inherited the world but also figured out better ways to survive and thrive.

ADHD AND CREATIVITY

ADHD is associated with higher levels of creativity, according to a study published in 1991 by researchers Geraldine Shaw of Georgetown College and Geoffrey Brown of the University of East Anglia in England. They found "a stable pattern of characteristics associated with ADHD and high intelligence."[7] Because of their "distractibility," these children often keenly notice things in their environment and think divergently.

Shaw and Brown bluntly stated that "those with attention problems . . . showed higher figural creativity." The reason, they concluded, was that "despite (or perhaps because of) their inability to focus attention normally, they are able to process and use large amounts of relatively scattered bits of information which appear to overwhelm, or to be ignored, by more verbally oriented [normal] children."

In another study published by the *Journal of Creative Behavior,* researcher Bonnie Cramond found that a "higher creativity score, sensation seeking, and use of imagery are common descriptors of creative individuals." She noted that ADHD children "have more internal distractions from fleeting sensory input" and quoted a 1992 study that "speculates that such spontaneous and diverse ideation may be part of the process that fosters more creative responses on a test of divergent thinking."

"In summary," Caramond wrote, "there is evidence to support the hypothesis that both creatives and those classified as ADHD show greater indications of mixed laterality and anomalies in cerebral dominance, more spontaneous ideation, higher levels of sensation seeking behavior, and higher energy and activity than do normal populations."[8]

The results of another study on ADHD and creativity were published by Cornell University's Stephen J. Ceci and Jayne Tishman in the journal *Child Development.* Titled "Hyperactivity and Incidental Memory: Evidence for Attentional Diffusion,"[9] the article explains a series of fascinating experiments determining the differences between the abilities of ADHD children and "normal" children relative to perception and recall. These differences may contribute to the marked creativity of Edison-gene children. They cite a series of studies showing that "it appears that hyperactive children's attention is more readily distracted than normal children's attention by the presence of task-irrelevant information. Hyperactive children engage in more diffuse (off task) eye movements, head-turns, and so on during learning than do normal children."[10]

This doesn't mean, however, that these children don't learn—on the contrary, they're learning more than their "normal" peers, in two different dimensions. "It is apparent that, despite their greater distractibility, hyperactive children's memory for task-relevant information is not impeded by the introduction of task-irrelevant stimuli."[11]

In one of the experimental models, non-medicated ADHD children and "normal" children of equal intelligence were given a series of 120 picture cards to memorize in two-second sequences. On the walls of the room in which the test was administered were six posters seemingly unrelated to the testing and the study. When the two groups of children were tested to determine how well they did in memorizing the 120 cards, "As anticipated, nonhyperactive children's free recall (M=6.32, SD=1.57) was superior to that of hyperactive children (M=4.7, SD=1.65)" with a p value of less than .001.[12]

"In contrast to their inferior recall of the targets," the researchers discovered, "hyperactive children recalled significantly more of the most extrinsic stimuli, that is, the six posters that were affixed to the walls of the testing room, recalling, on average, 2.79 extrinsic pictures, whereas their nonhyperactive peers recalled only .58 pictures."[13] Further, the ADHD children were more competent at knowing whether their memory of detail was from the 120 target cards or from the "irrelevant" six posters in the room. "Overall," the researchers wrote, "hyperactive children were significantly better than their nonhyperactive peers at discriminating the original stimuli, after controlling for response bias."[14]

The ADHD children also had higher levels of certainty (true

knowledge) of the target cards. "While both groups of children correctly detected approximately 84 percent of the original stimuli," they wrote, "hyperactive children had approximately 50 percent fewer false alarms (i.e., affirming cards that were not originally shown) than nonhyperactive children." Additionally, the researchers noted, "Not only were hyperactive children better at discriminating targets from distracters, when the latter were considered as a group, but they committed fewer false recognitions at each level of missing information than their nonhyperactive peers."[15]

THE BEADS: CLUE TO THE FIRST EDISONS

Dr. Richard Klein, a Stanford professor of anthropology, and Blake Edgar, a science writer, believe that the discovery of the forty-thousand-year-old ostrich shell beads indicate a clear transition point for humanity, reflecting genetic changes to our brains as well as the early stirrings of fully modern human culture.

In their book *The Dawn of Human Culture*, they note, "In our view, the simplest and most economic explanation for the 'dawn' [of human culture] is that it stemmed from a fortuitous mutation that [survived the bottleneck and] promoted the fully modern human brain."[16]

But what might be that "fortuitous mutation"? Is it possible that what we now call a genetic "disorder" is actually *the* positive adaptation—that "fortuitous mutation"—that led to the creation of human culture and modern civilization as we know it?

Part 2

The Present

*If we are to achieve a richer culture,
rich in contrasting values, we must recognize the
whole gamut of human potentialities, and so weave
a less arbitrary social fabric, one in which each
diverse human gift will find a fitting place.*

MARGARET MEAD

While the rapid spurts of evolutionary progress our species has made in the past half million years have apparently been driven most often by violent and sudden climate change, the past ten thousand years have been a time of relative climatic calm. The result has been the rise of cities and civilizations and the blossoming of human population from fewer than a billion when the United States was founded in the late eighteenth century to over six billion today.

Regardless of the changes that have befallen humans in the past or may hit us in the future, the institutions controlling our present are very much organized along the lines of, "This is the way it's always been; this is how we've always done it; and this is how we'll continue to do it."

And those who don't fit in, to paraphrase Robert Service, often find themselves noticed, diagnosed, marginalized, medicated, or cast aside.

4

Anatomy of a Diagnosis

[School is to be a factory] in which raw products,
children, are to be shaped and formed into
finished products . . . [m]anufactured like nails,
and the specifications for manufacturing will come
from government and industry.

ELWOOD P. CUBBERLEY,
DEAN OF SCHOOL OF EDUCATION,
STANFORD UNIVERSITY, 1905

The creatures that want to live a life of their own, we
call wild. If wild, then no matter how harmless, we treat
them as outlaws, and those of us who are 'specially well
brought up shoot them for fun.

CLARENCE DAY, *THE SIMIAN WORLD*

In 1855, seven-year-old Thomas Edison was first enrolled in school in Port Huron, Michigan. After just three months in public school, his teacher had reached the end of his rope with Edison's constant interruptions and questions. Suggesting that the boy's brain was "addled," he sent Tom home with a reprimand.

As one Edison biographer, Gerald Beals, notes on the Web site thomasedison.com, "If modern psychology had existed back then, the genuinely hyperactive [Edison] would have probably been deemed a victim of attention deficit syndrome and given a prescription for the 'miracle drug' Ritalin."

Of course, during Edison's time, the label Attention Deficit Hyperactive Disorder (ADHD) didn't exist. Children who had his same symptoms were simply the ones who didn't fit in. As Robert Service (1874–1958) wrote in his famous poem "The Men Who Don't Fit In": "There's a race of men that don't fit in, a race that can't stay still."

In the 1930s, following an East Coast epidemic of encephalitis (an inflammation of the brain), teachers brought to the attention of the medical industry the observation that some of the children who'd had encephalitis weren't able to pay attention well in school. This led to the creation of the diagnostic category of *Encephalitic Brain Damage* or EBD. As time went on and authorities began looking for children who weren't doing well in school, it was discovered that many children with attention problems in the classroom had never had encephalitis, so the EBD category was changed to *Minimal Brain Damage* or MBD. By the 1970s the use of the term "brain damage" was considered a bit stark, so the term was softened to *Minimal Brain Deficit* (still MBD), and the category of hyperactivity, hyperkinesis, or hyperactive syndrome was added.

HOW EDISON-GENE CHILDREN ARE DIFFERENT

Children with the Edison gene display three primary differences from those who do not have it.

They are constantly noticing everything in their environment, something called "scanning" in the forest or jungle, but in the classroom Edison-gene children are called *distractible*.

Mentally they're very fast on their feet and are able to make snap decisions. In the forest or jungle this ability helped in making the split-second choices that ensured survival, much as it helps today when playing video games or flying fighter planes or working in an emergency room. But in the classroom, Edison-gene children are called *impulsive*.

Requiring high-stimulation environments, Edison-gene children are *easily bored* when they're not given a challenge or something interesting to do. While in hunter days these people may have been the very best and most excited hunters, in classrooms they're called *hyperactive* because if what's happening in class isn't stimulating enough for them, they create their own stimulation.

ARE THEY DISORDERED?

My first exposure to hyperactive children came in 1978, when I was executive director of a residential treatment facility for abused and emotionally disturbed children. Noticing that most of the children who were referred to our facility brought with them the diagnosis of Minimal Brain Deficit (MBD) or Hyperactive Syndrome, I determined to learn as much as I could about these conditions. Senator Ted Kennedy was holding hearings about "hyperactive children" in Washington D.C. that year, and there was great controversy in the field.

A year earlier, Dr. Ben Feingold, a pediatric allergist at Kaiser Permanente Hospital in San Francisco, had published his book *Why Your Child Is Hyperactive*, suggesting that Hyperactive or MBD Syndrome might be, in part, an allergic type of response to the salicylate-based food additives that had begun to trickle into the American food supply in the 1950s and entered in a veritable flood in the 1960s and 1970s. Curious, I flew to San Francisco to meet with Dr. Feingold and began a study of his proposition by removing all food additives from the diets of our children. The study, which I published in 1981 in the *Journal of Orthomolecular Psychiatry*, concluded that while diet may play a role in hyperactivity, it isn't an exclusive role.

A decade later, my curiosity about what was then known as ADD became personal when one of my children was diagnosed with it after a tough year in school. That diagnosis led to the 1993 publication of my first book about ADHD, titled *Attention Deficit Disorder: A Different Perception*. The book offered a new perspective for high-energy, stimulation-seeking children and their parents who were, as I was, uncomfortable with the medical-model diagnosis of a brain "disorder." I wrote that though they are brain-wired in a way that doesn't respond well to the structure of our modern schools, they could think of themselves as the carriers of a behavioral skill set that would make them spectacular hunter/gatherer people.

ANTHROPOLOGY MEETS PSYCHOLOGY

This anthropological view of a behavior that psychiatrists and psychologists had laid claim to drew sharp criticism, particularly from a small group of psychologists who obtained funding and benefits from the pharmaceutical industry. At the same time, however, others in the field of psychology were suggesting it was time to revisit psychological definitions in a cultural context.

For example, Stephen J. Ceci, in his groundbreaking book *On Intelligence,* notes that, "A popular thesis in the anthropological research has been that different environmental demands associated with different cultures lead to the development of different patterns of ability across cultures."[1]

This point is largely lost on psychologists, however, who want to use the same tests and measurements for everybody, everywhere, regardless of background or upbringing. As Ceci notes:

> There are many reasons why psychologists have ignored the insights of anthropologists, but perhaps no single reason is more important than the clash of disciplinary values. Simply stated, psychologists and anthropologists have operated under differing assumptions about the nature of knowledge and scientific explanation. As a result, the rules of evidence can be quite different in the two disciplines.

Using the anthropological view, my "hunter versus farmer" hypothesis suggested that it would be useful to view these high-energy characteristics not as defects, but as a set of traits that might be very useful in the right setting, if properly understood. My book showed that what our society sees as problems can be seen very differently if viewed as skills that are useful in a hunting society. At that time, my idea of high-energy children being the genetic descendants of ancient hunters, explorers, and discoverers was just a story or a metaphor—but it was a *useful* metaphor: It helped rescue the self-esteem of children who'd been told they had "broken" or "disordered" brains, and it offered them (and their parents) a positive, useful way to view themselves and the world.

And it worked. In the years since then, a startling number of people—parents and children alike, as well as physicians and therapists on four continents—have written me to say that the metaphor has served them well.

FROM HUNTERS TO INVENTORS

Now, a decade later, new research has proved that my hunter/farmer idea is more than just a metaphor: It turns out there's solid scientific evidence that our high-energy children really do carry a new gene that first emerged when hunter people began to behave in a whole new way, at that time now called "the dawn of human civilization." This explains why the initial reframing was so effective for people: It was accurate, and parents sensed the truth in it even before the research arrived to prove it.

The impact of reframing our thinking extends far beyond those who have already been given labels such as ADHD or learning disability or hyperactivity. There are literally millions of children in America—perhaps tens of millions—who carry this gene and stand at an uneasy precipice: As a response to their failing or under-performing in school, they can be isolated and diagnosed and drugged, or they can be nurtured, inspired, and brought to their full potential.

The important question today isn't whether or not a child should be labeled (or what the label should be), but instead, how we can help each of our children grow into an effective, happy, healthy adult.

5

The Mystery of
Novelty-Seeking Behavior

*Every great advance in natural knowledge has involved
the absolute rejection of authority.*

THOMAS HENRY HUXLEY

John rushes out onto the dance floor, while Bill stands by the wall, not willing to take the chance that he won't find a dance partner. Susan goes skydiving for her thirty-first birthday, but her sister Amy won't even get on the roller coaster at the nearby amusement park. We take tests to determine if we're introverts or extraverts, quiet and shy or outgoing and curious, but what determines who's going to turn out how?

Nature versus nurture is the age-old controversy over the roles played by genetics and environment in the development of children to adults. It's important, however, to put this battle in context, because both our genetics and our environment can have a powerful effect on who we become.

As anybody knows who is familiar with the unique behaviors of different breeds of dogs, some components of how animals think and behave are genetically determined. Hitler tried to use this fact to suggest that different human races have different mental competencies and moralities, and he used Darwin's own words to support his case. (In his *Descent of Man*, Darwin implied that some human races might be more evolved than others, reflecting the Victorian-era thinking that sanctioned Britain's conquest, colonization, and exploitation of lands occupied by "inferior" or "primitive" peoples.) But nothing like Hitler's theory has ever been credibly demonstrated; the differences in human brains based on race are so tiny as to be irrelevant.

At the same time, however, we know that some traits such as novelty-seeking behavior are genetically transmitted from parent to child and exist in all races. In fact, novelty-seeking is one of the most thoroughly studied of such behaviors. And today we know exactly where much of it comes from. The story is fascinating.

THE "NOVELTY GENE"

The gene most closely associated with hyperactivity, sensation seeking, curiosity, and ADHD was thoroughly researched for the first time in the 1990s. It's called the DRD4 gene,* and it apparently contributes to these behaviors by controlling the brain's level of the neurotransmitter dopamine, the chemical that's responsible for the sensitivity of our thalamus and cortex to sensory stimulation. Variations of the gene mean that different people have different levels of dopamine.

People whose dopamine levels are genetically low seek out stimulation in the world. People with genetically high levels of dopamine tend to be more passive and less sensation- or novelty-seeking in their behaviors.[1] It's important to realize that there's no correct or incorrect level of dopamine. To a geneticist, the only question is, "What's best suited for survival?" And that depends entirely on the situation.

For scientists trying to figure out the biological basis of personality and behavior, 1996 was a banner year in whcih Richard P. Ebstein and his colleagues at Ben-Gurion University and Herzog Memorial

---

* Genetics terms such as *DRD4* can seem cryptic, but they do reflect their meanings. *DR* in this gene name refers to "dopamine receptor," a receptor being a feature in the brain that determines how a particular chemical is received. *D4* refers to a specific gene that affects dopamine receptors. The real significance of DRD4 is that in it we have finally discovered how a specific gene connects to our behavior: This gene influences how the brain responds to a specific neurochemical—dopamine—which affects how we naturally respond to our environment.

Hospital in Israel published in the journal *Nature Genetics*[2] the results of a fascinating genetic and behavioral study they'd completed examining how risk-taking and novelty-seeking behavior might be genetically determined. As the journal *The Scientist* noted,[3] they found a variation on the dopamine receptor gene among such people and therefore concluded, "These people tend to be extroverted, impulsive, extravagant, quick-tempered, excitable, and exploratory."

Another study completed by Jonathan Benjamin, Dean Hamer, and colleagues at the National Institutes of Health in the United States and published in 1996 in *Nature Genetics*,[4] found, as reported in *The Scientist*, "Those who scored highest in novelty-seeking, impulsive, quick-tempered, and fickle were more likely to have long repeats of DNA subunits in their D4 dopamine receptor gene." Both studies looked at these behaviors, according to *The Scientist*,[5] "through personality inventories that gauged four dimensions: novelty-seeking, harm avoidance, reward dependence, and persistence."

The attention of the scientific world was now riveted on the DRD4 gene. Because a gene can carry different variations or "repeats," it can encode for or against a particular characteristic. In 1998, a study was published in *Molecular Psychiatry* by Epstein, Levine, Geller, et al., that looked at the DRD4 dopamine gene and a serotonin promoter gene in two-week-old newborns. By "using the well-known Neonatal Behavioral Assessment Scale which was designed to evaluate the temperament of the newborn baby," the researchers reported they found "a significant association of the so-called 'novelty seeking' gene across four behavioral clusters pertinent to newborn temperament."[6]

Industry, sensing profit in these findings, got on the ball, and by the next year scientists had discovered that people with a particular variation of this gene were more likely to become addicted to tobacco, presumably because they enjoyed the "novelty" or sensation that the drug nicotine produces.[7] Thus the industry determined that tobacco ads should feature people being athletic, taking risks, and behaving in an extroverted fashion if it wanted those who were most easily addicted to identify with them.

THE NOVELTY GENE AND ADHD

Researchers in the field of ADHD were also intrigued by the work that had been reported on the DRD4 gene because novelty-seeking behavior closely matches descriptions of the behaviors that drive ADHD diagnosis, and, in addition, some studies had indicated that people with ADHD are at greater risk for addictions. Sure enough, by 2001, six different peer-reviewed studies had been published in scientific journals associating the specific 7R (seven repeats) allele (al-LEELE), or variation, of the DRD4 gene with ADHD,[8] and other recent research linked it with traits such as curiosity, inventiveness, and a willingness to take risks or strike out in unorthodox directions.

In 1996, *Molecular Psychiatry* published a paper titled "Dopamine D4 Receptor Gene Polymorphism Is Associated with Attention Deficit Hyperactivity Disorder"[9] that shows a clear association between changes in the DRD4 gene and ADHD. It was followed two years later by another paper in the same journal, titled "Dopamine DRD4 Receptor Polymorphism and Attention Deficit Hyperactivity Disorder,"[10] which reported that the 7R allele of the DRD4 gene could be found more often in ADHD-inattentive children than in controls.

Another paper with the self-explanatory title "Evidence That the Dopamine D4 Receptor Is a Susceptibility Gene in Attention Deficit Hyperactivity Disorder"[11] was published in *Molecular Psychiatry* that year as well. This banner year for the journal and for the fields of ADHD study and genetics was rounded out with the publication of "Association of the Dopamine Receptor D4 (DRD4) Gene with a Refined Phenotype of Attention Deficit Hyperactivity Disorder (ADHD): A Family-Based Approach."[12]

The following year saw peer-reviewed research published about the dopamine receptor gene in *Pharmacogenetics,*[13] *Neuropsychopharmacology,*[14] and the *Journal of the American Academy of Child and Adolescent Psychiatry.*[15] An excellent summary article of the research was published in 2001 in the *Journal of the American Academy of Child and Adolescent Psychiatry.*[16] While earlier research[17] had pointed the way to this gene, some of the world's best scientists have been finding clear associations between it and ADHD, and as I write this, several more research reports are on their way to publication.

But if the 7R variation of the DRD4 dopamine gene has a connection to ADHD, many people at the end of 2001 were asking why. Why would humans develop a genetic variation producing traits that could be interpreted as a disorder? It's estimated that 15 percent of Americans carry this variation, according to Epstein's study at Ben Gurion University. Even more puzzling, then, is why this gene so common. Normally, genetic disorders that have no value but instead cause problems are quite rare and show up only in genetically isolated populations. Why, then, would the ADHD gene be found among people all over the world? Finally, a more urgent question, perhaps, for Americans, who have the highest Ritalin consumption in the world, why is the gene suddenly becoming so active?

6

Genes Move Around
and Turn On and Off

Change is the nursery of music, joy, life and Eternity.
JOHN DONNE

One of the most common questions that people ask me when I speak about ADHD is, "Why is this such a big problem now if it wasn't when I was a kid or when my parents and grandparents were in school?"

The easy answer is that up until the past few decades, America was a world leader in manufacturing. There was a huge demand for people who could work in a factory making a whole range of products, from cars to clothes to shoes. Because labor was so much in demand, wages were high enough that a union job in a factory provided sufficient income for one working parent to support an entire family and put the kids through school.

But in the past twenty years in the United States, starting largely with George H. W. Bush's "New World Order" of international "free trade" replacing historic notions of "fair trade," and accelerated by Bill Clinton's support for General Agreements on Tariffs and Trade (GATT), the World Trade Organization (WTO), and the North Atlantic Free Trade Association (NAFTA), those jobs are gone. American and European factory workers no longer compete with each other in the world labor market; they now compete with fourteen-year-old girls in Indonesia, eight-year-old boys in Pakistan, and slave labor in China.

As a result, to earn a good salary in today's America, a high school diploma isn't enough. Only a professional job provides enough income to support a middle-class family on one salary. Thus, the pressure is on now to perform academically, and it's a pressure that's never before been felt in the Western world. Our children are feeling it, our teachers are feeling it, parents are feeling it, and doctors are feeling it: *Do something! Help my child get the best grades possible so he can get into college! If he has a hard time performing in school, there must be some pill that will help him!*

But this societal shift away from manufacturing doesn't really explain why ADHD is such a big problem now, because we're seeing not only more children failing than ever before, but also more kids behaving in a more hyperactive fashion than ever before.

THE GENETICS OF BEHAVIOR

If you took biology in high school, odds are you remember the story of the nineteenth-century monk Gregor Mendel, who first suggested that genetic codes determined the nature of living organisms. For about a hundred years, biologists and geneticists believed that Mendel had proved genes made up a fixed code, determined at conception, that remained the same during the lifetime of an organism.

But in 1983, Barbara McClintock won the Nobel Prize for medicine. It was a significant event for two reasons: She was the first female solo recipient of the prize since Marie Curie, and she explained for the first time how genetic mutations occur and what events or agents can produce them. In doing so, she may have knocked Mendel off his pedestal.

McClintock was the first to discover, back in the 1920s, while examining the genes of maize, that there were specific bumps and twists on specific chromosomes that represented a way to identify one chromosome from another. In doing this, she and most of the scientific community thought she was operating within Mendel's notion of genes as being fixed biological "programs" that determined biological outcomes.

But then in 1951, while looking at the consequences of potentially cancer-causing radiation such as that used in SPECT scans today, she discovered something new, which led to her Nobel Prize: When exposed to stresses in the environment, chromosomes can break and heal and/or rearrange themselves in response to the particular type of stress they encounter. Genes have elements that can transpose or move around: There is a system of *transposable elements* as well as specific elements called *activators* and *dissociators* that control mutations.

The result of McClintock's work was a final explanation of how and why, for example, the human immune system can produce over a million *different* proteins or antibodies in response to invading bacteria or viruses—even to those the body has never before encountered. If this process were entirely controlled by an unchanging human genome, simply controlling the behavior of immune cells would require more resources than the genome has available to it. It's mathematically impossible, given what we know so far about genetics. But the ability of genes to *change* in response to their environment provides an enormous flexibility—what geneticists call *plasticity*—to living organisms, and makes the functions of our immune system plausible.

While we know that the actual genetics of our immune system are capable of changing throughout our lives in response to our environment, as of this writing nobody has looked at whether the nervous system or other bodily systems are capable of such changes. If they are, it may help to explain why it's so much harder for a forty-year-old to learn how to operate computer systems than it is for a ten-year-old: Each generation shifts slightly its genetic data that allows it to adapt to the world in which it's growing.

TURNING ON GENES

A simpler model of genetics that we know to be accurate, though it doesn't account for how the immune system works, shows that our genes contain enormous amounts of latent ability just waiting to be switched on by environmental pressures.

For example, in June 2002, researcher Andrew Camilli of the Tufts University School of Medicine reported in the journal *Nature*[1] that the bacteria that causes cholera—*Vibrio cholerae*—has a gene that is switched on only when the bacteria encounters stomach acid. Because previous researchers hadn't known about this gene, they hadn't been able to figure out how or why the bacteria is so incredibly virulent in people but grows slowly on Petrie dishes in laboratories.

The gene for celiac disease functions in the same way. Many people of northern European ancestry carry the gene for this condition in which the body's immune system reacts to the gluten protein in wheat, rye, and barley as if it were cholera or some other pathogen. I had never had a problem with these foods until, at the age of fifty, I was in Australia and contracted dysentery from contaminated water. Although antibiotics eventually knocked out the dysentery, for the next year I continued to have symptoms of a milder cholera-like illness that went away only when I eliminated all wheat, rye, and barley from my diet. A genetic test showed I'd been carrying the gene for celiac disease my entire life, and it had been switched on or activated by the dysentery I contracted in Australia. (This is common—most people with adult-onset celiac disease discover it after a bout of food poisoning that won't go away.) Now, and most likely for the rest of my life, I must totally avoid bread, pizza, and so many of the other foods that are common in a typical Western diet.

The interesting point here is that it wasn't only one cell in my body that mutated or switched on—my entire immune system and digestive tract did. It was a systemic shift, complete and seamless, that involved my whole body. And it was one that was reflected in a gene I've carried my entire life, presumably inherited from one of my Norwegian ancestors. (Celiac disease is very common in Scandinavia.)

Additionally, there's a natural logic and internal intelligence to what my immune system did, even though it was slightly off the mark. It turns out that many pathogenic gut bacteria produce waste proteins that are chemically similar to a part of gluten, the main protein in wheat. When a pathogen is present, the immune system reorganizes itself to react to its proteins, but after they've been eliminated, it mistakenly thinks wheat gluten is an indicator of the continuing presence of intestinal contamination.

A similar process occurs in over 90 percent of all people of African or Asian ancestry and about 20 percent (depending on whose numbers you use) of people of European ancestry who have a condition called *lactose intolerance*, which causes them to experience gas or other intestinal distress when they drink milk or eat products that contain milk sugar (lactose).

For years, it was assumed that people with lactose intolerance lacked a specific gene to encode for the production in the stomach of lactase, the enzyme that breaks down lactose so that it's digestible. But in research conducted at UCLA and in Finland and reported in the January 14, 2002, issue of *Nature Genetics*, scientists who looked at the genetic profiles of 196 lactose-intolerant people descended from Finland, Africa, Europe, and Korea and other parts of Asia found they all had the same identical gene. "If [a genetic disorder] is found around the world, genetics tells us that it must be very old," said researcher Leena Peitonen, who chairs the Human Genetics Program at UCLA and led the study. "Perhaps," she added, "it was even in the genome of humans before they migrated out of Africa."

In fact, everybody has a gene that tells the stomach to stop producing the enzyme lactase when a person is weaned. But in northern Europe, where people eat dairy products daily, the gene doesn't get a chance to turn itself off—people there are, in effect, never weaned. But if they go a year or two without dairy products, even people of Scandinavian ancestry often find themselves incapable of digesting milk thereafter, because the switch of that gene has been flipped by the dietary change.

CODOMINANT GENES

Another model that illustrates whether or not a gene is turned on is that of genetic *dominance:* We all carry two copies of each gene, one that we inherited from our mother and one that we inherited from our father. If one of these genes is dominant, it will take over, or be expressed—the way brown eyes are most often expressed in the children of a brown-eyed parent and a blue-eyed parent—and the unused gene from the other parent will remain unexpressed, latent, or recessive.

But genes don't always have dominant or recessive characteristics— some are what's called *codominant.* When you have two codominant genes, they are *both* expressed.

An example of this is the blood type AB, resulting when a person inherits a gene for Type A blood from one parent and a gene for Type

B blood from the other parent. Because these genes are codominant, both are expressed; a person has both Type A and Type B blood at the same time, which we refer to as Type AB.

Dominance in dopamine and other neurotransmitter genes is still a very hotly debated topic. It's even possible that in neurotransmitter genes there exists codominance or instances of two competing genes being able to alternate dominance, depending on the environment or other factors. These theories are all on the cutting edge of genetic research.

TURNING ON EDISON CHARACTERISTICS

Combining these insights into how genes work with the explosion of the numbers of children taking Ritalin raises this question: If many of us carry the DRD4 gene, is it possible that an environmental stressor or activator is required in order to turn it on?

Could it be that in a sedate world, it remains dormant, just as my celiac gene did for fifty years, but that when the world is perceived to be more dangerous, or input becomes more rapid-fire (such as it does when we watch television or play video games), the nervous system reacts by turning on the gene in order to produce the adaptive, response-ready behavior?

At this point, nobody knows. If this is the case, however, it, along with the other variables we'll explore in the next chapter, could help account for the explosion in ADHD diagnoses.

7

Other Genes
and Influences

*In questions of science the authority of a thousand is
not worth the humble reasoning of a single individual.*
GALILEO

As with many other things in life, ADHD isn't simple, and therefore we can't confine it to a single gene. Actually, it isn't even a single condition—most scientists in the field are coming to the conclusion that the label is a "wastebasket diagnosis," that is, a giant category that encompasses many different conditions, with many—perhaps most—of them not being pathologies or illnesses at all, but just variations on the human condition.

As of this writing, there are forty-nine different genes that have been implicated in ADHD. While the DRD4 gene is still considered the major one, others color or shade the type of ADHD a person has, pushing them more towards hyperactivity or impulsivity or scanning behaviors.

There are other examples of such multiple-gene connections. In 1990, Dr. Kenneth Blum and associates found an association between the A1 allele variation of the DRD2 dopamine gene and alcoholism. It was a brief sensation in the newspapers, called "the alcoholism gene." But as Blum and others did more research into the DRD2 gene, they found the A1 allele variation played a role in a variety of compulsive and addictive behaviors, ranging from compulsive gambling to alcoholism to Tourette's syndrome. But for such behaviors to fully manifest, the presence of an environmental trigger is required (gambling, for example, must be available for a person to become a compulsive gambler), as well as the A1 version of the DRD2 gene and other associated genes arranged in particular ways to support the behavior.

As Blum and associates wrote in an *American Scientist* article about what they called the "reward deficiency syndrome" associated with the DRD2 gene:

> Needless to say, there is no such thing as a specific gene for alcoholism, obesity or a particular type of personality. However, it would be naive to assert the opposite, that these aspects of human behavior are not associated with any particular genes. Rather, the issue at hand is to understand how certain genes and behavioral traits are connected.

NEUROTRANSMITTERS AND PERSONALITY CHARACTERISTICS

Researchers have identified four primary personality characteristics that seem to be modulated or varied by differences in specific neurotransmitters, and thus by different genes that control the levels and expression of those chemicals. These four include *novelty seeking* (associated with dopamine and the DR genes, particularly DRD4, DRD2, and DRDT), *reward dependence* (also primarily associated with dopamine and these genes, although it can be modulated by receptors for opiates, nicotine, alcohol, and other addictive substances, and thus seems to be most associated with the DRD2 gene), *harm avoidance* (which seems to be most associated with the neurotransmitters serotonin and norepinephrine), and *persistence* (which seems to be most associated with dopamine).

The balance of dozens of different allele variations of each of perhaps as many as a hundred different genes, all providing subtle (or not-so-subtle) shadings and variations of the DRD4 gene, produces the broad spectrum of people you'd find if you were to line up a group of individuals all diagnosed with ADHD. No two would behave alike, and most would have totally different areas of strength and weakness in their physical, emotional, mental, and spiritual lives.

THE REASON FOR GENETIC VARIATIONS

Nearly all of these various genetic differences—the ones that have survived generations of natural selection—confer some sort of adaptive strength, which, while perhaps not useful to a person today, was at one time quite useful.

For example, the climate in which your ancestors grew up influences how your body converts energy to heat, according to new human genetics research published in 2002 in the *Journal of the National Academy of Sciences*.[1] Scientists have found that people whose ancestors lived in cold regions more easily produce internal body heat than do people whose ancestors spent millennia in tropical regions. And this genetic difference isn't as ancient as racial differences: People of Asian ancestry from North American arctic regions generate more heat than their cousins of Asian ancestry from southern Asia, even though the two groups share many similarities in physical appearance and a common ancestry prior to the crossing of peoples from Asia to North America between ten thousand and thirty thousand years ago.

The upside of this is that people who are genetically adapted to producing body heat easily do well in northern climates, and those who are not do well in southern climates But, wrote the study's authors, "[a]ncient regionally beneficial mitochondrial DNA variants could be contributing to modern bioenergetic disorders such as obesity, diabetes, hypertension, cardiovascular disease, and neurodegenerative diseases as people move to new regions and adopt new lifestyles."[2]

The downside, then, is that when "northern" people—including descendants of northern Europeans—live in southern climates such as that of Dallas or Miami, their body's natural desire for high-fat foods (which produce more heat than low-fat foods) puts them at risk. Similarly, people whose ancestors lived in tropical areas may not adapt as well to cold climates and may thus be at risk for disease because of that mismatch between environment and genetics.

CULTURE AND GENES

A large part of the human mental environment is what we loosely call culture. While genes change over time to adapt bodies to the environment, they also change to adapt minds to a culture.

John J. Ratey, M.D., assistant professor of psychiatry at Harvard Medical School and coauthor of the bestselling books *Driven to Distraction*[3] and *A User's Guide to the Brain,*[4] suggests that one reason why there are so many more children diagnosed with ADHD today than there were twenty years ago is because our culture is actually causing more children to develop ADHD brains: "I'm seeing a lot more ADHD now than twenty years ago," he told me in a November, 2002 interview, "and I think it's because there actually *is* more ADHD now than there was twenty years ago. I don't think it's just that there are more diagnoses."

The cause for the increase in ADHD, Ratey said, is found in our culture and technology: With television and video games and other elements in our rapid-fire culture, we're training children's brains to function with ADHD. "Overall, I think the nature/nurture business is really key," he said. Ratey continued:

> There is a huge impact of culture on how the brain finally gets shaped. And if you have the DRD4 7R allele and you also grow up in our changing environment, where you have the possibility of rapid stimulation, rapid reward, Game Boys, and the Internet, you're not going to learn to guide your attention very well—and that will have physiological developmental consequences. That may be why we're seeing 7 to 15 percent of kids being able to be diagnosed these days.

In the course of our conversation, I mentioned that I remembered, as a child more than forty years ago, sitting in front of a television screen at seven o'clock on a Saturday morning watching a test pattern for an hour, waiting for the cartoons to come on. I told him that I had to learn to wait—and that it was the same way with family meals. I concluded that such things as having to wait helped me learn patience and persistence.

"I watched the test pattern, too," Dr. Ratey said. He further noted:

Although you probably had the D4 gene and were seeking novelty, you still had to learn to wait for the test pattern to go away and for Mighty Mouse to come on, and those cartoons were slow and had a plot to them. But today they are so very, very different. Today the kids don't have to wait or learn to wait. Things were slower then, we were slower to develop, slower to feel rewarded, slower to get to the reward, so we had to learn to inhibit or control our restlessness, whereas today kids just don't.

My own take on it is that modern life really has an impact on training the orbital-frontal loop to put the brakes on and inhibit the limbic system, and that the loop is not nearly as well trained as it was when we were in school and had to do penmanship, for example. Now, versus ten years ago, there's a lot less playing with Legos because of the frustration associated with it, as opposed to playing with your Game Boy and if you lose, *ping*, you go right back to it and start the game over.

Does that mean that television—at least in its modern, rapid-fire, twenty-four-hour form—is responsible for ADHD?

"No," said Ratey. "I'm not saying the genes weren't there before. But that was a very different world that we grew up in." He concluded, "I really do think that the lack of institutions, the lack of frustration-tolerance training, and the lack of resiliency training—things that we all had back then but that kids today don't get—is a problem for today's children, that it has a major impact on today's children not developing inhibition."

But what about the other side of the Edison gene: the benefits associated with it?

8

Scientists Find the "Adaptive" Edison Gene

I managed to stop being stupid long enough to see
something that should have been obvious all along.
                                          SIR ALAN WALSH,
             INVENTOR OF THE ATOMIC ABSORPTION SPECTROMETER

Dr. Robert K. Moyzis's voice crackled with enthusiasm. "It's a wonderful example," he said. "It's maybe the first one in humans."

I'd reached him at his office at the University of California at Irvine, where he's the director of a genetics lab named after him. Moyzis is a scientist's scientist. Up until 1997, when he moved to the University of California at Irvine to run his own lab, he was the director of the Center for Human Genome Studies at Los Alamos National Laboratory. While there, he made several major discoveries in the field of genetics, which earned him both publication in some of the world's most prestigious scientific publications and the attention of geneticists around the world. He was telling me of research he'd done cooperatively with scientists at Yale University and the University of Beijing[1] that had just been published in the *Proceedings of the National Academy of Sciences of the United States*.

Looking at how frequently the 7R allele variation of the DRD4 gene (the one most often associated with ADHD) appeared in different human populations around the world, these scientists, among the top geneticists in the world, found two startling facts. The first was that

74

some groups had more people with the gene variation than others. The differences weren't defined so much by racial groups as by culture. For example, people in Asia had a low frequency of the gene variation, while Native Americans, whom we now know descended from Asian populations ten to twenty thousand years ago, had generally higher frequencies of the gene variation.

I asked Moyzis why. "We found that the frequency of the gene [was] being affected by culture, and I don't think there's any question in my mind that that's true," Moyzis said. He added that the biggest factors influencing the frequency of the gene were "clearly cultural norms, including who's even considered valuable to reproduce with."

But, I wondered, does that mean that the gene variation is less prevalent in cultures where ADHD is considered a disorder?

"It doesn't take much in the way of [cultural] bias," Moyzis said, "a very small 10 percent or so, even in terms of who's deemed preferable as a mate, and over not too many human generations you can radically change the allele frequency. Especially if it's ongoing. If your culture thinks one particular behavior is good versus another."

Parts of Asia are a good example. "A big enigma is why the frequency of the gene is very low in Asian populations while it's very high in the Native American populations that arose from it," he said. "This allele actually did exist in higher frequency in Asian populations at one time, and it has now been greatly reduced."

The reason, Moyzis suggests, could be that Asian agricultural cultures over the past eight thousand years have been hostile toward novelty-seeking and inventive behaviors. People wanted things to remain as they always were. The way the Chinese cursed a person was by saying, "May you live in interesting times." Moyzis added, "I could easily see how the gene frequency could be modified in such cultures."

But what about places where the gene is very widespread, such as the United States and Australia? That leads us to the second startling fact discovered by Moyzis's team:"Prior work had suggested that variants of this gene were associated with novelty seeking or Attention Deficit Hyperactivity Disorder." He continued:

Our major finding, to our amazement, [was that] unlike many disease genes that have been previously identified, where it was quite clear that the variant wasn't doing any good for the individual who contained it, [in this case] we have strong evidence for positive selection working on this variant.

Positive selection is what geneticists call a process by which evolution encourages a gene to stick around, and perhaps even increase in frequency in a population, rather than die out. It means the gene is doing something *good* for people. But how could ADHD be good? How could the 7R allele variation of the DRD4 gene do something *useful*? Moyzis had these thoughts:

We carry a history of our ancestors in our DNA, and we've been able to uncover the tracks of human migrations and whether or not a particular gene has been selected for. This particular variation is clearly a new mutation—new in the historical sense; it's still thousands of years old—but clearly to have the frequency it has in the current population, it must be doing something very good. That's a very unusual finding, that a gene that's clearly doing something very good is disproportionately represented in individuals who are deemed to have a disorder.

And, he said, it's a variation that produces a predictable result. He explained that in many of the studies done to assess differences among children or college students, including reaction time studies and spatial tasks, students with the "normal" gene variations appear at the middle of distributions, while those having the 7R allele variation appear at the extremes. Moyzis pointed out:

It almost seems that everything we do to look at differences among either kids or college students, including reaction time studies, you keep on coming up with really positive things, no matter what we look at. One of the last ones we did had to do with some of the tests the kids have been given. When I look at kids who have the normal variation they are almost boringly uniform. They're always right at the middle of these distributions. And it's always the 7R-allele kids who are out at the extremes. And that can be extremely good. Some of the brightest kids, especially on the spatial tasks, always end up being the 7R-allele kids; we never find the other kids out at that extreme.

I told Dr. Moyzis that I'd suggested a decade ago that kids (and adults) with ADHD actually carried a genetic toolbox of useful behaviors for a people, but that those behaviors weren't useful in an agricultural society. He agreed it was possible, saying:

When I saw this result, I got quite excited because I'm a molecular geneticist and it's always been a dilemma why high-frequency genetic disorders even exist—why do 3 percent or so of kids have ADHD—you would think these things would have been eliminated from the population. So when I saw this, it fit a general idea that a lot of us are beginning to have that the reason this disorder is so common is because the genes that predispose to them are doing something good. They have been under positive selection, and so now it's only in the context of a different environment or in combination with other genes that you have something that's considered to be detrimental.

He explained that there is speculation that individuals with the 7R allele variation are predisposed to having certain behaviors that are positive or beneficial in some environments, but that our current school system, which generally encourages particular behaviors and modes of learning, has deemed 7R-allele behaviors unacceptable. He continued:

And if that's what's going on here, then the implications are quite obvious. Maybe for certain classes of ADHD kids it might be more appropriate, rather than drug therapy or the other forms of therapy that are offered right now, to get them into a different mode of education. Nurture what's good about having this particular trait and see where that goes. That's certainly speculation at this time, but it's one implication of our work.

The study of Moyzis and his colleagues published in the *Proceedings of the National Academy of Sciences* noted at its end that, "It is possible also to speculate, however, that the very traits that may be selected for in individuals possessing a DRD4 7R allele may predispose behaviors that are deemed inappropriate in the typical classroom setting and hence diagnosed as ADHD."

BUT SOME SAY IT'S A DISEASE

I pointed out to Moyzis that in June 2000, at the Schwab Foundation for Learning, the chief proponent of the pathology model, Dr. Russell Barkley, had told an audience a very different story about the genetic condition called ADHD that's so strongly associated with the 7R variation of the DRD4 allele.

After using Einstein's Theory of Relatively as a comparison to his own ideas of ADHD as a disease, Barkley proceeded to debunk my hunter/farmer hypothesis. "Here's storytelling about ADHD," Barkley told the group, preparing it for the "hunter versus farmer" concept:

ADHD children are just leftover hunters from the Pleistocene era of human evolution and there's really nothing wrong with them. They're just the good old hunters from our caveman days being forced to live in a world of farmers and education. That is one view of ADHD that became very popular over the last decade and that is not a theory.

Having thoroughly established that my theory wasn't worthy of comparison with Einstein's theory—it's not even a theory, after all— Barkley went on about the dangers of giving children hope for their futures and improving their self-esteem. "That ['hunter versus farmer' non-theory] is a silly little idea for building self-esteem in ADHD children," he said with disapproval, "and I don't happen to believe that you should be building self-esteem by lying to people, by practicing small deceits, by creating little stories about the origin of a disorder so that you can craft it as if it wasn't a disorder."

He continued his assessment of the "hunter versus farmer" perspective, noting that the hypothesis suggests that "there's nothing wrong with ADHD. It's the environment that's the problem. ADHD is just a mismatch between little hunters where hunting is no longer needed by the environment."

Barkley then went for the punch line, the comment sure to draw a laugh from his audience: "Let me tell you something," he said. "The last person I ever want to go hunting with is an ADHD individual off their medication."

Having thus dismissed the "theory" of "hunter versus farmer" he revealed his own interpretation (italics mine): "*[W]e want a theory of a disorder.*"

IS IT A DISORDER?

"The really spectacular work is what Bob Moyzis has done," said Dr. James Swanson of the University of California at Irvine. (Swanson is not to be dismissed, either: His *curriculum vitae* points out that he "developed a laboratory school paradigm that has become a standard method for evaluating the efficacy of psychoactive medications for the treatment of ADHD children.") He continued with his assessment of Moyzis's work:

Moyzis is probably the top scientist in the whole university system. When you get people like that working on the area of ADHD, it's so different from even a couple of years ago. . . . This isn't just a "just so" story, it's not speculation; at the level of biochemistry it's documented. . . . The genetic form of this disorder is not really a disorder at all.

At UCI Moyzis decided to direct his considerable talents to understanding why the DRD4 gene has come to be so prevalent in the human genome, and looking at where it may be over- or under-represented in human populations.

Thus, Dr. Robert K. Moyzis, one of the world's leading geneticists who had just completed a massive study funded in part by the National Institutes of Health, suggested that based on what he'd read of the writings of the pro-pathology crowd, they didn't have a particularly good understanding of genetics. "It's been very convenient to have a drug treatment, and therefore very little research has been done on what's really going on here," he added.

His own observations were that there's a positive side to ADHD. "It amazed me," he said of his first research findings:

> You could clearly see different physiological differences between kids who have this variant and kids who do not in terms of reactions times and a variety of other things you can measure. There's really nothing wrong with these kids—they actually have faster reaction times than most people, which isn't surprising because dopamine is not only related to cognition but also to motor movement and other things. So we think that there's no doubt that this particular variant of this gene is doing positive things.

And might the positives be related to strategies and behaviors that would be useful for helping hunter people survive ten millennia ago, during times of severe climate change?

"I think what's going on, if you look at the molecular data, is a great example of balanced selection," Moyzis said. He continued:

> [Different] individuals have different strategies for life, and they're successful out in the wild whatever that was ten thousand years ago and nowadays for whatever reason. We're taking a certain fraction of these kids and saying that they're not adaptive, and I think it's that we're getting a little too narrow in our focus and I don't think that's particularly productive.

Asking him if he thought it possible that the 7R variation of the DRD4 gene was useful in hunter times, he said, "I definitely agree with your hypothesis. Based on the genetics and everything else, it makes good sense to me." Moyzis and his coauthors on the article in the *Proceedings of the National Academy of Sciences* also noted traditional evolutionary theory in support of their hypothesis:

As defined originally by Darwin, any advantage which certain individuals have over others of the same sex and species solely in respect of reproduction will lead to increased offspring. If individuals with a DRD4 7R allele have personality cognitive traits that give them an advantage (multiple sexual partners, higher probability for mate selection, etc.), then the frequency of this allele will expand rapidly, depending on the cultural milieu. Perhaps cultural differences can account for some of the observed differences in DRD4 7R allele frequency.[2]

In this regard, it appears the authors are suggesting a refinement of the rather simple hunter/farmer hypothesis I'd suggested back in 1993.

NOVELTY SEEKING

But the thing most responsible for this genetic variation spreading across the world, according to anthropologists, is probably the tendency of the variation of the 7R allele to push people toward novelty seeking, toward exploration of the unknown. "As modern humans colonized the earth, bearers of 7R were more likely to be movers so that populations far away from their ancient places of origin have, in effect, concentrated 7R," Harpending and Cochran wrote in a commentary in the same issue of the *Proceedings of the National Academy of Sciences of the United States* that had carried Moyzis's research.[3]

This, they say, would account for why the Asians who left Asia and moved to North America tens of thousands of years ago to become what we call Native Americans have a high proportion of the 7R allele variation of the DRD4 gene, while the Asians who chose not to move but stayed in Asia have a very low number of people carrying the gene variation. Back in 1993, citing similar logic, I had suggested that there would probably be slightly more ADHD found in North America among ancestors of Europeans than in Europe itself.

Moyzis suggested that it's not as simple as hunters and farmers, although that provides a beginning point for discussion. But the 7R allele on the DRD4 gene is almost certainly not the gene for agriculture, he told me. "I don't think this is the agriculture gene—this is something very different." Nonetheless, people with this gene were useful—rare as they may have been—even in agricultural societies. "You could even see in an agricultural society like Asia, where the frequency of this allele is low, that there were innovations in agriculture, too, and they probably came from the few individuals who didn't want to just go out and drop those rice plants every day."

It's possible, then, that the nonconformist hunters drove innovation even in the farmer's society.

9

The ADHD Gene and the Dawn of Human Civilization

All the means of action—the shapeless masses,
the materials—lie everywhere about us;
what we need is the celestial fire to change the flint
into crystal, bright and clear.

HENRY WADSWORTH LONGFELLOW

Prior to Moyzis's research tracking the genetics of ADHD, if someone suggested (as Klein did in *The Dawn of Human Culture*) that neurological change was the cause of cultural change, the idea was often discounted. In the past, it's been practically impossible to track genetic changes over time through conventional scientific methods. Changes in genes—particularly subtle changes such as variations in a single allele on a single gene—don't leave traces in the fossil record because DNA decays before fossils are formed. We've been looking at fossils for centuries, but still haven't found broad samples of ancient DNA that we could read to learn how people's genes changed over thousands of years. To do that, scientists thought up until 2002, we'd need a time machine.

THE TIME MACHINE

Moyzis and his colleagues, however, were able to create a sort of time machine by examining DNA from different modern humans in different parts of the world and comparing it with available evidence of which groups of humans migrated where and when.

The result is clear: The gene most closely associated with ADHD is also associated with what scientists call *novelty seeking* and many lay people would call a dimension of *"insatiable curiosity."*

But could it be responsible for even more than that? Is it possible that while curiosity (or distractibility) may have killed the proverbial cat, it may also have begun a chain of innovation that started with ostrich shell beads and continues right up to today with wild and crazy innovators in Silicon Valley?

THE NEWS HITS THE STREETS

When the research of Moyzis and his peers was first published in 2002, the University of California at Irvine issued a news release about it headlined "Attention Deficit Hyperactivity Disorder Related to Advantageous Gene."[1] The text of the release included the following:

> A variant form of a gene associated with attention deficit hyperactivity disorder (ADHD) indicates that the disorder is a recent affliction and may once have helped humans thrive and survive, according to a UCI College of Medicine study.
>
> The human gene study, which appears in the Jan. 8 issue of *Proceedings of the National Academy of Science,* suggests that behavior now considered inappropriate in a classroom may be related to behavior that once helped humans overcome their environment.
>
> Robert Moyzis, professor of biological chemistry, and his colleagues studied genes from 600 individuals worldwide. Among numerous new genetic variations of the receptor for the dopamine neurotransmitter, they found one linked strongly to both ADHD and a behavior trait called "novelty seeking," a condition often underlying addiction. Their analysis of the genetic variations also suggests that this variation occurred recently in human evolution between 10,000 and 40,000 years ago.
>
> "We found a significant positive selection for the genetic vari-

ation associated with ADHD and novelty-seeking behavior in the human genome," Moyzis said. "This study strengthens significantly the connection between genetic variations and ADHD. It also provides a clue as to why ADHD is so pervasive and may show us a way to provide more effective treatments."

The researchers found 56 variations, or alleles (al-LEELEs) of a gene called DRD4, which produces the receptor for dopamine, a neurotransmitter. One allele, known as 7R, was strongly associated with ADHD. By analyzing the variations in DRD4, they also found that the 7R allele was created recently and may have provided an evolutionary advantage at some time in human history. The study could not determine, however, if that evolutionary selection is still occurring.

Brain cells signal each other with a number of neurotransmitters, including dopamine. The dopamine system, among other things, controls movement behavior and may be involved in learning and responding to psychological rewards. It also has been implicated in addictive behavior. . . .

Between 10,000 and 40,000 years ago, anthropologists concur that humans were developing the first signs of complex societies, replete with agriculture, rudimentary governments and the creation of cities for the first time. Humans also were rapidly expanding and exploring the planet. These revolutionary changes in human societies may have changed the forces that selected for certain genetic traits.

"Our data show that the creation of the 7R allele was an unusual, spontaneous mutation, which became an advantage for humans," Moyzis said. "Because it was an advantage, the gene became increasingly prevalent. This is very different from other genes that predispose to genetic disorders, where the mutations are detrimental. We believe this helps explain why a disorder with such a strong genetic association is so common today."

The researchers are now working on determining how the genetic variations in DRD4 may actually predispose individuals to ADHD and other behaviors, and on examining the relationship between other complex genetic variations and ADHD.

Noticing that the time period of forty thousand years ago was mentioned twice in the news release, I was reminded of my earlier interview with Dr. Stanley Ambrose, who had discovered the ostrich shell beads in Africa in 2001. I'd spoken with Dr. Ambrose during the summer of 2002, the day before he flew back to East Africa's Rift Valley to continue his work, and he'd pointed to forty thousand years ago in Africa as being one of the most significant times in the history of the human race.

I originally interviewed Ambrose for another book I was writing, about how cultures move in cycles of boom and bust, but now his mention of that period sparked a burning question in my mind: Could it be, I asked Dr. Moyzis, that there's more than coincidence in the fact that the 7R allele variation of the DRD4 gene—the ADHD gene—appeared about the same time that humans first began to organize themselves into sophisticated societies?

"The fact that it arose right around the time that we like to think that modern civilization arose seems to be more than just coincidence," he said. "It's an interesting speculation."

At another point in our discussion, he came back to the idea that the DRD4 7R genetic variation implicated in ADHD may also be one of the "fortuitous mutations" that authors Richard Klein and Blake Edgar suggest, in their book, was responsible for "the dawn of human culture." Moyzis acknowledged that its tempting to speculate on these things, and that we don't yet understand these associations.

He pointed out that human genes among Africans show greater variation than among other races, indicating that all those humans who are not of African ancestry probably descended from a relatively small group of Africans who left the continent around the time the 7R allele variation in the DRD4 gene appeared forty thousand years ago.

> Because it [the DRD4 7R gene variation] arose around the time of this major expansion of human beings [out of Africa] and this major technology shift [of the ostrich shell beads and the creation of interdependent societies], you can easily see that if individuals with this gene exhibit some of the personality traits that current individuals have, maybe those were the ones who decided to do novel things in comparison to their more conservative neighbors.

Looking at the peer-reviewed study Moyzis and his colleagues published in the *Proceedings of the National Academy of Sciences*, I saw that they'd considered the possibility themselves:

> If the DRD4 7R allele originated 40,000 years ago, one might ask what was occurring at that time in human history? It is tempting to speculate that the major expansion of humans that occurred at that time, the appearance of radical new technology (the upper Paleolithic) and or the development of agriculture, could be related to the increase in DRD4 7R allele frequency. Perhaps individuals with personality traits such as novelty seeking, perseverance, etc. drove the expansion (and partial replacement).[2]

But then, in our conversation, Moyzis added that until all the research is in, which may be a while in coming, "It's hard to know at this point in time."

THE EDISON GENE AND DEMOCRACY

While the field of genetics is constantly growing and discovering more and more about how our bodies and brains came about as the result of our confrontation with worldwide catastrophic disasters, one thing is clear: We are all the descendants of survivors. Those who died out left no offspring, and as such, our characteristics that have been under positive genetic selection have helped the human race through difficulties and crises both large and small.

Consider an earlier time of difficulty in North America. On January 17, 1706, a young man who clearly possessed the Edison gene was born the fifteenth of seventeen children produced by his parents. As a biography of Ben Franklin published in 1929 notes:

> Some men acquire learning by the process of saturation, others by welding. Franklin belonged wholly to the former class and "did not remember when I could not read." At the age of eight he first went to grammar school, and the next year to a school for writing and arithmetic, where he found that he "made no progress."[3]

Thus, "at ten years of age he was put to his father's trade of soap boiling," and that was the end of Franklin's formal education.

Over subsequent years, this public school failure would come to be known as one of the world's greatest scientists, statesmen, and public servants. He was inducted into the highest scientific societies of Europe, was referred to during most of his later years as "Dr. Franklin," and was one of the Founding Fathers of his nation.

Yet he never held a job for more than a few years:

Interested in all that concerned the welfare of his fellow men, to the extent of making that interest his living creed, he founded in 1728 the Junto as a debating society; in 1731 he founded the Philadelphia library; in 1732 he began publication of *Poor Richard's Almanac*; in 1736, observing the appalling destruction of property by fire, he organized the Union Fire Company of Philadelphia; in the same year he was chosen clerk of the General Assembly of Pennsylvania; and the following year he was appointed postmaster of Philadelphia.

Four years later, in 1741, he published a monthly magazine. In 1744 he established the American Philosophical Society; and in 1747, against all the tenants of pacifist philosophy and the entrenched forces of Quakerism, he persuaded his unprotected city and province to drill a militia and arm itself against all foes. . . . In 1752, being made a member of the General Assembly of Pennsylvania . . . out of the troubles of the young state with the Indians he forsees and draws up, far ahead of other minds, a plan for the union of the colonies.

In 1757 he went to London as a [trade] agent from Philadelphia . . . [then returned] to America to reorganize the post offices of the colonies and to act on various commissions, and then again, is dispatched to London to arrange governmental changes in his state. . . . And always through these years, wherein the Occident shook, with the coming cleavage of the English-speaking nations, his ceaseless energy and vivacious mind were feeding the printing presses of England and America with pamphlets of politics and dissertations on science which changed the mental aspects of an age.[4]

Franklin became Pennsylvania's delegate to the Continental Congress, one of the draftsman of the Declaration of Independence, and a minister to France as the new nation entered the arena of international affairs.

> He had reached the psalmist's span of man allotted years when he returned to America. But the urge of service now relentlessly set his hand upon the loftier rung of international affairs. In 1775 he was appointed a delegate to the Continental Congress. By that body he was elected as one of the draftsmen of the Declaration of Independence, and in 1776 was sent as its minister plenipotentiary to France. . . . Recrossing that sea, for the eighth time, in 1785 he was elected president of Pennsylvania, an honor bestowed thrice on him.[5]

He died in April 1790. His biographer wrote, "Master of himself to the last he dealt efficiently with state matters a few days before his death; and watching with tired eyes the younger generation around him, he wrote, 'I seem to have intruded myself into the company of posterity, when I ought to have been asleep.'"[6]

In today's world, a child failing school at the age of ten would be diagnosed, medicated, forced into a behavior modification program to "take charge" of his different learning style. Then, his spirit broken, he would either learn to conform and fit in or be shunted into special education.

Had Franklin simply "fit in," King George III would have been very pleased—it's possible the American Revolution would never have happened. And the world might not have electricity or bifocal glasses or Franklin stoves, or even a public library or postal system.

Clearly, the practice of a number of our public schools and our psychiatric system to test, drug, and force our Edison-gene children to fit in is misguided. At its best, it destroys creativity and replaces it with functional mediocrity. At its worst, it keeps from the world the greatest gifts these children have to give.

But how do we raise Edison-gene children to fulfill their greatest potential?

10

Brain Development and the Edison-Gene Child

*Plasticity [of the brain] is a double-edged sword that
leads to both adaptation and vulnerability.*

J. P. SHONKOFF AND D. A. PHILLIP,
FROM NEURONS TO NEIGHBORHOODS:
THE SCIENCE OF EARLY CHILDHOOD DEVELOPMENT

Most of us think our brains grow as we get smarter and older. In fact, while a three-year-old has a brain with over one hundred billion neurons and over a trillion synaptic connections between these neurons, by the time he's a teenager, about half those synapses will have been pared away, chemically dissolved, and flushed out with the urine. How this pruning happens, and which synapses are wiped out, determines the kind of person a child will grow up to be.

There is much about raising a child that is a wonderful mystery. But today, we have access to important new information that our grandparents couldn't possibly have known. Research completed within our lifetime gives us new insights into how the brain develops, before *and after* birth. In this chapter we'll examine this new information. The research results are fascinating and teach us much about both how to raise Edison-gene children so that they can achieve their maximum potential, and what may stunt their development and full growth.

To help an Edison-gene child achieve his greatest potential involves several efforts, including: nurturing and supporting the child's sense of self, teaching discipline and limits, helping the child to heal from wounds that may have been inflicted by public schools and peers, and providing education in an environment that matches the way the child's brain works. Let's look at each of these more closely.

As the National Clearinghouse on Child Abuse and Neglect Information (NCCANI) notes in an October 2001 summary of research on brain development, the way we grow up is a function of both nature and nurture. "It appears that genetics predispose us to develop in certain ways," they say. "But our interactions with our environment have a significant impact on how our predispositions will be expressed; these interactions organize our brain's development and, therefore, shape the person we become."[1]

SENSE OF SELF

Children acquire their sense of self from a variety of sources. In an ideal world, most of a child's sense of who she is and where she fits in would come from her family and community. The healthy result would be that she'd feel important and wanted and would see early on the many places in her community where she could fit in and make a productive contribution.

In his book *The Biology of Transcendence*,[2] Joseph Chilton Pearce documents in extraordinary and precise detail how the entire experience from gestation to early childhood has a huge effect on the development of the brain a child will carry with her into adult life. In particular, a safe and nurturing environment for the mother during pregnancy and a safe and nurturing upbringing for a young child produce a youngster with a mental mechanism that is the pinnacle of what evolution has to offer. Such a child expresses the fullest potential with which all humans are born.

In this regard, through birth the Edison-gene child shares with all children the same developmental processes. But after birth, as he grows, he's more susceptible to those processes being harmed because of the hostility to his neurology that's built into our culture and institutions. In order to better understand the position of the Edison-gene child, here's a quick recap of the process of development.

A PROCESS THAT MIRRORS EVOLUTION

Back in the 1960s, *Life* magazine stunned the world by showing in utero photographs of a developing fetus. In the photos a single ovum or egg, fertilized by a sperm cell, quickly divides into two cells, then four, then sixteen, and so on until a discernable cellular mass is formed. As the spinal cord and heart emerge, the tiny fetus, complete with tail, resembles an early reptile or amphibian.

As a fetus continues to grow, the tail shrinks and the head grows, and the fetus appears to move through the stages of evolutionary development from reptile through mammal until, around the twentieth week, it resembles a modern human.

THE REPTILIAN BRAIN

The development of the brain itself, it turns out, follows the same bottom-up evolutionary path that humans follow from conception to birth.[3]

Shortly after development of the neural tube, the spine, brain stem, and earliest brain form, mirroring the brains found in reptiles. For this reason, this earliest and lowest of complex brain structures is often referred to as the reptilian brain or *R-brain*. It contains the components necessary for the fight-or-flight response, pursuit of food, and reproduction.

THE LIMBIC BRAIN

Over the top of the R-brain and extending from it, a second brain structure forms in the early months of fetal development that is physically and neurologically similar to structures found only in mammals, and so is sometimes referred to as the mammalian brain. But because it extends from the R-brain like a limb of sorts, it's most often referred to as the *limbic brain*.

The limbic brain is the center of our emotions, it turns out, which is why we can so readily identify with the emotional range of a cat, dog, or cow but don't seem to identify with a fish or alligator. The alligator doesn't have a limbic brain and thus doesn't have access to the emotions produced there, the ones we know so well. A cat or dog, however, does have a limbic brain and therefore can feel and express a range of emotions, from shame to joy to embarrassment and beyond.

The limbic or mammalian brain is wired to the heart, while the reptilian brain is wired to the gut, so that when we react to the survival issues of food or fear, for instance, we feel it in our stomach, whereas emotions such as love are associated with our heart.

THE "NEW" BRAIN

After the limbic brain is formed in a growing human fetus, another cortical structure forms around it. Referred to as the *neocortex*, or, literally, "new brain," it is the most highly developed and most recently evolved brain structure in mammals.

While the right hemisphere of the brain develops first in utero, and is tightly wired to the R-brain and the limbic brain, the left hemisphere of the neocortex, which in humans develops in utero a week or two later, has few direct connections either to the reptilian brain or the mammalian (limbic) brain. It must get its information about what's going on there via the right hemisphere, through a dense bridge between the two called the *corpus callosum*.

Although in early popularized versions, the right hemisphere (which controls the left side of the body) was said to be responsible for creativity and "feminine" strengths, and the left hemisphere was said to be more abstract, linear, and therefore "masculine," research done in the 1990s shows this to be an oversimplification.[4] A more significant difference is that the right hemisphere is more closely connected to the R-brain and the limbic brain, and is thus more directly involved in novelty and new learning, whereas the left hemisphere is the repository for automatic and rapid processing of information once it's learned.

THE UNIQUE PREFRONTAL BRAIN

In the front of the neocortex, just above the eyebrows and behind the forehead, are the two brain structures that are the most recent evolutionary developments in humans. (Some scientists place their development as recent as five hundred thousand to even two hundred thousand years ago.) These are the left and right *prefrontal lobes,* and they are unique to the highest apes and humans.

Research done as recently as the late 1990s[5] indicates that the prefrontal lobes are intimately involved in many of the higher functions that we identify as uniquely human, including our sense of future time and our ability to feel or experience states of divine transcendence.

THE BRAIN DEVELOPS AFTER BIRTH, TOO

The prevailing popular notion at the time of the publication of the *Life* pictures in the 1960s was that human development largely ended with childbirth—that is, a fully modern human baby came into the world, and needed only to grow and learn in order to become a healthy, functioning adult. The evolutionary processes mirrored in developmental processes ended with or before childbirth, we believed.

However, this belief—held from the Middle Ages up to the late twentieth century—turns out to be wrong. While a developing fetus's brain does form the reptilian brain first, and then the mammalian brain, and then the left and right hemispheres of the neocortex, and finally, the prefrontal lobes, a huge pruning of brain matter occurs just before birth, and just after birth, the development of entirely new prefrontal structures begins and continues until about age twenty.

THE FIRST PRUNING OF THE BRAIN

A few months before a baby is born, his developing brain contains millions of extra neurons and their associated structures. These extra brain cells exist throughout the brain—in the reptilian brain, the mammalian brain, and the neocortex, our respective seats of reaction, emotion, and reflection (including thinking and speaking).

It turns out that nature has packed the developing fetus with these extra cells so that she can selectively pare away millions of cells from regions of the brain in response to the world into which the baby is about to be born.

Once nature has determined what type of world the child—still in the womb—will enter, chemicals are released into the brain that selectively cause parts of the brain to die off and dissolve into the bloodstream. The result upon birth is a baby with a brain that has begun to be customized for the world in which he will live.

At birth, a baby's brain contains roughly one hundred billion neurons—all he will have for the rest of his life. (Though recent research indicates that some new neurons may be developed after birth, these are relatively few in number.) By age three, a baby's brain has reached about 90 percent of its adult size, even though his body has grown to only 18 percent of the size it will achieve as an adult.[6]

A three-year-old's brain has over one thousand trillion synapses interconnecting his neurons, a number that will be pared down to around five hundred trillion by the end of his teenage years and, absent alcohol or amphetamine abuse, remain relatively steady at that number for the rest of his life. This pruning process of discarding unused synapses is at the core of personality development, and much of it happens in response to the type of world in which a child finds himself.[7]

The Hostile-World Response

From just before birth, through childhood and the teenage years, right up to the early twenties, the shaping of the brain continues on a daily basis. If the body and mind sense that a child is living in an extremely hostile world where "fight or flight" will be the most important imperative, then the pruning of brain cells hits the neocortex and limbic brain hardest, while the reptilian brain remains intact.

This produces a person with a more sensitive startle response, quicker involuntary reactions, and a more finely developed sense of survival. What's sacrificed is a small portion of the person's abilities to deeply feel or think—but in the world of survival, nature evidently considers that a reasonable tradeoff. As Dr. M. D. DeBellis points out in a 1999 article published by the journal of the *Society of Biological Psychiatry*, "the overwhelming stress of maltreatment experiences in childhood is associated with alterations of biological stress systems and with adverse influences on brain development.[8]

The Safe-World Response

If, on the other hand, the body and mind sense before birth and throughout childhood and adolescence that the world is a highly nurturing place where there is little or no danger, then this pruning hits the reptilian brain hardest, leaving intact most of those extra cells in the more recently developed limbic brain, neocortex, and prefrontal lobes.

This produces an adult who isn't quite so adept at fighting or aggression but feels intensely and thinks more deeply. Because this scenario represents the preservation of the most recently developed parts of the brain and the sacrifice of the evolutionarily older parts of the brain, it's probably safe to conclude that this is the evolutionary direction in which nature would prefer humans move.

Thus, the large R-brain/small cortex human is slightly more capable of *survival* but isn't the most intellectually developed type of human that nature and evolution can produce, while the smaller R-brain/larger cortex human is more capable of thinking, reflecting, and planning but not quite as adept as fight-or-flight survival in a physically, mentally, or emotionally hostile world.

How the Brain Knows Which to Choose

Perhaps the most fascinating thing about all of this is the mechanism whereby nature knows how to prune a child's brain from the time before birth through the end of the teenage years to create a fighter or a thinker.

As Bruce D. Perry, M.D., Ph.D, of the *Childhood Trauma Academy* points out:

> The sequential and use-dependent properties of brain development result in an amazing adaptive malleability, ensuring that, within its specific genetic potential, an individual's brain develops capabilities suited for the "type" of environment he or she is raised in. Simply stated, children reflect the world in which they are raised. If that world is characterized by threat, chaos, unpredictability, fear and trauma, the brain will reflect that by altering the development of the neural systems involved in the stress and fear response.[9]

This adaptation begins in the womb. During the final three months of gestation, the growing fetus detects in the mother's blood the level of cortisol, a hormone produced by the body when it's under stress. The higher the cortisol level, the more the primate forebrain is pruned. The lower the cortisol level, the more the R-brain is pruned.

In the world of the savannah or jungle or forest, cortisol is produced as part of the fear and startle response a pregnant mother might experience living in an area that's regularly raided by hostile humans or saber-toothed tigers. Every moment of fear generates a bit of cortisol, and large shocks and full-out, run-away fear produce lots of it. Because it takes from eight to twenty-four hours for cortisol to clear the bloodstream, the fetus interprets many small doses of startle and one large dose of fear as equal evidence of a hostile outside world.

In the modern world, a mother living in a war zone or area of conflict (such as an inner-city ghetto or in a home with a violent spouse) could have continuously high cortisol levels. Another, more insidious source is a television in a mother's living space. As documented in Marie Winn's book *The Plug-In Drug*,[10] television producers and, particularly, advertisers, know that in order to capture the attention of a casual viewer and hold the attention of a serious viewer, they must produce a steady flow of startle flickers. Quick changes of camera angle, rapid changes in sound, punctuations in color and movement—all of these produce very small startle responses in the reptilian brain, preparing the body to react and riveting attention to the television just as surely as it would be riveted to a cobra or tiger. The effect of this is a continuous stream of low-level cortisol entering the bloodstream.

While maternal stress, such as that caused by maternal malnutrition or alcohol or drug abuse, can lead to significant changes in fetal brain structure prior to birth, the experience of stress throughout childhood and adolescence causes this process to continue at an even faster pace. Assuming the child is appropriately nourished and is not taking drugs, one of the most significant factors in brain development is a child's exposure to stress.

National Clearinghouse on Child Abuse and Neglect Information (NACCNI) notes regarding the neurological impact of child abuse, "One example of the effects of early maltreatment on brain and body functions involves the chemical cortisol. Cortisol is a hormone that helps the body prepare to cope with stress through its effects on metabolism and the immune system."[11]

In 1995, a cortisol marker for stress was found in the saliva of children, and this salivary cortisol was associated with alterations in brain development and behavior.[12] Interestingly, it was discovered that school-age children with unusually low levels of salivary cortisol were more violent. It appears that their brains and cortisol-producing systems had already been rewired by maternal stress, infant stress, and/or abuse as very young children; as a result, their systems "down regulated" to produce less cortisol in response to stress.

THE IMPACT OF STRESS

Research done in the 1990s and published by Dr. Allan Schore, one of the world's leading brain scientists, has shown that the most recently developed parts of the brain, the prefrontal lobes, begin their two most significant stages of development at the moment of birth—and that this growth continues into the early adult years of the twenties, when finally the prefrontals are fully formed.[13]

This trajectory of growth teaches us much about how to raise Edison-gene children to encourage them to achieve their maximum potential—and about those things that could stunt their development and potential, so that we can steer them clear on their way to adulthood.

THE BRAIN IN THE BIRTH PERIOD

If a baby sees a recognizable human face and is in proximity to the sound and sensation of a human heartbeat (as if he were breastfeeding) within the first few minutes of life, the prefrontals immediately begin their first stage of development. This is one reason why it's so important for mothers to hold and, if possible, breastfeed their babies within minutes of birth.

If a baby receives regular care and nurturing throughout the first year, the prefrontals continue to develop at a rapid clip. Their development during the first twenty years of life is a long-term parallel to the development of the rest of the brain during the nine months of gestation. During the first year or so until a baby begins to walk, the prefrontals develop thick interconnections with the sensory-motor parts of the brain.

THE BRAIN IN THE TODDLER PERIOD

During the toddler period, the connection process shifts to wiring the prefrontals to the limbic brain (which controls emotions) and the neocortex (which controls thinking). The *cyngulate gyrus,* the most recently evolved part of the reptilian brain and the area that is genetically programmed to control herding and social instincts, is particularly well wired to the developing prefrontals during this time, producing a new structure called the *orbito-frontal loop*, which is responsible for high social function. As this system begins to work, we see toddlers becoming interested in social interactions beyond their relationship with Mom.

THE BRAIN IN THE EARLY CHILDHOOD PERIOD

As the child enters what Joseph Chilton Pearce calls "the dream-like intuitive period"[14] from about four years of age through the fifth year, the prefrontals establish connections to the temporal lobe of the right hemisphere, just above the right ear, where sound and music are processed.

After that, and up until around the age of fifteen, the prefrontals continue to grow but direct their connections to the left hemisphere (responsible for more sophisticated language) and then to the rest of the brain.

Throughout this entire period, the prefrontal lobes are forming, in part based on the continual question of Mother Nature: "Is this a safe environment?" If the answer is no, as evidenced by cortisol in the bloodstream, then development of the prefrontals is slowed (and the child is more likely to remain at the fight-or-flight competence level). If yes, meaning there is little stress and few or no continuous startle flickers such as television in the child's environment, the research of Pearce,

Schore, Winn, and others shows that the prefrontals then form more rapidly and interconnect with the rest of the brain at the fullest and most aggressive rate that evolution has provided for and nature has intended.

THE BRAIN IN THE TEENAGE PERIOD

Thus, at about the age of fifteen, the first of two stages of prefrontal growth have finished. At this point, the prefrontals have become intimately interconnected with the rest of the brain's structures, acting both as regulator and initiator, activator and restraint.

A fully developed child at this point has a deep sense of time, excellent self-restraint, and a powerful notion of self, or what in pop parlance is called self-esteem. His ability to learn and to respond to the environment is as optimal as is genetically possible. And so the stage is set for the second phase of prefrontal development, which begins at about the age of fifteen.

A clue to this final prefrontal stage was given in the book *Higher Stages of Human Development*[15] by C. N. Alexander and E. J. Langer in 1990 (before researchers had verified the final stage of prefrontal growth). In it the authors point out how growth of brain capacity through childhood and adolescence isn't just linear but is virtually logarithmic. Tied into learning ability and a "knowing" of the world, these prefrontal processes are the quintessence of what it is to be uniquely human. They make an adolescent going through prefrontal brain growth particularly competent at learning new habits and behaviors, and seamlessly stitching those habits and behaviors into his sense of self for the rest of his life. (When this research was first released, it wasn't lost on the tobacco companies, political parties, or logo-driven consumer product industries, which suddenly woke up to the importance of the "teen market." Children who can be induced to become brand-loyal are usually lifelong customers because that information has been inserted into their minds during this critical stage of brain development.)

THE BRAIN IN THE
EARLY ADULT YEARS

But the second stage of the development in the prefrontal lobes seems to have an additional—perhaps higher—purpose: When children enter this stage at about age fifteen, they describe a feeling of expectation, a sense of something great about to happen over the next few years of their lives or in the world around them. This powerful sense of destiny or fate, for better or worse (depending on life's experiences up to that time), and the sudden arrival of *idealism* are the most visible signs that this growth process has begun.

As with the two hemispheres of the neocortex, the right prefrontal goes into its final stage of development first, followed by the more recently developed left prefrontal, and the process continues through the first year or two of the twenties.

At some point in the late teens or early twenties, this growth slows and the sense of expectation leaves, often with painful results, producing depression or cynicism in young adults. In societies rich with transition ritual, this is handled by a rite of passage and is appropriately processed emotionally. In our culture, graduation from college, marriage, or leaving a stint in the army are about as close as we can get to such a ritual (although these suffice for some young adults).

ADULT MEMORY OF THE STAGES
OF BRAIN DEVELOPMENT

What's of particular interest is that in the very recent studies done on these stages of brain development, very clear associations between the growth of brain structure and externally visible behavior or measurable mental processes are usually apparent.

The experiences of the baby at breast or the toddler are absolutely necessary to prepare the ground for the "magical child" stage of ages four through seven, but we don't remember these experiences because it isn't until about age three or four that the brain reaches a stage of development that provides a place for the storage of such "intellectual" memories.

Even the years from four to seven are remembered only as a magical, dream-like time, because the wiring of the prefrontals to the rest of the brain isn't sufficiently complete to give us access to intellectual processes approximating those experienced by an adult and thus memorable in an adult context.

INTUITION VERSUS INFORMATION

Our sense of practical and human "knowing" all happens after the age of seven, more or less, a point made by Rudolph Steiner (the founder of Waldorf schools) in arguing for why children shouldn't be "force taught" until at least the age of seven so as not to stunt earlier developmental processes that are not yet ready for the rigidity of a classroom. This is why schools in Sweden don't begin teaching children to read until they're about seven years old and is probably one reason why Swedish children—who graduate from high school at about sixteen—consistently outperform American children who have spent many more hours and years in classrooms.

But while all the earlier developmental stages of the brain, from pre-birth right up through the ages twelve to fifteen, are identifiable both internally and externally, only in a very small minority of people is there a noticeable external consequence of the development of the most sophisticated and evolutionarily recent part of the human brain. That may mark the difference between my high school physics teacher, who bragged that he received "average" grades and was thus a "grade rebel" in the system, and another "average" student named Albert Einstein.

Einstein, it's interesting to note, found his world-changing insights not in rational, linear thoughts but in a process he described using the terminology of what Pearce calls *transcendence*. Just as Mozart said that symphonies came to him in a brilliant flash, fully and completely formed (leading to days of hard work transcribing them from memory), Einstein also relied on his intuition rather than on rationality for his insights. He wrote, "The intuitive mind is a sacred gift and the rational mind is a faithful servant. We have created a society that honors the servant and has forgotten the gift."

THE LOSS OF INTUITION

Why have so many modern people lost access to what Einstein called the "gift" of our intuitive minds and are thus less capable of critical and deep thought? Why is our society rich in intellectual rationality but seems too often to be lacking in compassion, insight, and understanding?

When we go back to developmental neurobiology, we discover that building a brain is somewhat parallel to building a computer. A computer is made of obvious parts—the monitor, the power supply, the box and keyboard—and the more sophisticated parts of the computer's motherboard and its chips for audio, video, and processing function. There are its memory chips, which determine in speed and capacity via their interaction with the processor chip or "brain" of the computer, the ability the computer will have. If the memory chips are too slow in their ability to handle data, then no matter how fast or fancy the processor chip we build into it, the computer will never go faster or farther than the limits of the slower memory chips.

Similarly, every stage of brain development builds on those that come before it, all the way back to the first pruning of the brain in utero. The baby in utero has determined to some extent whether the world outside is safe or hostile. This process continues from birth into the early twenties, during which time half the total mass of synapses—over five hundred trillion—are pruned away and discarded.

At every stage the brain must decide which of the two poles—safe or hostile—to emphasize. On this foundation is built the earliest of the brain's structures, and these depend to a significant degree on the level of care and nurturing the child experiences with his mother. On this experience are built the toddler and later brain structures that depend on a child having nonhostile, supportive interactions with his father and mother, siblings, extended family, and the larger world. Throughout childhood, daily experiences such as stress in a school environment or living in a war zone continue to determine the nature and shape of the brain the child will have when he achieves adulthood.

If we want to produce children who are deep and thoughtful in their emotions and intellect, every step along the way requires that they receive full reward and nurturing and avoid more than the occasional burst of cortisol from an occasional brush with a tiger.

THE TRAGEDY OF LOST POTENTIAL

It's entirely possible—indeed, given recent research into neurobiology, almost a certainty—that our modern culture is producing children (and therefore, adults) who have not fully realized the brain/mind/heart intelligences for which we carry genetic blueprints. These children grow up to be adults who easily accept violence and even find appeal in quick, violent answers to complex problems. This may account, in large part, for why the twentieth century was the bloodiest in history, with over one hundred million humans killed in wars worldwide.

The children in our culture don't always have access to all they need in order to develop mentally, emotionally, and intuitively into the fully human beings that nature and evolution have set forth within our genetic makeup. We see this vividly in the statistics on child suicides, crimes committed by children, and the consumer culture, barren of meaning—particularly on television—that is projected at our children.

Exhaustive research presented by Schore, Pearce, and others shows that part of the reason has to do with both a lack of time-critical nurturing (a function, in part, of hospital births, bottle feeding, day care, early entrance to grade school, separation from family, long work hours for both parents, and divorce) and a cortisol-rich environment (ranging from the dangers of the ghetto, stressed parents, the constant cortisol-inducing flicker of a television in the house, and the daily ingestion of cortisol-producing stimulant drugs such as caffeine and amphetamine, to—perhaps most significant—stressful situations in school when a child's neurologically-defined learning style doesn't match the teacher's and school's teaching style).

INVASION OF THE LIZARD PEOPLE?

I have a friend who, in all seriousness, once took me aside to assure me that "the lizard people have taken over the United States."

"And who are the lizard people?" I asked. This friend has multiple graduate school degrees (including a master's degree in psychology) and a very high IQ, but recently, I'd begun to wonder about his reading habits.

"Lizard people!" he said. "Some people think they live under the earth and then zip into human outfits when they come up to the surface; others think they're some sort of incubus that inhabits the bodies of regular people, like in *The Invasion of the Body Snatchers*. But it's obvious they've taken over. How else would you explain the current state of world affairs? I'll bet that the president gets up every morning, zips on his human suit, and then starts his day. Have you noticed how sometimes his features seem like they're not quite right, like his smile is phony and might even slide off his face? It's the rubber suit he wears over his lizard body."

"And where are these lizard people from?"

"Again, there's some controversy," he said. "Some people think they're from a distant star, maybe explorers marooned here tens of thousands of years ago. Others think they're simply the first highly intelligent beings to have evolved on this planet, probably during the time of the dinosaurs, and it was when we started evolving that they figured out how to infiltrate us and take control of our societies. They became our first kings and leaders and are to this day. What we call *history* is really the history of the lizard people's control of the human race."

In a way, my friend may be partially right. From just before birth all the way into the early twenties, the brain is constantly facing the decision of whether to produce a mind that is more lizard (reptile brain–dominant) or more human mind (forebrain– or prefrontal lobe–dominant). Over five hundred trillion synapses are pruned away to leave dominant either one structure or the other, and all of adult life is then based on that dominant structure.

It's not surprising that hierarchical, power-based cultures, from warrior tribes to feudal societies to modern empires, are stressful places for most of their inhabitants. Even those individuals who rise to the top of the power and wealth structure experience regular stress because of their constant need to defend what they have.

Thus we see that reptile brain–dominant people are the ones best adapted to fight and claw and climb their way to the top of the social, political, and economic ladders—after all, that's what reptiles do best. "Survival of the fittest!" is their slogan. "Might makes right!" is their marching theme. Compassion and insight are for wimps: "Get while the getting is good!"

Those mothers and children hit by the greatest stresses are often at the most survival-oriented end of our social structure—the economic bottom. But the stresses echo all the way up the ladder, particularly in high-pressure households or among children exposed to high levels of advertising. Even though the changes induced at the level of the individual brain are subtle and small, when expressed over a nation of millions of people, their effects are amplified and become broadly visible.

ARE WE STUCK IN A LOOP?

It would seem that this is a never-ending loop, that once a culture enters into it, there's no clear way out. The culture restrains its members from developing into the most evolved state humans are capable of because each generation is birthed in stress, forming R-brain–powered brains instead of those powered by transcendence and intuition. Children who have been born in stress, whose neural pruning favors the reptilian brain, become the adults that control and maintain ever more rigid hierarchical and wealth- and power-centered governments, companies, and social institutions, and more and more violent and rapid-fire media. In this way, more stress is produced for new mothers and the next generation of developing children and young adults. And on the cycle goes.

When a society or nation goes into decline because of a loss or lack of resources, and fighting over the crumbs begins, the stresses in the culture produce more and more children whose brains defer to the survival mechanisms of the reptilian brain. These children, in turn, grow up to produce cultures that are less feeling, less intuitive, and more power-oriented—and, as is seen in both ancient and modern feudal societies, very stable and persistent. The culture feeds the neurology, and the neurology then sustains the culture.

TRIGGERING EVENTS

In *The Biology of Transcendence*,[16] Pearce suggests that some sort of triggering event drove societies worldwide into this cycle of domination, stress, and proliferation of children whose reptilian brains are dominant. This echoes the work of Schore in his book *Affect Regulation and the Development of the Self,*[17] and the similar work of others. The science behind it is solid. Stressors alter brain development, and the modified brain, in turn, has the potential to change culture in ways that make life more stressful.

There is no shortage of possible stressors: They range from war, cycles of global weather change, Riane Eisler's theory that the violence associated with eating domesticated animals has required a change in the brain, and the theory first presented by Walter Ong[18] in 1982 and Robert Logan[19] in 1986, and later brilliantly developed by physician Leonard Shlain in his book *The Alphabet Versus the Goddess,*[20] that the development of the alphabet created a rewiring of the brain, which led to hierarchical behavior when the alphabet was taught to children younger than seven years old.

Books have been written about how World Wars I and II were caused, in part, by late nineteenth- and early twentieth-century German childrearing practices that advocated violence toward children in order to break their wills and teach compliance. In the 1950s psychologist Erik Erickson wrote a brilliant analysis of how the early American Puritan practice of "breaking the will of the child" prior to the age of two led to a generation of violent, angry, and even paranoid Puritans who were so incapable of living and working together without strife that they sowed the seeds of the end of Puritanism.[21]

RAISING FULLY HUMAN CHILDREN

But the pattern can be—and is being—changed. In 1946, Dr. Benjamin Spock first published his groundbreaking *Baby and Child Care,* a book that contradicted the remnants of American Puritan conventional wisdom that believed that children, like horses, should have their will broken at an early age. Instead, Spock persuasively argued, children should be treated with respect and shouldn't be subjected to physical violence as a way of guiding or controlling their behavior.

Spock didn't have the benefit of the knowledge we now have about the impact of stress on the developing brain. He didn't realize that the growth of the uniquely human prefrontal lobes can be slowed or even stunted simply by angry words or regular spankings from Mom or Dad. But he intuitively knew that for children to grow to their full potential, they must, from the earliest age, have recognition of their humanity and personhood.

SCHOOLS MAY BE THE KEY

In the huge body of literature on stress, cortisol, and childhood brain development, there is virtually no mention of the single largest presence in a child's life: school. Thousands of studies have been done over the past fifty years on the consequences of child abuse and neglect, and on how substance abuse changes brain structures, but the only publication I have been able to find on the topic of the impact of school stress was published in India.

When I asked a physician and researcher about this (who asked that his name not be used), he said:

> I wouldn't touch that topic with a ten-foot pole. You can't get funding if there's any indication that your study is going to end up suggesting that our schools need to be changed in a way that may be more expensive. Government won't support it, industry won't support it, and true foundation support that's not promoting a specific agenda is nearly invisible. . . . If you want to do a study that will probably conclude that giving schoolchildren drugs is a good idea, I can get you cash tomorrow from a dozen sources, mostly in the pharmaceutical industry or the government agencies that respond to their lobbying. But even the people who criticize our schools as a device to support their advocacy of school vouchers don't want anybody looking into how much it might cost if we were to *really* provide both teachers and children with a high-quality, stress-free educational environment. Forget it.

We know about the impact of the hour or two the average family with a school-age child spends together. We've even begun to discover—although it's not widely publicized on television—the neurological impact of the four hours a day the average school-age child spends watching TV or playing video games. But when was the last time you heard about a study on the neurological impact of the six hours a day the average child spends in school?

Children attend state-run schools six hours a day, nine months a year, from, on average, ages five to eighteen—the largest chunk of time in the most neurologically critical developmental period of their lives. (Throw in day care and the amount of time becomes even more significant.) By simply looking at the time spent in school—and considering that it's the time of day of peak awareness and brain activity—it would be impossible not to conclude that school must have a huge impact on how a child's brain forms, on the neural pruning process, and on whether he ends up as an adult with a dominant R-brain or dominant prefrontals.

That said, I want to be on record as a strong supporter of public education and our public education system. There are many excellent teachers in our schools and much innovative work being done, but this institution that is so critical to a free society is under daily attack by radical so-called conservatives who want to privatize education, destroy teachers' unions, and starve government assistance to public education. While I philosophically object to "compulsory" education, I strongly agree with Thomas Jefferson that one of the most important functions of government in a democracy must be to provide a quality, comprehensive, and free public education—from the earliest years up through college—to any student who wants it. My goal is to improve public education, not destroy it.

SCHOOL AS TORTURE

I've noticed an interesting pattern in all three of my own children, in my three younger brothers, in many of the children we've had in our care, and even among the many teachers we've had as friends, acquaintances, or employees over the years.

The pattern goes something like this: When kids (and new teachers) start school for the first time, they're incredibly excited. They can hardly wait for the year to get underway—they believe it's going to be new, stimulating, and exciting, a wonderful opportunity and a great new experience. By the second or third year of school, however, both kids and teachers are beginning to balk. The teachers are tired and frustrated; the kids are stressed and wounded.

Somewhere in the middle of the thirteen years of their public school incarceration, some children begin to complain and rebel. And after their first decade of teaching, many teachers I have met have become complete cynics.

CONDEMNATION

Some of the nation's most well-promoted ADHD researchers have stated that people with attention deficit disorders have "stunted" frontal or prefrontal lobes, implying that these stunted prefrontal lobes are the cause of ADHD and similar problems involving self-regulation and self-control. They further suggest that the reason stimulant drugs help such people to increase their self-control is because they increase blood-flow to this particular part of the brain.

But the most recent science shows that these stunted prefrontals (and the lack of inhibition that comes with them) may well be the result of children being psychologically harmed by the mismatch between the way they learn and the way some of our schools teach. Scientists now know that when a child receives predominantly punishment, criticism, and other fear- and anxiety-inducing feedback from the world around him, the development of his brain's prefrontal lobes is stunted. Research demonstrates that such cortisol-producing negative input causes a child's brain to emphasize development of the survival-oriented R-brain and sacrifice development of the emotional and intuitive prefrontals involved in inhibition and higher function.[22]

So a child who's developing normally but may have some differences from others—perhaps she takes a bit longer to understand questions or to process language or needs to mentally rehearse her answers before giving them—may find herself in a school environment that doesn't tolerate these differences. Unlike the adult world, in school generally what is most valued is the ability to quickly memorize and instantly repeat things that may not even seem to have any value or context.

While a number of our schools emphasize rote memorization and test-taking, the real world rarely demands these as primary skills. Anyone who's been to a twentieth high school reunion knows that there are many surprises—late bloomers as well as people who did well in school but went nowhere in life. The fact is, very few careers require sitting in one place for hours a day, switching topics every hour or two, although our schools seem locked into this as their singular model of education.

One result can be that the child who functions differently is criticized or condemned for her learning style. The condemnation produces stress in the form of the disapproval of the teacher, the jeers of classmates, and the disapproval or concern of her parents, and this stress increases cortisol levels. This, in turn, slows development of her prefrontal lobes with their regulatory system and increases development of her instinctual, rapid-response R-brain. After a few years of this daily stress in school, the child's brain has been sculpted into something different from what it could have been: It's more functional for survival—fight or flight—and less functional for deep or long-lasting thinking processes. She now has attention deficit disorder.

SCHOOL AS WORK

Some of you may know how hard it is to sit, day after day, through a job you hate. A number of things could be making it difficult for you: Maybe your boss constantly puts you down—and your coworkers know it. Or perhaps you do your work poorly every single day because it isn't something you know how to do well, even though there are other jobs you can do quite well. Maybe you're a petite woman with exquisite handiwork skills who's trying to move hundred-pound sacks of cement all day. Or perhaps you have to solder miniature components on a circuit board but your fingers are thick and you don't see very well.

Imagine that everybody knows you're no good at your job and many of your coworkers make fun of you for it. Maybe your boss reminds you of it all the time and even regularly reports to your family on how poorly you're doing. But if, after all this, you try to quit this job, the police will come and get you and take you back to it; and when you protest, they say that you are being oppositional and give you drugs to eliminate your reaction or put you in jail. How would you (or do you) exist in such an environment? What kind of attitude do you have toward the world after a few months in this situation? How about after a few years?

This, in reality, is the world many of our children face each day: It's daily life for Edison-gene children in many public schools. On the first day of kindergarten, they're so excited to go to school that they can hardly wait. In the first days, weeks, or months, they love school.

And then the mismatch starts to show up, the difference between their learning style and their teachers' techniques. And they begin not to like school. They beg not to be sent, but they're sent anyway (with the best intentions). Being in school begins to hurt, to be unpleasant; they're being wounded by it. Whether it takes months or years, they begin to hate school. And out of those wounds come all sorts of problematic behaviors.

Of course, there are some teachers and some students who love our schools just as they are. Their genetic profile and neurology matches up perfectly with the instructional style required in most modern educational environments, and they have fun. But school becomes little more than imprisonment for those teachers who thought they could innovate to make their work positively transformational, and for those children who began by seeing school as a wonderful new opportunity for learning but then realized they would be criticized, punished, and given what they experience as painfully boring work to do for no apparent reason.

The predictable result for an Edison-gene child whose learning style is mismatched with our public schools' teaching style is stress and its accompanying flood of cortisol, hour after hour, day in and day out, year after year, through the largest part of a child's developmental years.

COMORBIDITIES

When Edison-gene children have trouble in school, they're often described as oppositional (argumentative), or having a bad attitude, or behaving as if they think the world owes them something. Having been treated as misfits and outcasts by the school, such children may have problems making and sustaining friendships among peers. These become additional diagnostic criteria for psychiatric conditions, and in the delightful language of the medical world, the new behaviors are called *comorbid conditions* or *comorbidities.* *

School can be hell if for a child who doesn't fit in and can't perform as well as his peers. The experience can leave scars that last a lifetime. In my experience, however, these comorbidities are a natural and predictable result of the daily wounding these children receive in the classroom environment.

APPLYING COMORBIDITIES
TO EDISON-GENE CHILDREN

Cultures determine which behaviors will be considered good or bad, which will be rewarded and which will be discouraged, and then they impose those determinations on their children.

When I went into the advertising business in the 1970s, I learned that the first job of effective advertising is to tell a viewer (child or adult) that he's incomplete or imperfect and thus unhappy. Television images flash so quickly between product shots and smiling faces that even pre-literate babies can get the idea: "You're unhappy now, but this product will bring you happiness."

An Edison-gene child faces a double whammy in that he's also confronted with a school system that says he must fit in with the teaching and testing style in common use in order to be accepted. Failure and the blame associated with it, Schore's research shows, can produce a stress-driven cortisol response that inhibits the normal maturation process of the prefrontals and other structures in the most recent (human) parts of the brain and strengthens the fight-or-flight R-brain.

The result is that the child's intellectual development is slowed— which produces more stress that further slows the process of brain growth, which leads to more developmental delays. Ultimately the child becomes clearly and definably both different from and developmentally inferior to his peers. The "different" part is something he was born with

---

* In everyday language, the word *morbid* connotes "dying," but in medical terms *morbidity* refers to how often something occurs, and *comorbid* refers to diagnoses that occur together.

and, in another time and place, could be a great asset to him. But the "developmentally inferior" part is a tragedy: It's the result of the mismatch between his learning style and the school's teaching style, and doesn't have to happen.

BREAKING THE LOOP

When Edison-gene children are misunderstood and endure years of stressful negative experiences, they are at particular risk for stress-induced developmental brain damage. When allowed to continue through school under such circumstances, it's just common sense to infer that they're at greater risk for drug abuse, promiscuity, antisocial behavior, relationship troubles, and a whole range of failures and problems in the teenage years and adult life—the range of problems that are usually attributed to their genetic difference, but in fact are more directly the result of that difference colliding with a hostile school environment.

It's particularly critical, then, to break the cycle of damage to these children as early and as quickly as possible, so their normal brain development can continue through their early twenties.

In later chapters we'll go into much more detail on the ways that Edison-gene children can be parented productively and effectively. But to close this chapter, here are two actions we can take: We can create for a child a new way of interpreting events and put a stop to any wounding he may be experiencing.

OFFERING A NEW STORY

To begin creating a new way of interpreting events, the first step is to offer a new story, a new way for the child—and the adults around her—to view what her behavior signifies: Instead of thinking of an Edison-gene child as having a genetic mental problem or "disorder," tell her—and yourself—that she is the descendant of the explorers who moved across the world discovering and populating new lands and of people like Thomas Edison, who invented all sorts of ways to make life better, healthier, or easier. Then tell her about the latest research that shows that this is more than just a story you've made up. Children love hearing this and begin to view their inner tendencies in a completely new light. Instead of being seen as an evil from within, the itch to be active begins to feel glorious. Think of the difference!

Point out the positives of his genetic trait: energy, enthusiasm, creativity, the ability to think on your feet, fearlessness. Suggest that such things are a skill set that will suit him well in adult life *if* he can learn to channel them well and to perform basic "farmer" tasks, reminding him that "You don't have to *change* how you are."

One of the most primal of human instincts is to form a tribe, an instinct that's subordinated only by the need for family. Tribes are rightly self-centered: I've sat with Apaches who made jokes about the Hopi, and with Hopi who told unflattering stories about the Navajo. Tribalism emerges in our culture in sports and sports talk—"my" team is better than "yours" is—and in politics. And it's powerfully visible among genetic and religious minorities in our culture. It holds them together, keeps them strong, keeps them going in the face of adversity.

Tribalism is healthy when one tribe says "our tribe is better for people like us than your tribe would be" but becomes unhealthy when one tribe says to another, "and therefore we have the right to invade or harm your tribe." Thus, frankly and openly, I'm recommending that you tell your child about the noble tribe of hunters, of Edison-gene people, she has descended from, and how, from her viewpoint, they're better than those farmers. (One of my son's proud possessions when he was struggling in middle school was a T-shirt made by Dave deBronkart, a friend of mine and the editor of many of my books) that said, "There's nothing wrong with me—you just can't keep up!" Tribal pride is not a bad thing: It's a social and psychological survival mechanism.

Read to her the biographies of famous people in history who may have had the Edison gene and talk about how they learned to play to their strengths and get around their weaknesses.

As for putting a stop to any wounding an Edison-gene child may experience, when you catch yourself wanting to criticize or punish him for Edison-like behaviors, reframe his actions in terms of the positive message you're trying to instill. Thus, "Johnny, quit running around knocking over the lamps!" becomes, "Johnny, you have a lot of energy! Someday you'll use it to change the world. But your energy shouldn't be indoors where there are so many things to break! How about going outside to play or finding some other way to let it out if you want to be inside?"

Much of time you won't need to be so explicit—but what's most important for a parent or other adult to realize is that you can't change a child's story for the child until you change it for yourself. This is not in any way a recommendation that inappropriate behaviors be over-looked or ignored. Instead, I'm suggesting that the consequences for such behaviors or the reasons for telling a child to change them be delivered not in a "bad child" way, but in the context of an Edison-gene story.

Out of this understanding, effective techniques for child rearing, discipline, and even good nutrition become clear.

11

The Edison Gene, Drugs, Exercise, and Nutrition

Better to hunt in the fields for health unbought
Than fee the Doctor for a nauseous draught.
The wise for cure on exercise depend.

JOHN DRYDEN

Interestingly, most of the research on the DRD4 7R gene shows that it occurs in about half of the children diagnosed with ADHD. The other half may have been diagnosed not because of novelty-seeking behaviors (indicative of true, genetic ADHD) but because of a wide variety of cultural, nutritional, psychological, environmental, and family factors ranging from growing up in a stressed-out family to mineral deficiencies.

As Dr. James Swanson, one of the world's leading ADHD researchers, told me:

Based on that [that half of children diagnosed with ADHD have the gene variation], there are two causes of the disorder. One is a genetic cause, in which the 7R allele has a major effect, but the other is probably due to some sort of environmental effect, which brings us back to the old MBD [minimal brain damage] definition of the disorder.[1]

In other words, about half the children diagnosed with ADHD actually have some sort of non-genetic challenge they're facing. The evidence indicates that malnutrition is at the top of the list of things that can alter in unpredictable ways how a child's brain works.

NUTRITIONAL DEFICIENCIES ARE RAMPANT

The *Earth Summit Report of 1992* documented an 85 percent loss of nearly all human nutrient minerals in world topsoil compared with soil samples from one hundred years ago, largely the result of a factory farming system that replaces (fertilizes with) only phosphorus, nitrogen, and potassium. This makes for plants that still grow large, but produce for humans a food supply deficient in nutrients essential to proper development of the nervous system. Similarly, a report published in the *British Food Journal*[2] documented over the span of fifty years an 81 percent drop of a single element (zinc) across the spectrum of forty different foods in the British food supply.

The U.S. Department of Agriculture (USDA) publishes on their Web site a study it did in 1997, which concluded: "A shortage of copper or magnesium in the diet may affect human behavior, according to scientists with USDA's Agricultural Research Service. The scientists say laboratory rats that didn't eat enough of these essential minerals were hyperactive and had either learning or memory deficiencies." The study documented how their results with rats can probably be generalized to humans. "Deficiencies of both minerals prompted the rats to be generally more active," the USDA Web site notes. "That's consistent with symptoms of magnesium deficiency in people who often experience tremors and disrupted sleep. The animals also turned in circles incessantly, similar to people who exhibit obsessive behaviors." They added: "Copper-deficient rats were slower to learn, and the magnesium-deficient animals had more difficulty remembering than their counterparts who got adequate doses of these minerals."[3]

Similarly, fatty acid deficiencies (most of the brain's mass is fatty acids) have been tied to learning problems and hyperactivity. For example, a study done at Perdue University and published in the April/May 1996 edition of the journal *Physiology and Behavior* concluded, according to a news story issued by Perdue, "that boys with low blood levels of essential omega-3 fatty acids have a greater tendency to have problems with behavior, learning and health consistent with attention deficit hyperactivity disorder or ADHD."

The Perdue researchers pointed specifically to omega-3 fatty acids, found in flaxseed oil and fish oils, as the most commonly associated factor. After looking at fifty-three boys with ADHD and forty-three "normal" children, the researchers discovered that "Approximately 40 percent of the boys with ADHD had a greater frequency of symptoms indicative of essential fatty-acid deficiency, as reported by their parents. Nine percent of the boys without ADHD had similar symptoms." John R. Burgess, assistant professor of foods and nutrition, said, "Evidence is accumulating that a deficiency of omega-3 fatty acids may be tied to behavior problems, learning and health problems."[4]

Perhaps most striking, in July 2002 the *British Journal of Psychiatry*[5] published the results of a randomized, double-blind, placebo-controlled trial of the effect of vitamin, fatty-acid, and mineral supplementation on the behavior of 231 violent young adult prisoners in the Aylesbury Prison. Those receiving the supplements committed 25 percent fewer offenses than those getting the placebo during the nine months of the study, and serious offenses were reduced by 37 percent among those taking the supplements. "The improvement in behavior was huge," said Bernard Gesch, a senior researcher at Oxford University, who was the director of the study. And, sadly, when the study ended and the supplements ended, the levels of violence among the offenders gradually rose to pre-supplementation levels.

Ironically, such supplementation is now illegal in many American prisons, where recent laws have been passed to prevent violent inmates from having access to exercise equipment or nutritional supplements that may be used for bodybuilding.

ENVIRONMENTAL TOXINS

On the other hand, too much of some compounds in urban air, such as lead and the new chemicals that have replaced it in gasoline, or mercury, which is found in rainwater downstream from coal- and oil-fired power plants and in most fish, can cause very specific types of subtle nervous system damage that are often misdiagnosed as ADHD.

Severe stress during childhood, particularly child abuse, will cause attention-deficiency symptoms, and it's well documented that long-term television exposure can rewire the brain to demand rapid-fire, fast-action stimulation.[6]

Unfortunately, such variables are rarely considered when a psychologist or physician is trying to determine if a child has ADHD. Instead, in probably 99 percent of cases, they observe only the child's behavior, compare it with the DSM (Diagnostic and Statistical Manual of the American Psychiatric Association, which defines mental illness in the United States) checklist, and recommend pharmaceuticals if the child qualifies for a diagnosis.

NUTRICEUTICALS

Old wives tales are funny things. Hundreds of years ago, while physicians were bleeding people with fancy surgical instruments and imprisoning "witches" for competing with them, the underground of healing women knew that a moldy potato would heal a wound faster than draining out a pint of blood. Centuries later, that mold turned out to be penicillin.

These women also knew that St. John's wort helped ease depression, and three hundred years later, studies now show it performs as well as modern antidepressants such as Zoloft.[7] Ginkgo, flax, and fish were, they said, brain foods, and likewise it turns out that ginkgo enhances cerebral blood flow, while coldwater fish and flaxseeds are rich in the omega-3, -6, and -9 fatty acids that the brain requires to operate efficiently because fats and fatty acids comprise about 70 percent of the brain's total mass by weight.

The discovery in the last two decades that foods and dietary supplements can have huge effects on mood and brain function has brought to the fore a brand new word: *nutriceuticals.* These are nutrient substances that have pharmaceutical-like effects. (In reality, because the nutrients have been around for millions of years and were a standard part of the human diet for most of that time up until recently, you could argue that they're really nutrients. (But to the pharmaceutical and nutriceutical industries, the word *nutrient* doesn't sound as compelling.)

To those outside mainstream American medicine, the relationship between diet and brain function is an area of interest. Although "research" funded by the processed-food industry claims to refute such a relationship, most parents and all naturopaths will tell you that a diet rich in fresh fruits, vegetables, and whole grains will bring about a big change in a child who's previously been subsisting on fast food, processed foods, and sugar-containing products.

This isn't rocket science. The moguls of the fast-food industry would never consider putting regular gasoline into their top-of-the-line cars, but somehow think that humans can run on whatever is tossed down the gullet. Unfortunately, many of the directors of our nation's largest fast-food and junk-food corporations also sit on the boards of directors of our largest media corporations and drug companies. Thus, while stories about very profitable drugs will make the news, stories about the value of the unprofitable benefits of the "eat healthy and take a few vitamins" lifestyle rarely make the news.

While most of the research on fatty acids and the brain has focused on the demonstrated ability of fish-oil or flax-seed–oil supplements to eliminate or reduce depression,[8] several books on non-pharmaceutical therapies for ADHD write at length about using these substances. Keeping in mind that hunter people ate and used every bit of an animal that they'd killed and consumed seeds that were whole and unrefined, thus getting generous amounts of these fats in their diets, it may be that "treatment" with these supplements is simply a way of reinserting an essential nutrient into the deficient Standard American Diet (SAD).

YERBA MATÉ: NATURE'S RITALIN?

According to the legend of the indigenous Guarani people of Paraguay, long ago the tribe had to move to a new location, but one old man was too sick to travel with them. So as not to slow down the tribe, the old man's daughter chose to stay behind and care for him, even though it would meant that they would die alone in the jungle.

The gods, however, looked down on this girl's kind behavior and decided to help her. They sent a beam of light to draw her attention to a bush growing nearby with the botanical name *Ilex paraguariensis*.

Intuiting that this was a message from the gods, the girl pinched off some of the bush's leaves and made them into a tea for her ailing father. It so revived him that he was able to get up and walk with her to rejoin the tribe. When they caught up with the rest of their people, the girl and her father shared the leaves of the bush the gods had shown her, and thus was born the tradition of drinking what is referred to by the Guarani tribe as *caá-y,* as *Chimarrão* in Brazil, and, in Paraguay, Uruguay, Argentina, and Venezuela, as *yerba maté.*

Over the centuries, maté has become virtually the national drink of Paraguay and Venezuela. Tribal people drink it in a traditional way: They put a couple of large pinches of leaves into a sacred clay pot the size of a fist, then pour cold water over the leaves. The tea sits for a while and then is passed from person to person for a sip. When the water is gone, it's replaced; it takes some time for all of the active alkaloids in the leaves to infuse into the water that's air temperature when it's added. In the cities, people prepare it just like tea, putting a pinch of cut and sifted leaves into a pot or cup and pouring boiling water over it.

Maté, like tea, contains over one hundred different alkaloids and nutrients. Unlike tea and coffee, however, it does not contain caffeine. Instead, its main active ingredient is a xanthine alkaloid known as *mateine.* Because mateine is chemically related to caffeine (they're both xanthines), it was assumed for years that the stimulant properties of maté were the result of caffeine. It has been only in the past decade that German research found there is almost no caffeine in maté, and that mateine has different pharmacological properties than caffeine.

The main claims made for mateine are that it doesn't elevate blood pressure, as caffeine does, and that it doesn't lead to a "crash" after taking it, the way caffeine does. Its effects come on more gently and last longer, and it's more mood-elevating and less likely to create nervousness. Little solid science has been done on this (most drug research is funded by companies who seek patents, and mateine is not patentable), although many people report this experience and it has been my experience over the years that I've been drinking yerba maté.

While nobody with an extensive knowledge of brain development would recommend giving any stimulant drug—including caffeine—to a child whose brain is still developing, many Edison-gene teenagers and adults find yerba maté to be a pleasant and less harsh alternative to caffeine that still perks up mental alertness and focus.

My favorite brew is to mix equal parts of green tea, St. John's wort *(Hypericum)*, and yerba maté. I put about a quarter teaspoon of the mixture into a large mug, cover it with boiling water, then sip it slowly throughout the day. (Because of the addition of St. John's wort, anybody who's taking an MAO inhibitor, anything that may interact with an MAO inhibitor, or an SSRI—any of a number of current antidepressants—should not take this mixture. Yerba maté itself is as safe as coffee or tea.)

DRUGS FOR EDISON-GENE CHILDREN

Much has been written over the years about the use of prescription medications for controlling the behavior of children with ADHD. There are arguments and counter-arguments about whether these drugs are helping children function in school or whether they're just making them docile. There are the assurances of safety, and the studies that show the neurotoxicity of stimulant drugs in both rats and in humans.

But let's boil it all down to the real issue: We have a school system that is being pushed to teach in one particular way and to the tune of standardized testing, requiring prolonged periods of rote memorization, and we have millions of children whose brains are wired to learn in a different way. As a society and culture, we have faced two possible responses to this: Change these schools or change the children.

The "special interest group" who advocates changing these schools is largely made up of the children themselves and the few parents who are willing to get involved or speak out. These people are almost never heard in the halls of Congress or state legislatures, and when they are, lobbyist's campaign contributions speak louder. These people don't write or publish papers in scientific or consumer publications and don't spend tens of millions of dollars a year in advertising. They don't send out their representatives to visit doctors regularly, plying them with gifts, and they don't sponsor the speaking tours of physicians, psychologists, or researchers to convince parents of the benefits of drug therapy.

This group of people has only lukewarm support from school systems and teachers unions; these institutions tend to resist change, particularly change that may be disruptive to their established systems and methods and require them to learn entirely new things. This group really has only one goal: to optimize the school for the child.

In contrast to this, the "special interest group" that advocates changing the child is the single most profitable industry in America. The pharmaceutical industry made over $30 billion in profits in 2001, all the time receiving so many government "research" subsidies and tax breaks that, according to Representative Bernie Sanders of Vermont, "the pharmaceutical industry pays an effective tax rate that is half of all other major industries."[9] Sanders adds:

> In 2000, the chairmen of Pfizer, William C. Steele Jr., received $40,191,845 in salary alone. During that same year the chairman and CEO of Bristol-Meyers Squibb had $227,869,513 in unexercised stock options, while the chairman and CEO of Merck and Co. had $181,252,976 in stock options. . . . Since 1990, the pharmaceutical industry has spent over $234 million on campaign contributions and $80 million on lobbying.[10]

That's an average of $2.5 million a *month* flowing into Washington from this one source—the pharmaceutical industry. Although $2.5 million a month is a lot of money, it's only one tenth of one percent of the industry's monthly profits.* How much influence would *you* have in Washington if you sent in one tenth of one percent of your paycheck to influence legislation? This gives a sense of perspective to the pressures faced by legislators, and to the relative influence of the individual in this world where the Supreme Court has ruled that corporations are "persons" who have "free speech rights" to give money to politicians (which was called "bribery" before this 1886 Supreme Court ruling).

---

* Two and a half million dollars per month equals $30 million for the year, versus $30 billion in industry profits in 2001.

Sanders also points out that drug companies use advertising dollars not only to shift public opinion, but also to influence legislation that may affect them. He notes:

> Incredibly, the drug companies have over six hundred paid lobbyists on Capitol Hill, more than one lobbyist for each member of the House and Senate. Some of their lead lobbyists are former Congressional leaders of the Republican and Democratic parties. The industry also spends millions to set up phony "consumer" organizations, such as Citizens for a Better Medicare, which lobby against serious prescription drug reform.[11]

The result of this imbalance in power between the group advocating for our children and the group advocating for the profits of a huge industry is this: In response to schools that fail to meet the needs of our "nonstandard" children, we as a society give chemicals to the developing brains of these children in order to neurochemically rewire them to be more school-compliant.

I propose that it would be a better use of our money to go into our schools and make changes or add resources to make them more child-friendly, such as better pay for teachers to attract the best to the industry, smaller classrooms, more modern instruction materials, and innovative educational programs.

MEDICATIONS BITE BACK

I've always been somewhat ambivalent about using synthetically manufactured drugs for ADHD. One of my children briefly took Ritalin, and I tried it myself, although the research about Ritalin and liver cancer and other side effects has always concerned me. I have said for years, however, that if we were to change our schools to become more stimulating environments, then the need for such medications could be eliminated for all but those few children and adults who may actually have some sort of environmental or developmental brain damage.

But now there's new research that's significantly raised my level of concern.

BURNING OUT BRAIN CELLS?

My curiosity about the possibility of brain damage from ADHD drugs started when the "ADHD is a disease" crowd cited a study done a few years ago that showed that the frontal lobes of children and young adults with ADHD were atrophied or less functional when compared to those of "normal" people.[12] In pointing this out, they were, of course, trying to prove the recently discredited theory that ADHD is a genetic disease that has absolutely no redeeming virtues and no value in the human genome.

When I tracked down the study, I found that 100 percent of the study's subjects with ADHD whose brains were scanned with PET scanners had been long-term users of Ritalin or other stimulant drugs. This raised in my mind the question: Did the brain atrophy occur as a result of the ADHD, or did the stimulant drugs cause it?

Interestingly, just over the past decade a number of researchers have been asking similar questions, although few have been noticed by the ADHD community because the results have had to do with other areas of science. For example, it's well documented that users of the recreational drug ecstasy (MDMA) suffer a long-term and probably permanent loss of brain cells (neurones) that leads to problems with short-term memory. But why and how? A study published in 2000 in the *Proceedings of the National Academy of Sciences of the USA* found that it was the contamination of ecstasy by amphetamine that was causing the brain damage, not the ecstasy itself. To quote the study: "These initial observations suggest that the sole use of ecstasy is not related to dopaminergic neurotoxicity in humans. In contrast, the reported use of amphetamine by regular users of ecstasy seems to be associated with a reduction in nigrostiatal DA neurones."

Another study published in the Spring 2001 issue of the *Journal of Child and Adolescent Psychopharmacology* (titled "Early Methylphenidate Administration to Young Rats Causes a Persistent Reduction in the Density of Striatal Dopamine Transporters") looked at how the brains of rats changed when, as youngsters, they were given methylphenidate (the generic name for Ritalin). The researchers pointed out that nobody had ever looked into the long-term brain effects of giving Ritalin to any mammal (including humans), saying that, ". . . until now, possible effects of this treatment [using Ritalin for ADHD] on brain development and the maturation of monoaminergic systems have not been investigated systematically."

The study found that doses of methylphenidate during the rats' period of growth analogous to human childhood led to a permanent loss of up to half of the neurotransmitter transporters in parts of the rats' brains in adulthood. The language was explicit: ". . . the density of dopamine transporters was significantly reduced after early methylphenidate administration (by 25% at day 45), and this decline reached almost 50% at adulthood (day 70), that is, long after termination of treatment."

A dozen or more other studies—most funded by anti-drug-abuse agencies within the U.S. government—have connected use of amphetamines with long-term loss of brain cells. Examples from the literature include: "Amphetamine-Induced Loss of Human Dopamine Transporter Activity";[13] "A Single Exposure to Amphetamine Is Sufficient to Induce Long-term Behavioral, Neuroendocrine, and Neurochemicals Sensitization in Rats";[14] and "Changes in Striatal D2-Receptor Density Following Chronic Treatment with Amphetamine As Assessed with PET in Nonhuman Primates."[15]

The National Institute on Drug Abuse even promoted stem cell research in the hope that it could provide cells to replace those burned out by stimulant drugs. On a National Institutes of Health Web site, they note: "Pluripotent stem cells offer a potential means of replacing neurons destroyed by drug abuse. This will be especially useful for individuals who have abused drugs such as methamphetamine, MDMA (ecstasy) and inhalants that have been shown in animal and some human studies to cause long-term, possibly permanent damage to selected areas of the brain."[16]

One of the most popular drugs for ADHD contains amphetamine, and pure methamphetamine in tablet form is also prescribed for ADHD children and adults. This makes sense, as Ritalin is in the same family of drugs and works by a similar mechanism—increasing dopamine. But, although research into such effects on Ritalin has not been done (largely because of a lack of interest or funding from the pharmaceutical industry), recent research funded by anti-drug-abuse agencies in the government "has shown that methamphetamine can have significant toxic effects on dopaminergic and serotonergic neurons in the brain. This is of particular concern because of the spreading use of this drug and may be related to the dramatic behavioral effects, including the development of psychotic-like behavior patterns that methamphetamine can have in some people. Pluripotent stem cells stimulated to develop into dopaminergic, serotonergic or other types of neurons, could offer a potential means of replacing neurons destroyed by drug abuse. In this way, we may be able to eventually reverse some of the debilitating behavioral effects of drugs such as methamphetamine."[17]

In the past few years, a startling number of adults who've used stimulant medications for years to treat ADHD have reported to me that their short-term memory seems very compromised. All have attributed it to aging, often making jokes about it.

But perhaps it's no joke. It's time for a dialogue on these studies and the troubling questions they raise, and for us to again revisit the issue of how we can improve our schools so that fewer children need medication to succeed.

DO DRUGS HELP OVER THE LONG TERM?

In a particularly interesting twist, recent research shows that children treated with drugs to help them through their schooling have no better outcomes as adults than children who experienced similar difficulties with their schooling but who didn't receive medication

This unexpected result even took the drug advocates by surprise. In his e-mail newsletter in June 2002, Dr. Sam Goldstein, who had previously coauthored direct attacks on my positions and been an outspoken advocate of Ritalin therapy (and who has also written or coauthored some excellent recent books on raising resilient children), wrote:

> Despite optimism by professionals and researchers years ago that treating ADHD in childhood led to improved outcome in adulthood, current research has not supported this perception. In fact,

the research suggests that relieving the symptoms of ADHD may not necessarily contribute to increasing the likelihood of positive outcome in the adult years.

A similar conclusion was reached in a 2001 evaluation of sixty-two different studies on Ritalin completed in the United States. As mentioned earlier in this book, the study, published in the *Journal of the Canadian Medical Association* and titled "Long-term Effectiveness of Ritalin Questioned," found that in American studies, "the quality of the research was poor" and "a publication bias may have suppressed studies questioning the drug's effectiveness."[18]

Goldstein suggests this solution: "By making tasks interesting and payoffs valuable, we have discovered that children with ADHD function dramatically better." Pointing out the benefits of high-stimulation school environments, he suggests a critical component of "treatment" for children is to help them develop resilience. "Children with such a mindset are empathic. They communicate effectively. They learn to problem solve, develop a social conscience and, most importantly, are self-disciplined." Thus, Goldstein concludes, we "may assist children with ADHD in developing the internal skills necessary to function more effectively in future life."

THE LOSS OF PLAY

Play is critical to the normal physical and mental development of all animals, including humans. Look at how kittens roughhouse with each other. While they're clearly building muscle mass as they play, what's not so obvious is that the process of play drives rapid development of their brains. Every play time produces hundreds of thousands to millions of new neural connections, building their skills and their self-confidence and constructing their view of the world and their place in it.

And yet the past few decades have seen a radical change in the amount of play children participate in, particularly once they start the school years. Instead of playing, they watch television or use video games for hours each day. Their parents may not allow them to go outside for fear of strangers, while schools have cut back on physical education classes, and those that survive involve little in the way of pure play but are instead rigidly achievement-oriented in order to satisfy the demand for objective and measurable testing criteria.

Positive emotions and achievement—which suppress or diminish cortisol—are now known to be absolutely necessary for a young brain to develop to its full potential. Play provides both, while television, video games, and achievement-oriented, worklike physical education classes provide little of either.

Similarly, regular and sustained physical activity such as walking or playing is necessary to bring the emotional parts of the brain to optimal function through several different brain mechanisms. Exercise stimulates production of endorphins, neurochemicals that create a positive mood (they're responsible for the "runner's high"). Endorphins also enhance the production and use of dopamine, which creates a sense of well-being.[19]

In addition, play and exercise give children a sense of mastery, of certainty that they can accomplish things they set out to do. As Martin Seligman found in his studies of dogs who learned to be helpless when shocked (see chapter 14), people who are in situations they can't escape from and or in which they do poorly or are punished will become depressed and give up. On the other hand, when people experience accomplishment as the outcome of their efforts, they gain self-esteem and motivation. Thus, exercise may provide an island of competence or accomplishment for an Edison-gene child in a school that doesn't suit his learning needs, as well as give the benefits of oxygenating the brain and keeping the body fit and healthy.

EEG NEUROFEEDBACK

One of the most promising new therapeutic interventions for children who have difficulty paying attention in school or other environments is called *EEG neurofeedback*. In several recent studies, it has been shown to be far more effective than even Ritalin in improving study skills and attention during classroom time.

EEG neurofeedback works by placing external electrodes on a child's head to monitor the brain's electrical activity, and then allowing the child to play a video game, using his own brain waves to drive the game. The principle of the system is that there are specific types of brain waves that are produced when a person is using focused attention, and different types of brain waves that are produced when a person is distractible or daydreaming. Whenever the child is producing focused, concentrated brain waves, the video game on the screen shows him winning (there are a variety of screen displays, from car races to fighter planes to simple lines that go up or down). Often there is also auditory feedback, with friendly sounds that indicate when the child is winning and buzzers or negative sounds that indicate when he's drifted off.

The mechanism by which EEG neurofeedback works is nothing new: It's called *learning*. The more the child "wins" the game, the more he experiences being in a focused state. He also notices, from the feedback on the screen and through the speakers, what it feels like inside his mind and body when his attention wanders, and learns to catch himself at such moments and return to a focused state.

Modern cultures have a long tradition of using biofeedback devices to train young people to attend and concentrate. In Christian traditions, rosaries and prayer beads have been used for millennia—when the faithful's attention drifts away from the prayer, the "biological feedback" of feeling the next bead acts as a reminder to return attention to the task or prayer at hand. Similar devices are found in Buddhist, Muslim, and Hindu cultures.

Another form of biofeedback is the family meal. In traditional European and early American cultures, mealtimes—particularly dinners—required the entire family to get together, and children had to learn to monitor external social cues to control and calibrate their behavior. Because family approval is so much more essential to a child than is the approval of a teacher (or even a peer group, at least at early ages), children learned to notice their attention.

Since the era of television and the trend, begun in the 1980s, to export well-paying industrial jobs to developing countries, which has led to the necessity of two incomes per household, the family meal has all but vanished in most homes. Whereas in 1960 in most of the industrialized world, a single wage-earner could raise a family with the paycheck from a forty-hour-a-week job, today more than half of all families must have two incomes to maintain the same standard of living. Additionally, half of all children in America now live in a single-parent home, and that parent is usually at work during the day. The result has been an epidemic of latchkey kids who come home to an empty house after school and find the evening meal a hurried affair that exhausted parents squeeze in between coming home from work and beginning the evening's round of household chores. The traditions of prayer, meditation, and after-dinner family time have been all but forgotten. The result is that our children no longer have opportunities to learn how to pay attention during boring times when they're growing up.

EEG neurofeedback fills in this gap by very quickly training children to notice their states of attention and inattention. Whereas the mind can still drift off for seconds or even minutes during a family meal, when a computer is monitoring brain waves and giving feedback within a ten-thousandth of a second of the brain's drifting, the brain quickly learns exactly how to control its attention mechanisms. The result is that approximately forty half-hour to one-hour sessions of EEG neurofeedback can produce a permanent and lasting improvement in a child's ability to attend to and learn from tasks and situations he finds boring.

EXERCISE: THE OPTIMAL "TREATMENT"?

More than two thousand years ago, Plato suggested that in addition to exercising our mind by studying or engaging in a "strenuous intellectual pursuit," we must make an equal effort to exercise our body daily to bring "to order" the system of the mind/body.[20]

On August 19, 1785, Thomas Jefferson advised a young friend, Peter Carr, about the importance of studying the classic authors such as Homer, Euripides, and Sophocles. But, Jefferson said, it is necessary to always balance this mental work with the physical activity of walking. He wrote:

> In order to assure a certain progress in this reading, consider what hours you have free from the school and the exercises of the school. Give about two of them, every day, to exercise; for health must not be sacrificed to learning. A strong body makes the mind

strong. . . . Games played with the ball, and others of that nature, are too violent for the body, and stamp no character on the mind. . . . Never think of taking a book with you. The object of walking is to relax the mind. You should therefore not permit yourself even to think while you walk; but divert your attention by the objects surrounding you. . . . Walking is the best possible exercise. Habituate yourself to walk very far. The Europeans value themselves on having subdued the horse to the uses of man; but I doubt whether we have not lost more than we have gained, by the use of this animal. . . . There is no habit you will value so much as that of walking far without fatigue.

I would advise you to take your exercise in the afternoon: not because it is the best time for exercise, for certainly it is not; but because it is the best time to spare from your studies; and habit will soon reconcile it to health, and render it nearly as useful as if you gave to that the more precious hours of the day. A little walk of half an hour, in the morning, when you first rise, is advisable also. It shakes off sleep, and produces other good effects in the animal economy.

The result of Jefferson following his own advice was that his body and mind were both sharp and functional up until the week of his death at the age of eighty-three. Biographies of Charles Dickens indicate that he, likewise, walked between one and *twenty* miles daily, and that his most productive writing periods were also the periods during which he walked the most. Jefferson, Dickens, and Plato believed that daily moderate exercise made the mind work better, and all viewed that as perhaps even a more important benefit of exercise than the improvements in physical health. Modern science seems to be backing them up.

Dr. John H. Greist and colleagues did a fascinating study in the late 1970s comparing exercise and several forms of psychotherapy as treatment for moderately depressed adults.[21] They divided a group of men and women into three groups: those who went jogging only three to four times a week with a psychologist who was also knowledgeable about how to run without creating injuries; those who underwent time-limited psychotherapy with psychiatrists without exercise; and those who underwent time-unlimited psychotherapy without exercise. All of the patients were measurably depressed at the beginning of the study, according to Symptom Checklist-90 (SCL-90) and Research Diagnostic Criteria.

At the end of the study's ten weeks, all but one of the running patients—who had received *no* psychotherapy whatsoever—had recovered from their depression (the one exception was a woman who didn't think she was physically fit enough to run; during the sixth week, however, she began walking, and within two weeks her symptoms were relieved, too). During the entire course of the therapy, all of the people exercising steadily moved from the beginning point of "quite a bit depressed" to only "a little bit depressed" at the end of ten weeks, and to "not at all depressed" when a follow-up study of the same people was done a year later.

By contrast, the people undergoing psychotherapy, particularly time-unlimited therapy, showed some improvement in the first two weeks of therapy, but by the ninth week of therapy had registered as being more depressed than when the therapy sessions had begun, and in the one-year follow-up study, were found to be still "moderately depressed." At virtually every stage of measurement during the entire ten weeks of the study and during the following twelve months of follow-up, the people who exercised experienced greater improvements in their emotional and mental health than did the people undergoing either form of psychotherapy.

Other, earlier studies had found similar results. For example, a study by Folkins, Lynch, and Gardner[22] found that 76 percent of men who engaged in regular "competitive athletics" had "mature [psychological] defense patterns," compared with such maturity existing in only 23 percent of men who didn't engage regularly in sports. These earlier studies, however, looked at people who were already exercising, so they may have been contaminated by sample bias; it's possible that mentally fit people were more likely to engage in physical activity.

Greist's study, however, fit the pieces together, as have other studies since: When people engage in regular physical activity—particularly walking or jogging—they become emotionally healthier, their minds work better, and their intellectual capacities increase.

Of course, these results are logical. The brain is part of the body, just another organ, and just like the muscles, it needs a healthy blood flow and ample oxygen to function. Exercise improves the elasticity of veins and arteries, increases capillary blood flow, and boosts the levels of oxygen and other nutrients available to every organ in the body.

As the BBC pointed out in a 1998 program on the importance of play and physical activity for children, "In the U.S., one in 18 school children suffers from ADHD and half are being treated with the psycho-stimulant drug Ritalin. The number of children with the disorder has risen by a huge 600% since 1990 and the U.S. has five times more cases than the rest of the world put together."[23]

The program went on to quote several experts about the importance of both play and exercise in giving children the ability to sit still and pay attention when time for class comes. The report quoted a team of international experts who looked into schools in the state of Georgia and concluded, the report said, "that children were more likely to fidget and lose attention the longer they were deprived of exercise."

It is critical for children to play with one another, according to developmental specialists, because it's through play that children learn social skills. As children are increasingly isolated by the replacement of after-school play with television, video games, and computers, and are increasingly constrained by the elimination of play in schools,[24] their social skills suffer and the stage can be set for lifelong problems with relationships.

The BBC report also pointed out that with increased emphasis on testing and a diminished focus on physical education or any time for play between classes, the amount of play and activity children experience in modern schools is lower than in times past. They quote expert Professor Alan Fridlund as saying that thus children are "doubly victimized" because their play time is reduced *and* they are punished for the resulting and predictable fidgeting that comes as a result of a lack of physical activity.

In addition there are the very real medical problems that accompany the doubling of childhood obesity rates in the United States in the past two decades as a result of both an increase in the time children spend with television, computers, and video games instead of engaging in physical play, and a change in dietary habits from such cultural changes as the introduction of soft-drink vending machines in schools. If these current trends continue, the next few decades will see an epidemic of adult deaths from heart disease and diabetes. And some deaths may not wait; as was exposed on a recent network news magazine show, children as young as ten are having heart attacks as a result of their steady diet of junk food and lack of exercise.

As youngsters, we were created by nature to be walkers and runners; to range the savannahs, the plains, the forests, and the jungles in search of food; to build neural interconnections and develop our young brains by interacting with the physical world and playing, just like the young of every other mammalian species. Schools and activities that deny children physical play time stunt their physical, emotional, and mental growth.

Although our public schools are steadily moving away from time set aside for play and more and more toward time spent on rote memorization for standardized testing, homeschooling parents and many alternative schools are placing strong emphasis on children getting the physical exercise and play time they need. This may well be one of the variables in why homeschooled students score so much better on college entrance tests and perform better overall in college: Perhaps their brains are more well-developed and they're emotionally more stable and healthy.

Play is particularly important for the Edison-gene child, who is genetically wired to be an explorer, a pioneer, or an active member of a hunting party. Play satisfies the body's genetic need for novelty and brain's need for oxygen and nutrients. To optimize the brain development, physical stamina, and mental resilience of an Edison-gene child, throw out the TV and encourage him or her to exercise and play.

12

Providing Discipline and Structure for the Edison-Gene Child

*I was taught to ask for proof, that it was good
to distrust authority. You need to have the courage
to disagree. There are times in your life
when you should be a radical.*

JAMES D. WATSON

Edison-gene children need a special and specific type of upbringing to reach their full potential, and in this chapter we'll visit a variety of techniques to nurture them to happiness, fulfillment, and even greatness.

In farming and industrial cultures, children are taught from an early age to work. Children raised among aboriginal agricultural societies begin working in the fields as soon as they're capable—sometimes as early as three years old. In his novels, Charles Dickens documented the transition of this practice into the industrial era, and today, according to the Industrial Labor Organization (ILO), over 250 million children around the world work as slave laborers, ranging, according to Human Rights Watch, from "four year olds tied to rug looms to keep them from running away" to "children who work long hours, often in dangerous and unhealthy conditions, [and] are exposed to lasting physical and psychological harm."[1]

In the developed world, the transition from carefree childhood to a regimented environment tightly controlled by adults happens between the ages of three and five, as children are moved from their family's care during the day into pre-school and then kindergarten. The conditioning for a lifetime of patient, determined, cubicle-friendly labor, starts before a child is only partially neurologically developed, thus increasing the probability that, regardless of the enthusiasm or idealism of teachers, by the time the child reaches adulthood she will be a compliant worker and a relatively unquestioning citizen, just as German philosopher Johann Gottlieb Fichte envisioned when he invented modern compulsory education.

NURTURING THE HUNTERS

In order for our Edison-gene children to achieve their full potential, they need a different type of upbringing, and clues to it are found in the lifestyles of hunter peoples all around the world. In the literature of anthropology about the child-rearing habits of such peoples, however, we find startling differences from the way children are raised in agricultural and industrial societies.

In west-central Africa, south of Chad and Sudan and north of the Congo, lies the former French colony of Ubangi-Shari, which became the Central African Republic upon gaining independence in 1960. The Republic is home to numerous tribal people, including the hunting Aka and the farming Ngandu, and Dr. Barry Hewlett of the University of Washington at Vancouver spent several decades investigating the differences in the child-rearing practices of these two tribes who live in close proximity to each other.

"The hunter-gatherer way of life is dramatically different than life in the West, or even life in [small] farming communities," Hewlett told *Science News* writer Bruce Bower in 2000.[2] His research found that mothers among the Aka held or touched their children 99 percent of the time, mostly by strapping children to themselves while they foraged for food or interacted with the community. The agricultural Ngandu mothers held or touched their children 79 percent of the time, while the comparison group of American and European parents held or touched their children 18 percent of the time.

The result, according to Hewlett, was twofold. First, the Aka children fussed and cried considerably less than did the Ngandu or the European and American children. But second, and perhaps most important, when Aka children grow up into Aka adults, they view the natural world and environment in which they live along with people they meet as safe and worthy of their trust.

Much of this difference in cultures can be accounted for by the fact that hunter peoples generally spend a maximum of two to five hours a day, on average, dealing with what we call the necessities of life—hunting or foraging for food, constructing shelter, preparing clothing, and so forth—and thus have much more time left to spend with family and children. Numerous observers have chronicled this in detail: for instance, Elizabeth Marshall Thomas in her book *The Harmless People;*[3] Laurens van der Post in his many books about the Bushmen of the Kalahari desert; and Colin Turnbull in *The Forest People.*[4]

In *Stone Age Economics*, Marshall Sahliins says:

Hunter-gatherers consume less energy per capita per year than any other group of human beings. Yet when you come to examine it, the original affluent society was none other than the hunter's—in which all the people's material wants were easily satisfied. To accept that hunters are affluent is therefore to recognize that the present human condition of man slaving to bridge the gap between his unlimited wants and his insufficient means is a tragedy of modern times.[5]

Psychologist Robert Wolff, author of *Original Wisdom,*[6] a book about the years he spent in the 1950s and 1960s among the Sng'oi, a hunter people of the jungles of Malaysia, told me in a 2002 interview:

Children in indigenous and aboriginal societies are raised by doing, our children must learn by being told, in words. . . . Community in their world is close, intimate, intense. Our children learn social "skills" by being told.

To me the biggest difference between how, for instance, I see my grandchildren being raised and how I grew up [more than eighty years ago] is that today's children grow up in a world that is basically dangerous and incomprehensible, unfriendly for an individual—and becoming an individual is stressed from the day they are born. Practically at birth babies are stuck in a box.

In indigenous societies, children are handled and cuddled and held for at least two years and probably longer. They grow up knowing that they are loved, and that they belong. Their parents, in my experience, never scold, never punish, never expect anything from a child other than to grow to be him- or herself.

Our children from day one have to learn to be on their own [in a crib], they have to learn how to fit in, they have to be constantly scolded and reminded not to do this or that. . . . The difference is enormous![7]

As Claude Levi-Strauss pointed out in his book *The Savage Mind,*[8] when boys from hunter cultures in New Guinea were taken from their tribes and sent to mission schools in the early years of the last century, and there were taught to play soccer, they thought the game was over when both teams had achieved the same score.

In 1998, I visited a school in the Australian Aboriginal community of Lockhart River in northern Queensland, and one of the teachers there told me of a similar ethic among the Australian Aboriginals. "They prefer not to compete, even in sports," he said. "They'd much rather cooperate and help each other."

Tanzanian writer Robert Lawlor spent years researching the aboriginal people of Australia and nearby areas and wrote a brilliant book, *Voices of the First Day*, about his findings. Aboriginal hunter child-rearing practices were similar to those of the Aka of western Africa. Lawlor writes:

Without exception, the earliest Europeans to catch a glimpse of traditional Aboriginal camp life noted the boundless joy, exuberance, and independence of the children. No other people seem to be as lenient or indulgent toward children as the Australian Aborigines, and many anthropologists have declared it to be the most child-centered society they have ever observed. . . . Children are never allowed to cry for any length of time; the parents and the entire clan see that their discomforts are quickly soothed or alleviated.[9]

Lawlor notes that:

It is considered a great personal defeat for an adult to lose patience and slap a child. If punishment is definitely called for, as in the case of one child threatening another, it can only be carried out by the natural mother or father. If someone else, even close kin, tries to reprimand a child, an intense clan dispute is bound to ensue.

This philosophy of being available to a child and meeting her needs continuously extends, in Aboriginal society, throughout a child's developmental years, in a way that would have made Maria Montessori proud. Lawlor continues:

Aboriginal childhood education rests on the conclusion that the sense of individual motivation is the universal characteristic of infancy, and what needs to be cultivated is a s sense of relatedness.

As a child matures, he or she is increasingly introduced to obligations to kin and society and, later, to the spiritual mysteries of the Dreaming. As a result of this natural progression, adult Aborigines are extremely mild-mannered, easygoing, and relaxed and have none of the armored defensiveness of the Western personality structure.[10]

REWARD/PUNISHMENT VERSUS INCLUSION/INTERDEPENDENCE

In hierarchical societies that operate along lines of power and control—as do those in much of our modern industrial world—the primary model for motivation is that of reward and punishment: Reward people when they do what you want, and punish them when they don't.

But reward and punishment isn't the most effective way to motivate or control the behavior of others, particularly Edison-gene children, and is used in our culture because the better option is available only to small groups, small businesses, and families: *inclusion and interdependence*. These are the hallmarks of tribal cultures, especially hunter cultures. In our culture, you find them at the core of functional small businesses, local communities, and emotionally healthy families. In such organizations, people feel a sense of inclusion; they're part of the family, community, or business and are thus motivated to behave in appropriate ways and contribute to the common good. Continuous social interactions reinforce the interdependence of all, and in so doing, also reinforce appropriate behaviors and minimize those that are negative.

In a typical family, a reward and punishment system may consist in part of Johnny getting paid when he takes out the garbage every week. On the surface, this system seems to work. But on a deeper, more structural level of family dynamics, it introduces a disconnection between Johnny and his family. He's participating not because of his sense of inclusion or interdependence but solely to get the reward.

While rewarding children isn't in and of itself a bad thing, it prevents them from the deeper and more meaningful experience of being part of a family whose members depend on each other for the family as a whole to function well. If Johnny takes out the trash because he's a member of the family, and being a member of the family means all members help in their own ways so life is better for everybody, then his sense of connection and meaningful interaction with the family deepens. Similarly, he receives a weekly allowance and other benefits of family life not because of any specific things he has done, but instead because in an interdependent community or family, everybody shares in the bounty.

This shift from reward/punishment to inclusion/interdependence provides Johnny, through his family experience, a basis for a lifetime sense of security and safety, and increases the odds that as an adult, he'll be more of a cooperator than a dominator.

SEPARATING PERSON FROM BEHAVIOR

I was in the local food co-op recently, and about four feet from me a two-year-old child in a shopping cart reached out from the cart and grabbed a bag of dried sweetened pineapple pieces. "Mine!" he said, tossing them into the cart.

His mother's reaction was immediate. She grabbed the pineapple from the cart and put it back on the shelf, then turned and glared at her son. "Don't be a bad boy!" she commanded, wagging her finger in his face.

His reaction looked to me like a mixture of pain and pride; the former from mother being unhappy with him, and the latter from some inner knowledge of identity, confirmed by her words. He reached into the cart and grabbed a can of soup, glancing at me, his audience, and prepared to throw it on the floor. Mom intervened by roughly grabbing the can and again demanding that he not be bad, this time giving him a slap on the hand. I found my cookies and moved away as the little boy began looking for a new audience for his behavior.

Whenever we react to a person's behavior—particularly a child's—we can do it in either of two primary ways. One addresses the individual's personhood and ties it to his behavior, and the other addresses his personhood and disconnects it from his behavior. This is a critical distinction.

People who think they *are* their behaviors are caught in a continuous loop: In order to define themselves or to feel okay about themselves, they must continually bounce their behaviors off other people. Most people who start with this as children also become early and vulnerable targets for the advertising industry, whose primary message is that you are your possessions (when they're selling consumer goods, a message more often directed at men) or that you are your body (when they're selling cosmetics, clothes, and weight-loss programs, messages more often directed at women).

The power of this industry and its messages were made explicit in 1999 when the result of a three-year study of teenage girls on Fiji was released. The schoolgirls, living in the remote community of Nadroga, had never before been exposed to television, but in 1995 the community was wired to an incoming satellite feed and most of the houses in the community received free televisions from the government. They could tune in to American and European programming as well as a few local shows.

Before the introduction of television, according to a 2002 BBC report on the study,[11] the Fijian girls were happy with their bodies and the percentage who vomited to control their weight was zero—the same as in most traditional communities around the world that are not exposed to television. Three years later, however, 11 percent of the schoolgirls in Nadroga were regularly vomiting to control their weight, 69 percent were on some sort of diet, and 74 percent said that they thought of themselves as "fat" and/or "ugly."

Harvard's Dr. Anne Becker, one of the researchers, wrote of their findings in the *British Journal of Psychiatry*: "The impact of television appears especially profound, given the longstanding cultural traditions that previously had appeared protective against dieting, purging and body dissatisfaction in Fiji." Television and advertising are such powerful shapers of young lives and minds that it's particularly critical in those families that choose to keep a television in the house that its children have the resilient sense of self that the minority of Fijian girls had, allowing them to resist the predations of modern consumer culture.

In each parent/child interactive situation in which the child is defined by his behavior, the "I am" center of his personhood becomes disconnected from any state of inner centeredness. Happiness and self-assurance come only with doing or getting, and have no relationship to simply being, to "I know who I am, and I'm larger and deeper than what I do or what I own or what my body looks like."

The lack of this important self-knowledge begins with parents or the media telling children that *they are their behaviors*. Thus the alternative to saying, "Don't be a bad boy," is to say, "If you do that, we won't be able to continue shopping." For a more severe behavior, it may even be, "I love you so much that I'm not going to let you do that." It brings the core of the interaction back to the community of parent/child and doesn't speak at all about the child as a bad or good person.

BREAK THE PATTERN WITH A POSITIVE MESSAGE

The child in the supermarket also reminded me of one of the best lessons in childrearing that Louise and I ever learned. A friend of ours, an NLP (Neurolinguistic Programming) practitioner and psychologist, shared it with Louise over twenty years ago.

One of our children was in the habit of throwing fits in the supermarket, demanding things and shouting loudly when the demands weren't met. We'd tried both placating and punishing, and neither worked; the behavior just continued. Our friend had a two-part suggestion. "Do something unexpected," he said, "and do it in a way that reinforces both your love *and* the idea that life can be fun."

We started by priming our child during the day, talking about how much fun Louise was going to have shopping in the afternoon. "Would you like to have fun with me at the store?" she asked our four year old. "Yes!" was the enthusiastic reply.

When they got to the store and were going through the aisles, our child began to throw the predictable fit in the predictable place. At that point, Louise had a shopping cart only half full of food. "Oh," she said, "I thought you wanted to have fun with me here. But if it's not fun for both of us, it doesn't work, and it's not fun for me if you're throwing this fit."

She propelled the cart—complete with demanding child—to the service counter in the supermarket, where she said to the startled clerk, "I came to the supermarket to have fun shopping with my child, but my child doesn't want us both to have fun, so I'm going to leave these groceries here, drop my child off at home, and come back alone to finish having fun shopping."

"Okay," said the clerk, nodding the way people do to the inmates in an asylum.

Louise picked up our child from the cart, drove the two of them home, came into the house, and said to me, "Our child wasn't willing to let us both have fun at the supermarket, so will you baby-sit while I go back to the store to have fun shopping?"

"Of course," I said, watching our child's astonished expression. "I hope you have a lot of fun!"

"I will," Louise said cheerfully as she went out the door.

It was the last supermarket fit we ever experienced, and the story highlights one aspect of how many hunter/gatherer tribal children are raised: Interactions are cooperative and positive, even as the adults clearly define the parameters of behavior and the values that underlie those parameters.

WATCH FOR ISLANDS OF SUCCESS

I remember watching Geoff Guest, a seventy-five-year-old half-Aboriginal horseman in northern Queensland, Australia, teach a young Aboriginal boy how to tame and ride a wild horse they'd just caught a week earlier. As the horse skittered back with a wild look in his eye, Geoff slowly walked up to it, gently talking and holding out his hand, until he was finally close enough to touch the horse on the side of its neck. He made contact briefly and then quickly but smoothly backed away from the animal, still talking soothingly.

"It's to get him used to you," Geoff said to Billy,* the ten-year-old boy who was watching him. "Now you try it."

It took Billy a half-dozen tries before he could touch the horse. The first few were clumsy and did more to frighten than to reassure the horse. But through it all, Geoff simply kept repeating positive advice and instructions to Billy, never once pointing out his failures or mistakes.

Finally, Billy succeeded in touching the horse, and ran back toward Geoff with an inquiring look, wondering what Geoff's response would be. Geoff behaved as if Billy had just done the most important and wonderful thing Geoff had ever seen in his life. He mentioned it several times during the afternoon when they were cleaning up the corral. Over dinner, he told his wife, Norma, and the other boys at the program about Billy's amazing accomplishment. He made sure everybody knew.

Billy was a young man who'd been sent into Geoff's care by the court because he'd repeatedly stolen things from the store in his community, had broken into a house, and then had beaten another child so badly that the child required hospitalization—all this by age ten. He was one tough kid, the master of antisocial behavior whom foster families and the child welfare system had given up on. But under Geoff's care, this young man discovered something he could do that was exceptional by any standard—train and then ride a wild horse—and he could do it well. As Billy achieved mastery in one domain, it quickly translated into competence in other areas of his life: He became more social, more empathetic, more trusting, and more willing to tackle his schoolwork, which quickly became another area of competence for him.

* I've changed the boy's name to protect his privacy.

THE IMPORTANCE OF MASTERY

Psychiatrist Milton Erickson was famous for his "ordeal therapy," as chronicled in numerous books including *Uncommon Therapy*[12] by Jay Haley. People would come to Erickson for issues ranging from impotence to phobias to insomnia, and very often, before taking them on as patients, Erickson would give them an ordeal, a difficult task to perform, such as spending an entire night scrubbing the floors of their house or climbing Squaw Peak (a small mountain near Erickson's home in Phoenix), in order to "prove their commitment" to working with Erickson. More often than not, people "magically" got better after undertaking the ordeal.

In the years since Erickson's death, many in the field and a number of books have speculated about whether his ordeal therapies were based on placebo effect, carried some subtle hypnotic component, or were meta-systems for people to work out issues at the unconscious level. While all are no doubt pieces of this enduring puzzle, the most likely explanation for why Erickson's method of forcing accomplishment in one area of life translated into psychological healing in others is found in Martin Seligman's book *Learned Optimism*.[13] Seligman's work with dogs, which he describes in his book, shows that depression can be *learned* at almost any time in life, as can optimism. And in almost all cases, optimism and competence in life come from a person achieving mastery in some domain of their lives.

As seen in Seligman's research and the literature on exercise and depression cited in chapter 14, it doesn't matter whether a person's mastery of process or technique stemmed from a problem area in their lives. Usually it didn't, but once people achieved mastery in one area—even if it was simply in daily exercise—then they quickly became competent in other areas. (I believe this is one of the reasons why people have hobbies, and why hobbies are so demonstrably therapeutic; they represent areas or domains of total self-control, competence, and mastery. The feelings of mastery experienced in the hobby then translate into work, relationships, and other areas of a person's life.)

I remember well a time when one of our children was struggling in school but had become an expert in skateboarding. Louise went out with a video camera to videotape his skateboarding.

"Why are you encouraging that dangerous behavior?" I said, incredulous.

"Because it's something he's good at," she replied, demonstrating the wisdom that has made her such a great parent and coach. "He needs successes in his life right now, and he needs recognition for them. This is the only success he has, so I'm going to make the most of it."

Her recognition of his skateboarding success corresponded—probably not coincidentally—with an improvement in his school-work. So look for areas of competence in a child's life, and then honor, praise, and nurture them. Encourage a hobby, even if it's collecting comic books (our children took up skateboarding and horse-back riding, but many parents aren't comfortable with such risky endeavors). Remember that Thomas Edison's mother *encouraged* her seven-year-old son when he insisted he preferred to play with chemicals and electricity over going to school.

TURN OFF THE TELEVISION

Author and psychologist Robert Wolff shared an interesting story with me while I was writing this book:

> The brightest of my grandchildren is the son of a Polynesian mother who nursed him till he was three, who constantly touched him, held him, and still does. He is very secure in who he is, and that he is loved. He is rarely scolded. He is now in Hawaiian school (taught in Hawaiian), and speaks four languages fluently: Hawaiian, Marquesan, French, and English. He is five years old. I would estimate his IQ to be at least 150.
>
> I also saw an interesting change in him when he began to watch TV. Before then, he would entertain himself for hours with sticks and a rock. Now he is more moody, hangs passively in front of the TV. Yes, definitely a change in personality. But fortunately his parents allow him only an hour, I think, of TV a day. Away from the TV he is pretty much his old self.[14]

Television is, in many ways, a drug. Consider for a moment what makes a substance a drug of abuse:

- A drug of abuse is a distillate or derivative of a natural substance but not the natural substance itself. Heroin, for example, is derived from morphine, which was originally derived from the fluids of the opium poppy. Cocaine is extracted from the leaves of the coca plant using solvents. In their raw states, neither poppies nor coca leaves are particularly toxic or mind-altering, but when they're distilled in these ways, they acquire both properties to an intense degree.
- A drug of abuse alters emotional state or mood in a way that is considered pleasant (which is why people continue to use them).[15]
- A drug of abuse creates a craving for more of itself. The more powerful the drug, the more likely it is that people will consume it daily; weaker drugs can be more readily resisted, consumed only occasionally or socially.
- A drug of abuse will alter in significant ways the lives of those addicted to it as they try to make sure they have regular access to the substance.
- A drug of abuse will *permanently* alter the brain function of either a child or teenager exposed to it because the brain of a young person is still physically and psychologically forming. So far this has been demonstrated in laboratory experiments with heroin, cocaine, amphetamine, and nicotine.[16]
- The addictive potential of a drug of abuse is measured most often by a behavior called *chipping*, which is defined as occasional, social, or experimental use of a drug (versus the regular and/or daily consumption that marks addiction).

For example, the majority of people can chip mildly addictive drugs such as marijuana and alcohol, while cocaine and heroin are harder to chip without developing addiction. The most addictive drugs available in our modern world are cocaine treated with a pH-altering substance such as ammonia, which shifts it from its natural acid form to a more powerful and more rapidly absorbed alkaline form (called "freebase" or "crack" cocaine); and tobacco treated with a substance such as ammonia to shift its nicotine from its natural acid form to a more powerful and rapidly absorbed alkaline form (as tobacco companies do to the tobacco in cigarettes by adding ammonia as a "flavoring," creating, essentially, "freebase" nicotine).

Now consider television in this context:

- Television presents a distilled derivative of real life. We see in ways that wouldn't be possible in real life; we look down from the sky, then zero in on a face for a close-up, then zoom across a landscape. In real life, problems often take years to solve and sometimes can't be solved at all, but on television all problems are neatly wrapped up in a show's thirty or sixty minutes. Our actual experience of reality is smooth and continuous, as we see, hear, feel, taste, and smell in a regular and seamless way. On television, however, reality is chopped into camera shots that rarely hold for longer than five to seven seconds.
- Television, as numerous studies have shown, alters brain waves in ways that are comparable to the alterations produced by both narcotics and hypnosis.[17] Through this process, they also produce a rapid shift in mood, generally flattening affect and separating people from the ennui or pain of everyday life.
- Television alters the behavior of children exposed to it for long periods of time in ways that suggest long-term or permanent changes in such children's brain structure.
- Television—even in small doses—creates a craving for more in susceptible individuals, as was discovered in the Fijian studies and as is so often the experience of those who have a television in their home.
- Television can induce people to alter their lives significantly to maintain access to it, including changing their eating and sleeping patterns, foregoing social interaction, reorganizing their living space, and assuming debt to purchase bigger and better TVs and access to more channels.

Think about it: For all practical purposes, television meets the same criteria as an addictive drug such as the nicotine in tobacco.

Now consider the power the tobacco industry would have if their drug, in addition to addicting people, was also able to change those people's opinions. If by smoking a particular brand, you could turn a person from a Democrat into a Republican, from a customer of Sam's Diner into a habituate of McDonald's. Television can do this.

Interestingly, on television you rarely see people watching television, although if you were to go door-to-door in the developed world on any given evening, the vast majority of the people you'd find would be watching their screens. The television industry presents not only a distillate of reality, but a highly skewed one at that. We don't see people doing those things that most of us do, and we are induced to feel or believe things that don't reflect reality. Numerous studies have shown that the more television people watch, the more likely they are to be fearful, isolated, and convinced that crime is worse than it really is.[18]

A report published by the American Psychological Association explicitly says that "Psychological research has shown three major effects of seeing violence on television: Children may become less sensitive to the pain and suffering of others; children may be more fearful of the world around them; children may be more likely to behave in aggressive or harmful ways toward others.[19]

A quarter century ago, pioneer thinker and researcher Marie Winn wrote a book about the effects of television known at that time. Titled *The Plug-In Drug*, it became a classic and has recently been reprinted in an updated edition. In the original book, which I've owned all these years and have often shared with others, she observed:

> Real addicts do not merely pursue a pleasurable experience one time in order to function normally. They need to repeat it again and again. Something about that particular experience makes life without it less than complete. . . . Not unlike drugs or alcohol, the television experience allows the participant to blot out the real world and enter into a pleasurable and passive mental state. The worries and anxieties of reality are as effectively deferred by becoming absorbed in a television program as by going on a "trip"

induced by drugs or alcohol. And just as alcoholics are only vaguely aware of their addiction, feeling that they control their drinking more than they really do ("I can cut it out any time I want—I just like to have three of four drinks before dinner"), people similarly overestimate their control over television watching. Even as they put off other activities to spend hour after hour watching television, they feel they could easily resume living in a different, less passive style. But somehow or other, while the television set is present in their homes, the click doesn't sound. With television pleasures available, those other experiences seem less attractive, more difficult somehow.[20]

The title of a *Scientific American* magazine article summarizes three decades of research: "Television Addiction Is No Mere Metaphor."[21] In August 1999, the American Academy of Pediatrics took the unprecedented step of publicly saying children two or younger should watch *no* television whatsoever: Watching television deprives babies of critical contact time with humans.

Psychologist Richard DeGrandpre argues in his extraordinary and thought-provoking book *Ritalin Nation* that many of the symptoms children are drugged for in school are caused by early exposure to television and other aspects of our rapid-fire culture. Television-raised children are impulsive and impatient, he says, because "listening is usually a waiting situation that provides a low level of stimulation."[22]

In his brilliant books *In the Absence of the Sacred*[23] and *Four Arguments for the Elimination of Television*,[24] author Jerry Mander documents numerous cases in which the cultures of indigenous peoples have been devastated and the children of such peoples damaged by the introduction of television into their communities (which has sometimes been forced upon them by governments who were lobbied by corporate interests). Television, it seems, hits hunter/gatherer people particularly hard; perhaps, because their minds are more sensitive to the subtle environmental nuance of something moving through the bush or jungle, they are more vulnerable to the rapid flicker of the television's neurological drug.

For many families with Edison-gene children, eliminating the television from the house—a seemingly radical step but a rapidly growing movement in the United States spearheaded by homeschooling groups and organizations like www.whitedot.org—has been a godsend, as these children become more curious, develop critical thinking skills, interact more and more competently with others, and begin to read voraciously.

13

Alfred Adler's Principles for Raising Children

Peace is neither the absence of war nor the presence of a
disarmament agreement. Peace is a change of heart.
RICHARD LAMM, FORMER GOVERNOR OF COLORADO

I mentioned earlier that my first exposure to ADHD was in 1978 when I was executive director of a residential treatment facility for abused and emotionally disturbed children. During my years in that position, I learned a tremendous amount about how to deal with troubled children, lessons that apply equally well to more normal children. But it's our Edison-gene children who are among the most vulnerable, for the many reasons already mentioned, and so it's particularly important to review our childcare practices in light of both their challenges and their potentials. One of the primary child care manuals we used when I ran the program for emotionally disturbed children was a book titled *Children: The Challenge* by Rudopf Dreikurs,[1] on the application of the psychological techniques of Alfred Adler to childrearing. It's particularly valuable for helping Edison-gene children achieve their full potential.

Entire books have been written about Adlerian childcare principles, with *Children: The Challenge* being among the best of them. The core principle of Adler's work is often referred to as *logical consequences* (as opposed to punishment). In a similar vein, Michael Popkin, Ph.D., president of Active Parenting Publishing[2] in Marietta, Georgia, produces a powerful and truly transformational set of videotapes based largely on Adlerian child rearing and logical consequences.

Because Adler's principles on child care are so powerful and timeless, I thought it would be most useful in this book to summarize them and then fill in the outline with some commentary based on my own experience working with and raising Edison-gene children. I've adapted the following outline of Adler's concepts from a more detailed article written by Henry T. Stein, Ph.D., of the Alfred Adler Institute of San Francisco.[3] The headings have been derived from Dr. Stein's words; the text is my commentary on his outline.

PROMOTE MUTUAL RESPECT

We learn our worldview as children, mainly from observing our parents and how they interact with us. When children are respected by their parents and see daily interactions between themselves and their parents based on that respect, they learn this critical skill—the importance of respecting others, particularly others weaker than themselves, and the importance of self-respect.

As we observe adults in the world who easily and casually disrespect others for "reasons" of nation, race, economics, education, gender, sexual preference, and so forth, it's easy to see the consequences of raising a child in a power-based home where children and parents don't have a relationship of mutual respect. (And when such people become national leaders, the consequences can be terrible on a large scale, as the world has seen repeatedly.)

Edison-gene children are far more often the victims of what they experience as disrespectful and disapproving behavior directed at them by parents, teachers, and even peers. Therefore, it's particularly important to provide these unique children with alternative respectful models of behavior, and to encourage their own self-respect.

ENCOURAGE

Adler noticed that a child most often misbehaves as a way of trying to get or accomplish something, whether it's a candy bar or simply to be noticed. As such, he concluded, this was a last-resort behavior, meaning that the child had given up on more positive ways of getting what he wanted because he'd observed that they weren't working.

It's so easy to ignore children until they misbehave and then react by either punishing them or giving them what they want. In doing so, we reinforce for them the notion that the last-resort behavior of misbehaving is an appropriate first resort for getting what they need or want—and thus set them up for a very difficult life. If we instead encourage children whenever we see them moving toward or engaging in any sort of positive activity, even the smallest and least significant activity, we teach them to trust and respect their own instincts for appropriate behavior, give them a sense of belief in their own abilities that will serve them for a lifetime, and help them clearly understand that misbehavior truly is a last-resort behavior, worthy of turning to only when all else has failed.

FOSTER SECURITY

In modern American culture, we tend to think that security comes from *things*—a good job, a home, a car that runs, the respect of our peers, a spouse or family who loves us. But these are actually externalizations of an inner security. Without this inner sense of security, no amount of possessions, money, or even relationships with others will make a person feel secure. (Literature and movies are filled with the almost archetypal figure of the insecure rich person, desperately trying to fill their need for security by acquiring more and more things or compulsively going through serial relationships.)

According to Adler and Stein, "It is only possible to achieve it [security] through the experience and feeling of having overcome difficulties." This may explain the recent study finding that the single largest variable that predicted success in graduate school—more important than high school grades, socioeconomic status, wealth, race, or the neighborhood in which a person grew up—was the percentage of the tuition that the student herself paid. Those who paid most of their own tuition had the highest grades; those whose tuition was paid by parents had the lowest grades and were most likely to drop out. Security, it turns out, is a gut-level feeling that must be installed through learning, and the only way to learn it is to take on challenges and successfully meet them.

Adults, then, must constantly be on the lookout for challenges that are within the realm of an Edison-gene child's competence—neither so easy that they're boring, nor so difficult that they're unattainable—and then structure opportunities for the child to take on the challenge and meet it successfully. This means not interfering, not paving the way, not making things easier. And it also means not criticizing when an Edison-gene child faces a challenge and fails but instead quickly helping the child find another, different challenge that she can successfully meet.

An Edison-gene child who has confronted and conquered challenges will grow into a secure adult who can take on nearly anything and succeed (as did Thomas Edison). An overprotected child who is always guaranteed success because of parental intervention will grow into an insecure adult who is overly dependent on, and vulnerable to, stronger personalities who may seek to exploit or abuse her.

AVOID REWARD AND PUNISHMENT

Reward and punishment disconnect a child from a sense of family and community. They turn every opportunity for mutual interaction into a "what's in it for me?" situation. Children who are over-rewarded often grow up to be adults who believe the world owes them a living, and who see others as objects to manipulate to their own ends. Children who are over-punished—a common situation for "Dennis the Menace"–type Edison-gene kids—often grow up to be adults with a distorted and cruel sense of what justice is.

Behaviorists object to this observation by pointing out that the real adult world is filled with rewards and punishments, from paychecks to tickets for speeding. While that's true, it's also true that only the unfortunate people raised in a world of extreme reward and punishment go to work only for a paycheck and hold to the speed limit only to avoid a ticket. Most emotionally healthy people instead find meaningful jobs they enjoy and drive at the speed limit because it's the reasonable and safe thing to do.

USE NATURAL AND LOGICAL CONSEQUENCES

Natural and logical consequences are at the core of Adlerian child-rearing principles. Natural consequences don't require adult intervention, whereas logical consequences do. A *natural consequence* to a child leaving his bike out in the rain is that it rusts and no longer works. A parent might say then, "I'm sorry you made that choice. Now you don't have a bike that works." And leave it at that. Children raised with natural consequences grow into responsible adults well prepared for the real world of our culture.

A *logical consequence* is an alternative to power-based parenting in that the parent's response to the child allows the child to experience the logical result of his own behavior. If a child persists in playing a video game when it's time to do his homework, the video game must be put away until the homework is finished. If a child throws a fit at the store, she's removed from the store and can't go back until she agrees to behave.

The key to administering logical consequences is never to let punishment-based, disappointment-based, or anger-based emotions enter into the picture. Raw punishment, disapproval, and anger create confusion and fear in a child and will produce an adult filled with anxiety that unpredictable and terrible things may happen at any time for no particular logical reason. Edison-gene children are particularly vulnerable to this because of their experience, throughout life, of being a square peg in the round hole of our society.

Children raised with punishment often grow into adults who arbitrarily and irrationally make decisions about which rules to follow, which to bend, and which to break—and thus have a life of consequences they can't understand (and often blame on others).

On the other hand, logical consequences help a child realize that his actions have very specific consequences, that those consequences have a pattern to them, and that pattern can be understood and predicted through logic. As an Edison-gene child raised with logical consequences grows up, he easily and quickly figures out the rules of society, school, work, and other social institutions, and can make rational and reasoned choices about when to follow and when to bend or break those rules to achieve a specific purpose.

ACT INSTEAD OF TALK IN CONFLICT SITUATIONS

When parents try to negotiate with children in conflict situations, they're immediately communicating to the child that they're open to compromise and the situation isn't clearly one of behavior consequence. Discussion instead of action also teaches a child that it's possible to "talk yourself out of trouble"—and bright Edison-gene children are legendary for their ability to fast-talk their way out of things. (It's a survival skill many develop early on.)

When a parent instead simply takes action—without anger or any other explicit or implied emotional content—an Edison-gene child learns that in this world there are consistent and predictable results to choices and behaviors. This is the sort of invaluable lesson a child will carry into adulthood.

USE WITHDRAWAL AS A COUNTERACTION

Withdrawing from a situation is different from using the cold shoulder as punishment. Withdrawal means a parent has determined the child is trying to provoke a power struggle or is making unreasonable demands (and knows they're unreasonable). Once the parent has made her point—clearly and without heat—and knows the child understands it, if the child persists in trying to debate the issue or engaging in the behaving, sometimes the best thing to do is simply to go elsewhere, leaving the child to realize, "Gee, I guess that didn't work."

A good example of this is another strategy that Louise figured out when our children were young: She'd take a book along with her and if the kids got into a fight in the back seat, she'd pull off onto a side street, turn off the car, pick up the book, and begin reading. When the kids asked what was going on, she'd say, "Until you stop your fighting, I'm just going to sit here and read and enjoy myself." The fights usually ended very quickly.

Keep in mind that this is totally different from using the very destructive emotional weapon of withholding attention or affection from a child as a way to control their behavior or win a power struggle.

WITHDRAW FROM THE PROVOCATION, NOT FROM THE CHILD

There's a subtle but vital distinction between disengaging from a child and disengaging from a child's negative behaviors. Doctor Spock pioneered the Adlerian idea that we should, as much as possible, praise good behavior and ignore bad behavior.

The reason is that all of us, all the time, are doing one of two things: moving toward pleasure or moving away from pain. We use these as essential motivation strategies in life and build elaborate self-talk around them. I've observed that adults who seem paralyzed in life, who have a hard time getting up in the morning or difficulty undertaking new projects or relationships, are those who use "moving away from pain" as their primary motivation strategy. To get themselves to do anything, they imagine the worse thing that will happen if they fail to do it and then use that painful image to scare themselves into, for instance, getting out of bed. While this works over the short term, it's exhausting and self-defeating over the long-term.

On the other hand, people who use "moving toward pleasure" as their primary motivational technique find getting up in the morning a joy, look forward to going to work, and enter new situations with a sense of adventure and positive anticipation.

While there are times when each strategy is important, in childhood we learn the primary one we'll use in most situations throughout life, by observing the way our parents motivate us. Children whose parents use punishment or emotional withdrawal as a way to get their children to behave become, as adults, pessimistic moving-away-from-pain people. They live in a world of inner turmoil that can be changed only by active outside intervention through techniques such as Solution-Based Therapy and NeuroLinguistic Programming (NLP). And, sadly, because Edison-gene children are so often "getting into trouble" or "not fitting in," they bear a disproportionate amount of criticism and punishment, even in early life. It's easy for them to pick up moving-away-from-pain strategies, and turn these into unfortunate lifelong habits.

However, parents who choose to withdraw from their children's negative behaviors (ignoring the bad as much as possible) and actively and enthusiastically engage them in their positive behaviors (rewarding the good whenever possible), help their children to grow up to be optimistic, can-do people with a core moving-toward-pleasure motivation strategy.

Finally, parents who withdraw from both behavior and child can produce insecure children who will grow to be adults who seek out love by acting compliant.

In support of this principle of Adler, one of the important points that Dr. Stein makes is this: "The less attention the child gets when he disturbs, the more he needs when he is cooperative."

DON'T INTERFERE IN CHILDREN'S FIGHTS

Both sibling and peer fighting are the means children use to learn how to resolve conflict. While they may appear one-sided (older versus younger child, for example) and provoke our adult sense of fairness, the reality is that children learn lifelong strategies in this way for dealing with those both less powerful and more powerful than they are. This is critical learning, particularly for Edison-gene children, and a parent who constantly intervenes on behalf of the smaller or weaker child prevents that child from learning adaptive strategies (including negotiation, withdrawal, and creating strategic alliances) for dealing with others who have more power.

When parents readily intervene in their fights, children also learn that fighting is a quick and simple way to get their parents' attention. This isn't particularly useful for either the parents or the children, and certainly not a skill we want our Edison-gene kids to carry into adulthood.

FIGHTING REQUIRES COOPERATION

There's truth to the old saying that "it takes two to tango." Recognizing this, parents are wise never to try to play judge and jury in determining who is "responsible" for a fight: It's always both children. When our kids were growing up and got into fights, both were sent to their rooms to cool down (a logical consequence). When one or the other would complain, "But she started it!" our response was always, "It doesn't matter who started it, it takes two to keep it going. You can both go cool down." In relatively short order, our children learned not to bother fighting around us.

Another strategy we used was to simply say to our children, "If you're going to fight like that, please go into another room to do it, because I'd like to enjoy this book I'm going to read until you're finished. Let me know when you're done." When the fighting no longer accomplished the usual goal of getting our attention, and never got either Louise or me to take sides, the children figured out pretty quickly that fighting wasn't a useful attention-getting strategy. This led them to try more useful and successful strategies, like engaging in conversation, playing games, asking questions, and so on.

The obvious exception to this principle is when one child continually and often surreptitiously brutalizes a weaker child, apparently just for the "joy" of causing pain. This behavior, like that of the child who abuses animals, is a sign of childhood mental illness, and must be responded to with immediate professional intervention.

TAKE TIME TO TEACH ESSENTIAL SKILLS AND HABITS

Children are not born knowing the rules of our culture. Be it table manners, interpersonal interactions, or conflict resolution, children need to be explicitly trained in the skills of functional community participation. And, as any parent of one can tell you, Edison-gene children often need even more attention and training than their "normal" peers.

Waiting until children misbehave in front of company to teach them lessons is humiliating to the child and counterproductive to the parents' social time. Make a point of using family meals, alone time, and other appropriate opportunities to overtly and explicitly teach your children how society expects them to behave and how to most functionally get what they want in the world.

NEVER DO FOR A CHILD WHAT HE CAN DO FOR HIMSELF

In the Dale Carnegie course, there's an exercise that involves standing in front of the class and reciting, in a loud voice and with animated gestures: "I know people in the ranks who will stay in the ranks.

Why? I'll tell you why. Simply because they *don't know how to get things done!*"

One of the most important skills we learn as children is how to accomplish things. The short-term benefits of accomplishment are a feeling of satisfaction and parental recognition. The long-term benefit is that a new skill has been learned that will help your child be one of those who lifts herself "higher than the ranks" to be a person of accomplishment. This is particularly critical for Edison-gene children, who so often have an overabundance of failure experiences in public schools.

Over the years I've talked with many high achievers and it seems they basically fall into two categories: those who are achieving for unhealthy reasons (and, thus, can never get enough money, power, or recognition), and those who are achieving for healthy reasons (and, thus, make positive contributions in the world but also enjoy their lives). My theory is that the former are still trying to impress parents who failed to acknowledge their childhood accomplishments, whereas the latter are those whose parents delighted in their accomplishments. (Those who rarely accomplish anything are often the ones who had life handed to them on a silver platter, or were those unfortunate children who were never encouraged or given opportunities to find their own areas of unique competence.)

DON'T OVERPROTECT

A child looks to her parents for information about what she is capable of doing. This happens in a thousand ways, both subtle and explicit. Even the expressions on parents' faces or their tone of voice tell a child that they think she is either capable or incapable of whatever she may be setting out to do.

Within the limits of safety and rationality, when we let our children push the boundaries of the world for themselves, we also help them to discover their own abilities. They'll naturally discover, through their own trial and error, where their boundaries of capability are, and as they grow up, they'll find that those boundaries change as their abilities grow.

When parents are overprotective, they stifle this natural, healthy, real-world learning process. Instead, children learn to look to authority figures to tell them what they can and can't do, and in adulthood will be more easily swayed by authority figures in our culture who may not have their best interests at heart.

Thomas Edison's mother, although alarmed about the dangers of the laboratory he built in their home at the age of ten, nonetheless allowed him to have and use it (although she moved it to a less flammable part of the house). Allowing children to take chances—and praising then when they succeed—while giving them the space to learn their own lessons from their failures will produce self-confident, responsible adults.

AVOID BEING OVERLY RESPONSIBLE

Natural and logical consequences are life's best teachers. A few weeks ago, I sat with a group of parents who were discussing their Edison-gene children's challenges in school. One mother commented on how her child hadn't been doing his homework, and his teacher called to let the parent know.

"And how are you and Jimmy going to work that out?" the mother asked the teacher on the phone.

Shocked, the teacher said, "But I thought you'd do something."

"I'm not his teacher, and I'm not him," the mother answered. "I'll leave it to you two to work out."

"But then he may fail!" the teacher said.

"That's not the end of the world," the mother said, reflecting on all the ways she was working with her son on in-home social skills, such as keeping his room organized and exercising some control over his social life. "If you can't motivate him to do his homework, I don't see how that's my problem."

The other parents in the room were shocked. What if Jimmy didn't make it through high school? How would he get into college? How would he get a good job?

"I'm more interested in him growing up to be a person who's responsible for himself," the mom said. "If he flunks out of high school, he can always take a GED and go to junior college. Even Harvard will take kids from junior colleges if they do well enough. If he's determined to get into college, he'll do it. In the meantime, I want him to learn that he can do things for himself. And if he has to fail as part of that learning, so be it. Henry Ford had seven bankruptcies before he succeeded; Thomas Edison had thousands of light-bulb failures. Sometimes we learn the most from our failures, and I'm not about to deprive my son of this valuable learning opportunity."

Alfred Adler couldn't have said it better.

DISTINGUISH BETWEEN POSITIVE AND NEGATIVE ATTENTION

When Edison-gene children misbehave to get attention (as they so often do), it's nearly always a symptom that their attempts to get attention through positive behaviors have failed. (Everybody would rather be praised than punished.) Negative attention-getting behavior should be a red flag to parents that they need to spend more time with their children in ways that will give their children opportunities for accomplishment, win-win fun, and praise. Over time, as children begin to know that their positive behaviors will get them the attention and approval they naturally crave and need, their negative behaviors will recede into the background.

In addition to this, one core NLP concept is that "all behavior has at its core the goal for a positive outcome." A corollary to this is that when people try to take behaviors we have away from us, we'll resist ferociously because we feel like a part of us or a potentially important resource of ours is being stolen.

Understanding this, it's important not to try to "take away" negative behaviors from children, but, rather, to put them in context. If a child is angry or violent, instead of telling him not to be angry or violent, it's far more useful to say, "That's a pretty good display of anger, and when you grow up there may be times when it's important for you to be able to have self-righteous anger. But right now, in this situation, I'd suggest you may want to try negotiation (or something else) instead. For example . . . ."

UNDERSTAND THE CHILD'S GOAL

According to Adler, all behavior (child or adult) has a purpose, and this purpose is generally derived from some very straightforward categories. A parent reacting to behaviors without first trying to understand the purpose the child is trying to achieve is like the mechanic who doesn't understand why the engine is making a funny noise but decides a new coat of paint would sure make the car look better.

Before parents choose their response to a child's behavior, it's useful to first have either a clear understanding or at least a good and reasoned guess as to the behavior's goal. (Notice I said "goal" and not "cause." This isn't an attempt to play Freud and go back into old traumas and other such things; instead, we want to deal with present behavior and present goals, which will translate into future abilities.)

Dr. Stein suggests that children's misbehavior can generally be organized into one of four broad goals. The child is usually unaware of his goals. His behavior, though illogical to others, is consistent with his own interpretation of his place in the family group:

1. **Attention-getting:** He wants attention and service. We respond by feeling annoyed and reminding and coaxing him.
2. **Power:** He wants to be the boss. We respond by feeling provoked and get into a power contest with him, e.g., "You can't get away with this!"
3. **Revenge:** He wants to hurt us. We respond by feeling deeply hurt, e.g., "I'll get even!"
4. **Display of inadequacy:** He wants to be left alone, with no demands made upon him. We respond by feeling despair, e.g., "I don't know what to do!"

If your first impulse is to react in one of these four ways, you can be fairly sure you have discovered the goal of the child's misbehavior.

A child who wants to be powerful generally has a parent who also seeks power. It's axiomatic that wounded children grow up to be wounded parents who, in turn, produce wounded children. According to Adler and Stein, when a parent has unresolved issues around power, he'll often act them out by creating power contests with his children. Stein notes that, "The use of power teaches children only that strong people get what they want." The result of this is that the child never learns negotiation, cooperation, innovation, and dozens of other strategies, and grows into a psychologically and emotionally lopsided, power-centered adult.

Even if your first instinct (because of the way you were raised) is to use power in your relationship with your Edison-gene child, let that be your cue to try something else. The result will be an improved and closer relationship with your child, and a good lesson to your child about other strategies she can use as she grows into adulthood.

A HABIT IS MAINTAINED IF IT ACHIEVES ITS PURPOSE

This is the Adlerian corollary to the NLP notion that all behavior has as its goal a positive outcome. The simple way of stating it is that there's always a reason why people do things. And when that reason goes away, unless the person has engraved the behavior so deeply in his psyche that it's become a habit (which, too, can change) then the behavior will go away, too.

The main driver of negative behavior, or what Stein calls "bad habits," is when it predictably, consistently, and repeatedly gets attention. Even if the attention is a dirty look, a harsh word, or a slap, in the world of an Edison-gene child, any attention is better than no attention at all. Children are helpless and dependent beings and, as John Bowlby pointed out in his books published between 1969 and 1988,[4] their need to attach themselves to their parents or caregivers is so strong that they'll even withstand abuse and punishment to meet it.

Thus, the goal of parents is to prevent them from having to go to those extremes and provide them with the positive attention they need for normal brain and emotional development. If provided adequately and consistently, the negative habits and behaviors will fall away.

MINIMIZE MISTAKES

By "minimize mistakes," Stein and Adler don't mean "don't make so many mistakes," but, instead, "don't pay much attention to mistakes."

This is true both for our own mistakes as adults (which our children are watching carefully) and our children's mistakes. It's the adults and children terrified of making mistakes who never seem to go anywhere in the world (because they're always planning, in order to avoid the mistakes) and are defensive about being "wrong."

Mistakes, after all, are essential to the learning process and one of our most important and valuable teachers. By behaving as if our own and our children's mistakes are opportunities for learning (rather than opportunities for punishment), we create "learning machine" Edison-like children who are unafraid to take on new challenges in the world because they now know that if they make a mistake they'll learn from it and move on to a new, higher plateau. In NLP there are two famous predicating assumptions: "There are no failures, only feedback," and, "There are no mistakes, only outcomes."

I remember a story that one of my first bosses, a man named Tom Jones, general manager at WJIM-TV in Lansing, Michigan, told me when I was just seventeen: There was a young man who worked in a bank, and he wanted one day to be the bank manager. He went to the bank's president and told him of his ambition and asked what he had to do to end up in the president's chair twenty years down the road. The bank manager took a puff on his cigar as he thought about the question, then said, "Don't make any mistakes."

"But how do I avoid making mistakes?" the young man asked.

"Get experience," the bank manager said.

"And how do I get experience?"

At which point Jones smiled at me and said, "And the bank manager leaned back, took a big puff on his cigar, and said in his most serious voice, 'Make a hell of a lot of mistakes—and learn from them.'"

One of the greatest gifts we can give our Edison-gene children is the knowledge that mistakes aren't bad things, but instead are learning opportunities—thinly disguised gifts.

TRY A FAMILY COUNCIL AND HAVE FUN TOGETHER

Stein's final Adlerian advice is that every family should regularly meet in a way that gives every member of the household an opportunity to express him- or herself. In many indigenous cultures, a sacred object or "talking stick" is often passed from person to person, and only the person with the stick is allowed to speak. While the stickbearer speaks, everybody else can only make noises of agreement or disagreement.

Stein recommends that every meeting be goal- and future-oriented, rather than dwelling on the past. As he says, "The emphasis should be on, 'What can we do about the situation?'" Many families find weekly meetings useful. In our home, we used Friday night, whenever possible, as a time both to light a candle for the world in a brief, spiritual ritual and to talk about our family issues. And most indigenous hunter peoples have a tradition that, while different from American democracy, is useful in families as well: Decisions are made only by complete consensus, rather than by majority rule. Without total consensus, the disagreeing member may feel left out, and may even work to sabotage the goal of the group.

Another critical element in building a sense of family is to play together. Families that call family meetings only when there's a problem will soon discover that the meetings are dreaded; they become a heavy weight or a reminder of negative feelings. After a while, just the act of calling the meeting itself will be enough to make people anxious or unhappy.

Be sure, then, that the numbers of times you meet to play as a family—whether for Scrabble or for a night out at the movies or a weekend of camping—is at least equal to (and ideally several times more than) the numbers of times you meet to discuss problems.

THE EDISON-GENE FAMILY

Given that the Edison gene doesn't exist in a vacuum—it's inherited, after all—odds are there's not just a single individual in a family with it. Of the thousands of Edison-gene children I've met, only a handful of times has it not been fairly apparent to me which of their parents also carried the gene.

Families with several members who are impulsive, distractible, energetic, and have a low threshold for boring meetings means that it's important to have regular rituals (such as our Friday night candle lighting) to keep things on track. It also means that all members of the family usually need to work on learning to listen carefully, to practice patience, and to discover ways to turn blame into a perception of opportunity.

In my experience as a parent, as the founder of a school for ADHD children, and as the executive director of a residential treatment facility for abused and emotionally disturbed children, the tools in this chapter are absolutely the most important and useful in helping raise an Edison-gene child to fulfill his or her greatest potential—along with, of course, finding an appropriate educational environment that's helpful, nurturing, and accommodating to a child's learning style.

14

Educating the Edison-Gene Child

*I had a terrible education. I attended a school
for emotionally disturbed teachers.*

WOODY ALLEN

*In our dream . . . people yield themselves with perfect
docility to our molding hands. We shall not try to make
these people or any of their children into philosophers or
men of learning or men of science. We have not to raise
up from among them authors, educators, poets, or men
of letters. We shall not search for embryonic artists,
painters, musicians, nor lawyers, doctors, preachers,
politicians, statesmen, of whom we have ample supply.
That task we set before ourselves is very simple . . .
We will organize children [of the working class] . . .
and teach them to do in a perfect way the things their
fathers and mothers are doing in an imperfect way.*

ROCKEFELLER'S EDUCATION BOARD,
OCCASIONAL LETTER NUMBER ONE, 1906

In 1965, a psychologist named Martin Seligman and some of his colleagues decided to expand a little on Pavlov's dog experiments. They were going to use a sound, just like Pavlov's bell, but instead of giving the dog the reward of food every time the bell rang, Seligman would instead gave the dog a brief but painful electric shock. The dog was suspended in a hammock for the experiment so he could be carefully observed during what was known in behaviorism circles as the "learning phase."

The idea was that the dog would come to associate the sound of the bell with the electric shock. Once the association was made, Seligman assumed that the sound of the bell alone would be enough to bring about some sort of "moving away from pain" response on the part of the dog.

So after giving the dog a few rings of the bell and a few shocks to train him to equate the sound of the bell with pain, Seligman and his colleagues put him into a box with two dog-sized compartments—one of which contained the apparatus that administered the electric shock—separated by a low fence over which the dog could easily see and even jump. The much-anticipated moment had arrived. The results could be predicted, of course: With a ring of the bell, the dog would jump out of the compartment with the shocking apparatus and into the safe compartment.

So Seligman rang the bell. And the dog didn't move. He rang the bell again, and again, the dog didn't move. Maybe the dog needed to quickly relearn the lesson, so Seligman rang the bell and gave the dog a shock at the same time. Still the dog didn't move but just stayed in place and cried.

The researchers thought that maybe this dog was odd. So into the same compartment they put a dog that had never been trained to associate a shock with a bell, and then rang the bell and gave him a shock simultaneously. With a yelp, the dog jumped into the safe side of the box. They moved him back into the dangerous area and this time only rang the bell. The dog jumped again, knowing that when he heard a bell, he might feel a shock.

But what about the first dog? Why wouldn't he jump?

LEARNED HELPLESSNESS

After repeating the experiment a few times, Seligman discovered the key to the process: While he was hearing the bell and receiving shocks, the first dog had been held by the hammock strap and was therefore unable to move. Because he couldn't do anything about his situation, he gave up trying. Later, when presented with an opportunity to do something, he didn't take the opportunity because he had developed what Seligman called *learned helplessness.*

I would say that Seligman's dog had lost hope.

And this brings us back to the Edison-gene child. He's stuck in a classroom where the bell is the teaching style and his difficulties in school are the shock that comes every day, day after day, year after year. Some of these children learn helplessness, just as Seligman's dog did. They give up. They become passive and sad and fearful. They blame themselves for their failures. As they grow up, they become professional victims. Like Seligman's dog that cried when he was shocked but remained where he was, they complain about their lives, proclaim to the world that they are the victims of a brain disorder, and perhaps ease their hopelessness with alcohol, drugs, sex, or clinging, dependency-based relationships.

But fortunately, our schools are not able to restrain children with ADHD as fully as Seligman's harness restrained his dog. Our children have opportunities outside of school to prove to themselves and others that they aren't failures or stupid or lazy. They can skateboard with the best of them. They can play video games and wrestle and throw a baseball. They can fight and flirt and dance.

Sometimes they shift their values and beliefs from the realm of schoolwork to some other realm that earns them acceptance and success. They become excellent class clowns. They learn to throw spitballs with deadly accuracy. They learn to hide out academically or to cheat. They learn that the adults who are telling them how they should be, who are offering rewards with one hand and shocks with the other, are the enemy. They become very good at telling off the adults around them. Psychologists refer to this as an "oppositional comorbidity," as if it were an infection these children have been harboring all their lives that has been waiting for the right moment to materialize.

Sometimes, though, these children still have hope. They look out into the world and see that, unlike schoolwork, there *are* things they just know they could do well. They could be great fighter pilots, the top of the top guns, or brilliant cops who could out-Dirty Harry Clint Eastwood. They could invent and build and lead. They could save the world.

They could—if they believe, that is, that they're not *really* brain-damaged, that they're not *really* psychiatrically disabled or disordered, that they're perhaps different but not defective. Those who believe they're totally broken will give up, just like Seligman's dog. They'll make the stats, fill the jails, and live desperate and tragic lives.

We can help them believe they're different in wonderful ways.

REFRAMING IDENTITY = SUCCESS IN LEARNING

When I first came up with the idea that ADHD might be an adaptive genetic mechanism that's useful in some spheres, but not in others, I wasn't looking for good science. It made sense to me that it may be good science, but I was proposing it mostly as metaphor. I wanted to give hope to my son and others I knew with this diagnosis—a *useful* way to look at themselves and the world.

My own hope was bolstered when, in 1997,[1] Peter Jensen, M.D., and his colleagues wrote the article titled "Evolution and Revolution in Child Psychiatry: ADHD as a Disorder of Adaptation," proposing that our "response-ready" children may have been ideally adapted to some past human environment but are not not so well suited to today's schools. They even went so far as to suggest we stop calling these children "disordered":

> In reframing the child who has ADHD as "response-ready," experience-seeking, or alert and curious, the clinician can counsel the child and family to recognize situations in modern society that might favor such an individual, both in terms of school environments as well as future career opportunities (e.g., athlete, air traffic controller, salesperson, soldier, or entrepreneur). Also the clinician can "frame" the effects of behavioral treatments as teaching the "response-ready" child to extend his or her range of skills toward increased task focus, motor and impulse inhibition, self-awareness, and problem solving. In addition, the parent and child can adopt the reasonable goal to assist the child through school without allowing his or her difficulties in that setting to erode self-esteem and motivation to do well in more adaptive societal niches. The child and parents are encouraged to seek sit-

uations and potential success areas where "response-ready" traits are more adaptive.[2]

To the relief of parents, therapists, physicians, and educators around the world who had embraced the hunter/farmer metaphor, in 2002 scientists at the University of California Medical School and Yale University, working under a grant from the National Institute of Mental Health (NIMH), published a study of the DRD4 gene across six hundred individuals on five continents. This study explicitly stated that the gene that seems to play the largest role in ADHD, as demonstrated in six peer-reviewed studies so far, is, to use their word, "adaptive."[3]

Unfortunately, this reality hasn't yet occurred to our government, which is lobbied hard by pharmaceutical company-lobbied government or to our woefully under-funded schools.

GOVERNMENT STUDIES
PRONOUNCE ON MEDICATION

Several years before the University of California/Yale study, however, NIMH sponsored entirely different research. Two weeks before Christmas in 1999, NIMH and Columbia University held a press conference at the Columbia University College of Physicians and Surgeons. The purpose of the event was to roll out the results of a huge new study that purported to prove that medication was more effective than psychotherapy in improving the academic results of schoolchildren with ADHD.

Their press release summarized the study: "Including nearly 600 elementary school children, ages 7–9, the Multimodal Treatment Study of Children with Attention Deficit Hyperactivity Disorder (MTA) randomly assigned them to one of four treatment programs: (1) medication management alone; (2) behavioral treatment alone; (3) a combination of both; or (4) routine community care."[4] In summary, the study claimed it had "demonstrated, on average, that carefully monitored medication management with monthly follow-up, with input from teachers, is more effective than intensive behavioral treatment for ADHD."[5]

Reading the detailed report on the study, I found it startling how closely it resembled the old story of the man who looked for a lost key under the lamp post because that's where the light was brightest, even though he'd lost the key elsewhere.

The MTA study was done by some fine scientists, several of whom I highly respect and know have the best interests of children at heart. The government paid top dollar for their talents to be sure the study succeeded—a total of eleven million dollars spent over a fourteen-month period, with 579 children observed and evaluated at six different sites around the United States.

The stated goal of the study was to determine once and for all whether behavioral therapies, medication, or a combination of the two was the most effective way to treat children with ADHD, which, on its surface, seems like an important and laudable goal.

But in my humble opinion, the study explicitly and intentionally chose not to look at the single key ingredient in school success or failure for ADHD children.

THEY IGNORED THE ENVIRONMENT

When one of the physicians who participated in the study presented it at a conference I attended in 2001 in London, he made a startling comment about what they had to do in order to get teachers to participate in the study (teachers were one of two observer groups of the children who decided whether medications or therapy were more effective).

Most amazing, in addition to paying the teachers to participate, he said, they also "promised" the teachers that the study would, in no way and under no conditions, evaluate the teachers, their teaching style or materials, or the schools. The study included no inquiry into the effects of classroom size. Nor were issues to be raised about curriculum or children's learning styles. The sole question was whether drugs or behavior modification psychotherapy were better at making children perform in our schools as they are.

I sat in the audience dumbfounded. Our schools aren't working, and are, in fact, wounding our children, as we can see by a doubling in the child suicide rate over the past twenty years. I've personally spoken with the parents of at least a dozen children who have committed suicide over the past decade—and every single one, without exception, had been failing in school. While this isn't, of course, the only cause of suicide—and the failure in school is often a symptom of deeper problems—it's nonetheless so clearly a factor that I hold our public schools responsible for many of our child suicides. The only nation in the world with a higher child suicide rate than the United States is Japan, and it's also the only nation in the world with "tougher" schools than the United States. And, perhaps most revealing, child suicide among the poor in America isn't exploding the way it is for the middle class: poor children not only have lower suicide rates, but are also often more resilient then middle-class children, as I documented in *ADD Success Stories* and as Dr. Sam Goldstein documents in his books and essays on resilience. As New York State's Teacher Of The Year John Taylor Gatto so well documents in several of his brilliant books, in Sweden, where children begin school at about the age of seven, complete school by age sixteen, and spend less than half the time U.S. children do with homework, the child suicide rate is among the lowest in the world.

What's more, an overwhelming body of evidence has been produced in the past five decades showing that among different children there are multiple and different intelligences and different learning styles, and that many children who utterly fail in public schools can be highly successful in alternative educational settings.

Yet the assumption of the MTA study was that our schools are fine. Instead of including such factors as teaching styles and materials, the study merely focused on which of two methods (medication or therapy) is most effective at getting a group of Edison-gene children to conform to our schools exactly as they're set up.

THE STUDY PROVED RITALIN DOESN'T IMPROVE LEARNING

A number of professionals have criticized the study for other reasons. One nationally known psychiatrist pointed out that the only form of behavioral intervention used in the study (to no effect, as it turned out) was based on the theories of Russell Barkley, which are grounded in the assumption that when children don't succeed in school and end up being labeled as having ADHD, they themselves must be defective and in need of being "taken charge of."

Other critics have pointed out that the study showed that neither medication nor therapy produced significant and measurable improvements in the spelling or math skills of the children with ADHD. (Oddly, this information was only referenced in a note to "Table 4" in the published outcome of the study.) Medication, it appears, made the children more likeable by their teachers but doesn't improve their grades. The same was true for behavior modification psychotherapy—that didn't work either. When measured by grades the children were still not performing.

There are also those who suggest that because several of the researchers in the study received funding from big drug companies (including Richwood, Bristol-Myers, Solvay, Wyeth-Ayerst, Glaxo, and Eli Lilly) in other arenas of their research and because parents and teachers were told in advance of the study that the drugs the children were receiving were effective in treating ADHD (the word *effective* used to describe the medication was italicized in the literature given to parents and teachers before the study began), that right from the start everybody participating in the study was hopelessly biased toward the outcome.

And, indeed, the "blind" observers in the school (those people who didn't know which children were taking drugs and which weren't), were not, according to the study's published results, able to discern a difference between the medicated children and those treated with behavior modification. In this regard, the MTA study pointed to, and in some ways mirrored, problems with previous studies.

However, many studies have been done in the United States over the past few decades—most funded by drug companies—that conclude Ritalin produces benefit to children with ADHD. The proponents of the pathology model of ADHD love to point to the sheer mass of these studies, saying, for example, that the "scientific evidence . . . is overwhelming."*

But in 2001, a group of Canadian researchers at Children's Hospital of Eastern Ontario in Ottawa decided to evaluate sixty-nine of the best-known and most well-promoted of those studies, which involved 2897

---

* The International Consensus Statement, a letter signed by seventy-five psychologists and physicians stating that ADHD is a disorder, published with a news release in 2002.

participants with ADHD. Their conclusions were explicit, as reported in the November 27, 2001 issue of the *Canadian Medical Journal:*

> [T]he quality of the research was poor—in particular, few studies compared Ritalin with a placebo—and . . . a publication bias may have suppressed studies questioning the drug's effectiveness. Only nine of the studies lasted more than four weeks, leaving some doubt about Ritalin's effectiveness and safety when given to children over longer periods of time.[6]

BUT IT MAKES THE TEACHERS HAPPY

It's important to keep in mind the beneficial lessons of the MTA study. It showed, with little doubt, that in our modern factory-model schools in which teachers are overwhelmed by large class sizes and very real student needs, and children are treated like items on an assembly line, psychoactive drugs do effectively modify children's behavior in a way that teachers appreciate. It showed that techniques for behavior modification are not particularly effective in producing these teacher-valued changes in behavior; in fact, they were largely discontinued during the last months of the study for that reason.

And, perhaps most important, it showed that if we turn away and refuse to look at how our teachers and schools can better serve our children, we'll just have to rely on the results of several million successful children from homeschooling and private schooling in the United States (where there are over three million homeschooled children) and across the world to inform us.

LIGHTING A FIRE FOR LEARNING

As modern public education exists now, it isn't working for Edison-gene children. But how did it get to be as it is now, and what lessons can we learn from this? More important, if our educational system isn't appropriate for Edison-gene children and, in fact, is often destructive to them, what are the alternatives?

The poet William Butler Yeats once wrote, "Education is the lighting of a fire, not the filling of a bucket." It was a philosophy largely in line with the system of education pioneered millennia ago by Socrates, whose students were constantly challenged to think ever deeper about the subjects before them, until they found meaning and interest in them.

The truth is that nobody can teach anything—not in the sense of reaching out and putting knowledge into another person's mind in a way that's guaranteed to make the knowledge stick. Instead, context and opportunity are provided in which people can learn. When minds are receptive and hearts are engaged, then learning is a rapid, easy, painless process that is virtually unstoppable.

No matter how "learning disabled" a child may be, the reality is that every child, regardless of intellect, has been continuously learning from the moment of birth (and probably even before then). As NLP trainer Rex Sikes says, "Children are learning machines."[7]

EDUCATION AND TESTING CORPORATIONS

Many aspects of modern education, such as its use of testing and mandated standardized curriculum—show a complete lack of understanding of how children learn. When, on January 9, 2002, George W. Bush told a Washington, D.C. audience that we must "demand excellence" in education, he wrapped that demand in his "No Child Left Behind" plan, which would guarantee a doubling of testing activities in schools nationwide.[8]

While on the surface this may seem like a good thing, two important points should be brought to the public's attention. The first is that in 2001 over $400 million in tests and test scoring services were sold to schools nationwide by private corporations, the largest being a corporation that does hundreds of millions of dollars of business with schools every year and whose CEO is a generous contributor to political campaigns.

By no coincidence, most recent education laws have at their core one primary directive: Schools must buy more tests from this and other test-selling corporations. The "No Child Left Behind" law mandated more than $500 million in *additional* test purchases, doubling the revenues of the politically active testing industry. The bottom line is that testing is profitable for the large corporations that sell tests to schools (and that donate money to politicians). It's not particularly useful for the educational process—it doesn't help teachers teach, and it doesn't help students learn. In this regard, we can see that the Bush "No Child Left Behind" plan is actually part of the neoconservative's agenda to turn the public commons—in this case, education—over to private for-profit corporations, particularly those who fund Republican campaign efforts.

The second point is that this authoritarian thinking in education— that we can "demand" learning from children or force learning upon them—often simply doesn't work.

I remember well a comment I heard over twenty years ago, when I was flying to Africa with comedian and civil rights activist Dick Gregory. We were somewhere over the Atlantic, talking into the wee hours about politics. At one point, he said, "I don't understand why we think we have to run all over the world forcing things down people's throats with the barrel of a gun. When you have something good, you don't have to force it on people. They will steal it!"

The same is true in education. When a teacher is passionate about a topic, that passion is contagious—as the movie *Stand And Deliver* so eloquently shows in its portrayal of the real-life story of South Central L.A. math teacher Jamie Escalante. If a teacher can light the fire for a particular topic within a child, nothing can stop that child from learning.

HOW MODERN EDUCATION CAME ABOUT

The years from the late 1700s through the mid-1800s were a time of enormous social ferment in the United States and Europe. American farmers rose up and overthrew the world's most powerful empire. French peasants rose up and beheaded the king and queen of their nation. Prussia (now part of Germany), which had considered itself the most powerful military force in the world until that time, was defeated by a ragtag band of volunteer farmer-soldiers under the leadership of Napoleon.

Although there was a small mercantile class, most people of the era were either very rich or very poor (the middle class as we think of it today emerged in the United States and Europe only after World War II, largely as a result of the progressive income tax which somewhat leveled the income playing field), and the very rich were becoming increasingly worried that the very poor might rise up and take their heads.

The traditional tools used to keep the rabble (to use John Adams's favorite term for working-class people) in line had been the whip, the rack, and the threat of prison. But the uprisings that started in Americas in the eighteenth century and spread across Europe through the nineteenth century and even into the early twentieth century alarmed the ruling classes and royal families. The traditional tools weren't working; the rabble were demanding rights and freedom. They were thinking for themselves and demanding political participation and power.

In the 1760s both King Frederick II of Prussia and Empress Maria Theresa of Austria took the advice of Ernst Wilhelm von Schlabrendorff that Austria and Prussia develop systems of compulsory education. Just as the system the German philosopher Fichte helped birth throughout greater Germany in 1819, this system had several features specifically designed to keep the working class in line:

1. **It was compulsory, enforced by the power of guns and prisons.** Other than a brief, failed experiment by Plato thousands of years earlier, compulsory education had never been tried in the Western world. If anything, it seemed counterintuitive: Why force the rabble to become better educated? Well, the first goal of this system was to cause impressionable children to learn early on that their first loyalty—and their greatest respect— should be to and for the state, instead of their family. If the state had such power, it must be greater than their mothers and fathers. The state was thus to be feared.

2. **It was linear, rather than holistic.** From the earliest foundations of civilization and the education systems of Aristotle to the apprenticeship systems of the Middle Ages that produced geniuses such as Michelangelo, education was an all-of-one-cloth process. The teacher was mentor, the children participated in the teaching and learning, and subjects were integrated (as in real life) rather than split apart. But the German philosophers reasoned that in order to produce good soldiers or factory workers, it was necessary that students become linear thinkers who would

do what they were told without looking at the larger picture. Critical thinking was to be unlearned; students were to be trained in linear thinking. To accomplish this, Fichte argued that topics must be split from one another, with each being taught by a separate instructor.

3. **It was timed.** To prepare children for a life of factory work at this time when the Industrial Revolution was taking on speed, the foundational thinkers of what we call modern education decided that children must learn to start and stop their activity at the ring of a bell. As L. Mumford noted in 1955, "the clock, not the steam engine, is the key machine of the modern industrial age." Children must learn to do what they are told only *when* they are told.

4. **It was graded.** The Industrial Revolution brought with it the idea of an individual product from an assembly line either "making or failing the grade." Shoes in a shoe factory, for instance, were either up to the grade or not. Those not up to the grade were variously rated to determine whether they should be sold to the poor as "seconds," taken apart and recycled, or discarded. When thinkers in this era threw out the Socratic notion of students as equals in the educational process, students came to be viewed as items on the assembly line of education and socialization, to be inspected and then graded by the narrow criteria of the school and its system—a system finally and fully institutionalized in England in the late 1800s by William Farish.

5. **It had no give-and-take.** In 1740, the Prussian philosopher Johann Hecker proposed that in order to create a populace who would not question authority, children in school must be forced to ask, "May I ask a question?" before actually asking it. The way to ask "May I ask a question?" he suggested, was to raise the hand. The give-and-take at the core of the Socratic teaching method was discarded: It produced independent thinkers, which was not the goal of this new form of education. Instead, in Hecker's mind, education flowed in a single direction, from authority/teacher to empty vessel/student, and Hecker's system was institutionalized in the German schools in the early 1800s.

6. **Its content was controlled.** Perhaps one of the most appealing aspects of this new form of education was that, like items produced on an assembly line, it could be standardized. If the government could control what children learned, it could teach them the importance of not questioning the government itself. It could inculcate them with values and beliefs that supported the existing power and economic systems. It could, in short, make them good citizens who would never again consider revolution.

GERMAN SCHOOLS COME TO AMERICA

In the first hundred years of its history, America had never embraced a system of compulsory education. But the opening of the West and the Civil War shook the leaders of the new nation to their core: Factories in the East couldn't get enough reliable labor (strikes first began to hit industry in the years during and just following the Civil War), and the whole of the South had risen up against the federal government and fought a miserable and bloody war for independence. There was concern all across the nation about the future of the Republic.

Horace Mann and others had gone to Europe to observe firsthand the Prussian compulsory education system. They came back, impressed that compulsory, linear, authoritarian, state-run education was *the* way to create social stability. With a nation of properly educated people, there would never again be a revolution and the likelihood that the threat of the rabble engaging in strikes and other actions to undermine authority would be dramatically diminished.

Mann and others began to preach their doctrine of compulsory education across the nation, but at first no government was willing to bear the cost. Then came the collision in Boston of the Catholics and members of the Order of the Star Spangled Banner.

AMERICAN EDUCATION AND
THE CATHOLIC PROBLEM

From the time of the Irish Potato Famine in the 1840s through the end of the Civil War in the 1860s, several million Irish people immigrated to the United States, and most of them ended up in the Boston area. The power structure of the region had been Anglo-Saxon Protestant since the days of John Adams, but in a twenty-year period the population had shifted to a majority of Roman Catholics.

In part in reaction to this, members of a Protestant secret men's club called the Order of the Star Spangled Banner began to run for political office and to appoint individuals from their ranks to judgeships. Eventually, the order had enough members in political office that it came out of secrecy and proclaimed its control of the Massachusetts legislature and governor's office.

One of the first official acts of the "Know-Nothing Legislature" of 1854 (referred to as such because the secret password of the Order of the Star Spangled Banner was "I know nothing") was to pass a constitutional amendment barring Catholics from voting. It failed ratification when submitted to the people for a vote.

The legislature further ordered compulsory education of Catholic children, and that the Protestant King James Bible would be read daily in the state-run schools. The Catholic Problem was finally solved.

BACKLASH AGAINST THE AUTHORITARIAN MODEL OF PUBLIC EDUCATION

After the implementation of enforced compulsory public education in Massachusetts and its subsequent success at pacifying the populace, other American states began to institute similar programs.

By the end of the nineteenth century, the federal government got into the act. After railroad magnates initially opposed public education for fear they'd lose their bottom-rung workers who cleared roadbeds and laid track, the first U.S. Commissioner of Education, William Torrey Harris, wrote a reassuring letter to railroad scion Ellis Huntington, assuring him that the emerging American public education system was "scientifically designed" in Germany "not to over-educate" but to produce instead socially compliant workers. With this letter, Harris apparently changed their minds.

As the focus in America shifted from a discussion of compulsory, authoritarian education to a debate about its state-controlled content, some American educators raised voices of alarm. John Dewey, in his 1915 book *Democracy and Education,* said that "education is not an affair of telling and being told, but an active and constructive process." However, Dewey said, this "is a principle almost as generally violated in practice as conceded in theory."[9]

Across Europe, too, educators were speaking out strongly against the system itself. In Italy, Maria Montessori developed an alternative system; in Germany, Rudolf Steiner came up with his Waldorf Schools; and parochial and private schools experienced a boom that has extended to today's full-blown homeschooling movement in both Europe and America. All of these movements began in response to the exact same problems that Edison-gene children face today in some public schools.

MARIA MONTESSORI

In 1901 Maria Montessori, a physician born in 1870, was given responsibility for a school and institution for retarded and insane children in Rome. Instead of treating the children in the traditional fashion, she demanded that the staff address them with respect and encourage them to explore their own interests. The transformation of the children in her care was so dramatic it led Dr. Montessori to develop a philosophy of education that was largely at odds with the German system that had so recently been adopted across Europe and America.

In 1907 she started her first "children's house," which became the model of Montessori education. She wrote the first detailed description of her techniques and philosophy in 1916 in a book titled *The Montessori Method.* In her 1949 book *The Absorbent Mind,* she brilliantly summarized the core of her educational philosophy:

> Ours was a house for children, rather than a real school. We had prepared a place for children where a diffused culture could be assimilated, without any need for direct instruction. . . . Yet these children learned to read and write before they were five, and no one had given them any lessons. At that time it seemed miraculous that children of four and a half should be able to write, and that they

should have learned without the feeling of having been taught.

We puzzled over it for a long time. Only after repeated experiments did we conclude with certainty that all children are endowed with this capacity to "absorb" culture. If this be true— we then argued—if culture can be acquired without effort, let us provide the children with other elements of culture. And then we saw them "absorb" far more than reading and writing: botany, zoology, mathematics, geography, and all with the same ease, spontaneously and without getting tired.

And so we discovered that education is not something which the teacher does, but that it is a natural process which develops spontaneously in the human being. It is not acquired by listening to words, but in virtue of experiences in which the child acts on his environment. The teacher's task is not to talk, but to prepare and arrange a series of motives for cultural activity in a special environment made for the child.

One of the best Montessori teachers I've ever known is an extraordinary woman named Anne S. Perrah. Anne took the extraordinary step of asking her children to create two make-believe islands—one for hunters and another for farmers—and for each child to choose one of the two on which to live. Once populated, the islands quickly developed unique and elaborate cultures, and this experiment and class project has been going on for several years now. It's produced wonderful learning for the children and startling insights for the teachers at Anne's Montessori school. Anne has created a fascinating presentation on it, with a documentary movie in the works.[10]

Montessori schools are among the most effective and useful environments for children with the Edison-gene, as their success all across the world testifies.

RUDOLF STEINER

Rudolf Steiner grew up in the 1860s and 1870s in the Austrian countryside, where he was exposed to the new model of education sweeping Austria and Germany at that time. Deeply concerned with understanding the spiritual basis of thought and philosophy, he reacted strongly and negatively to a school system that was exclusively centered in the domain of the mind and excluded the hands, the heart, and the spirit.

Responding to this, Steiner developed a philosophy of education embodied in what he named Waldorf Schools, the first of which he opened in 1919 in Stuttgart, Germany. In Waldorf Schools, *doing* is emphasized as much as *learning*—in fact, the two are considered inseparable. There's tremendous emphasis on physical activity; on children acting out what they are learning; and on children putting into practical application, in multidimensional ways, what they are studying—things that in our experience at the Hunter School are tremendous aids to learning for Edison-gene children.

Another aspect of Waldorf education is understanding the process of learning itself and the concepts and context of thought and understanding. Steiner's goal was to create an educational system that would produce a well-rounded individual and allow a child to express all of the genius and potential with which he or she was born.

The result for Steiner was a disaster. His philosophies in general and his school system in particular were considered a direct affront to the authoritarian government of Germany. Hitler—who used Germany's compulsory education system very effectively to indoctrinate German youth in the right-wing ideals of Nazism—was so offended that in 1922 he and the Nazi party targeted Steiner for persecution. (Steiner died in 1925, and the Nazis had enough national power to begin to officially close his German Waldorf schools in 1935.)

Like the Montessori movement, the Waldorf School movement has spread around the world. Like the Montessori philosophy, the system Steiner developed focuses heavily on the individual child and on building a relationship between teacher and pupils. And as in the Montessori system, many children with the Edison-gene thrive in Waldorf schools.

FREE AND ALTERNATIVE SCHOOLS

The 1960s saw the publication of several seminal works that spawned entire movements in education. Probably the best known are a book titled *Summerhill,* after the British school of the same name founded in 1921 by A. S. Neill, and the writings of now-deceased educator John Holt (author of *Why Johnny Can't Read*). These new educational movements were philosophically grounded in the idea that children should learn rather than be taught, that as long as they were following their own curiosity and they were in control of the process, the outcome would be maximum academic success and minimum emotional wounding.

The results were often erratic, and sometimes brought out the worst, rather than the best, of our culture in the ferment of the late 1960s and early 1970s. On the other hand, in his teenage years two decades later, my son attended an Atlanta alternative school in which the student council ran most of the functions of the school, in keeping with the alternative school movement's philosophy. This environment suited Justin well, and his academic performance took off brilliantly.

The alternative school movement around the world has learned much from the lessons of the 1960s and 1970s. Today's alternative schools tend more toward a child-centered but education-driven philosophy, and are often among the best options for Edison-gene children.

HOMESCHOOLING AND INTERNET SCHOOLING

When our youngest child was thirteen, she decided that public school was largely a waste of her time and that she wanted to get on with finishing her education and having it out of the way. On her own she found the Oak Meadow School on the Internet (www.oakmeadow.com), and asked Louise and me if she could attend it from home via the Web. We agreed to try it for six months, and the result for her was wonderful.

The Internet has also become a powerful support center for parents who are homeschooling. In the 1980s, I started the Homeschooling Forum on CompuServe, when our daughter began homeschooling through Oak Meadow. As of this writing, it's still operating at http://go.compuserve.com/homeschool and is one of hundreds of online communities that support and provide resources to homeschooling parents and students.

Other parents around the country are forming their own networks for homeschooling their children. One that I know of in Baltimore, for example, has several groups of five families per group that meet in the home of one of the families each day of the school week. Thus, each family who is homeschooling plays "teacher" only one day a week. This dramatically reduces the time burden of homeschooling (particularly for two-wage-earner or single-parent families), while exposing the children in the group to a variety of teaching styles and interests.

Another trend that's picking up popularity is to give kids a break from school for a year. This process, called "unschooling," gives kids a chance to get their developmental needs met and lets them have a year without the daily cortisol and stress of our factory-schools. As one of the better unschooling Web sites notes regarding students that have been diagnosed with learning disabilities:

> Once these children are at home and have "deschooled" for a year or so, their parents begin to wonder if some large part of the learning disability they've been told about might not be school-induced. In households where child-led learning is practiced, the child begins to learn naturally, learning what he needs when he needs to, and the stress of mastering a specific skill such as handwriting or multiplication tables at a specific age is gone. The child begins to unwind and blossom.[11]

BUT WHAT ABOUT SOCIALIZATION?

The most common question that people have asked us over the years since our daughter began her homeschooling experience is, "What about her social needs?" It's a question that every homeschooling parent has heard.

Somehow, we've come to believe that public school is the optimal environment for children to learn social skills and have their social needs met. The reality is that schools can function as kingdoms, with rigid hierarchies of power and status reflected both in the administration and among the students. While in the real world few of us ever have to worry about cliques or "in crowds," they're often present in school social situations, usually driven by consumerism: the kind of clothes a child wears, the kind of home a child lives in, the kind of car parents (or students themselves) drive.

Additionally, while school does offer some opportunities for social experience (which can be painful for some children—even those at the top of the social hierarchy), the time available for such interaction might be minimal. During class time in the majority of American classrooms, children are expected to sit down and shut up. Between classes they're hustling to move from room to room before the bell goes off. Before school, most children are struggling to wake up or make it in on time. This leaves after school as pretty much the only functional social time schoolchildren have.

Interestingly, after school was when our house would fill up. The kids who were our daughter's friends but were in public or private schools would congregate at our house (or at others, although ours was often the most convenient because we were usually home) for the real social time.

The question "What about her social needs?" implies that fulfilling children's social needs can somehow be denied them. I suppose it's possible in some dysfunctional cults or extremely remote rural communities, but our experience has been that it's easier to stop gravity than to prevent a child from being social and having friends. Whether she attends a school building and has to sit quietly with hundreds of other children during the day doesn't alter this biological and neurological necessity we all inherited from our mammalian ancestors.

WHY HOMESCHOOLING WORKS
FOR EDISON-GENE CHILDREN

It's interesting to note a September 2000 article in *Time* magazine[12] that says Stanford University accepted twice the percentage of homeschoolers who applied (26 percent) than they did children from private or public schools, and that the average SAT score of homeschooled children accepted to Wheaton College was fifty-eight points higher than their freshman classmates.

Harvard's director of admissions, Marlyn McGrath Lewis, commented about how impressed Harvard was by homeschooled students, who are comprising increasing percentages of Harvard admissions, year after year. Overall, according to *Time,* homeschoolers scored a full 81 points higher than the national average on SAT tests, and their national ACT average was 22.8 compared with a public/private school average of 21.[13]

Homeschooling is one of the very best options for Edison-gene children because it can be so easily customized to their needs and doesn't require them to comply with educational environments that are hostile to Edison-gene attributes. It was the educational choice that Thomas Edison's mother made for him the second time he was kicked out of school at the age of eight. It has worked for millions of children, and universities like Harvard are publicly stating that they not only seriously consider homeschooled or non-public-schooled children but some actually give such children higher rankings in their consideration for admission because such children are more often motivated, competent learners.

THE EDISON GENE
THROUGH THE COLLEGE YEARS

The adaptive nature of the Edison gene is often not as apparent in the early school years as it is in college, where students are more free to pursue their passions and control their own schedule and can pick and choose among instructors.

For those Edison-gene children who intend to pursue a college degree, the best advice is to look to the smaller, nontraditional colleges instead of large universities, at least for the first year or two. The first years of college involve studying the basics in any discipline, and at large universities, the classes are usually huge, obligatory, and often taught by professors, teaching assistants, or instructors who may only marginally care about teaching their topics to students. In such an environment, Edison-gene children often find themselves bored, disconnected, and doing poorly. It's often only in the last two years of pursuing an undergraduate college degree at a large university that students find themselves in classes that are smaller, especially focused on their areas of interest, and taught by people involved in and passionate about their topic and who are eager to translate their excitement to others.

Many Edison-gene children successfully complete their first year or two of college at a community college, where classes are smaller, schedules are flexible, costs are low, and it can be easier to achieve high marks. Further, applying to many universities as a second- or third-year transfer student can sometimes mean that the competition is nowhere near as intense as it is for a slot in the freshman class.

There are also colleges and universities that offer the kind of highly customizable and flexible educational programs, both at an undergraduate and graduate level, that are ideally suited to Edison-gene students. Hampshire College and Antioch College were pioneers in these programs in the 1980s (and still offer them), although now they are far easier to find at other institutions, including an increasing number of accredited colleges and universities that offer distance or online learning degree programs.

FIND A MENTOR OR A COACH

Hunter peoples didn't (and don't, with regard to such peoples still in existence) have schools—all education (and they had a vast range of things to learn) was accomplished by what we would call mentorship. An expert adult took responsibility for training a younger person in that adult's area of expertise, whether hunting, gathering, healing, midwifery, building shelters, making tools, preserving hides, conducting relations with other tribes, or any of the many other functions in these complex and ancient societies.

Similarly, modern Edison-gene children often thrive when they have a mentor or a coach, a role model who's achieved success in the field to which they aspire and who can check in regularly with them to keep them inspired and on-track.

Encourage your Edison-gene child to find such a mentor or mentors and participate in the process of looking for them if practical and appropriate. Regardless of what your student aspires to become—a physician or an entrepreneur, a soldier or a salesperson—the encouraging and guiding hand of a wise elder will make a huge difference.

15

Edison-Gene Girls and Women

The especial genius of women I believe to be electrical in movement, intuitive in function, spiritual in tendency.
MARGARET FULLER

Male as Hero story is a false model for women. Imitating this model can keep women from becoming who they truly are. . . . There is another perspective, another hero's journey . . . the hero is a she. Unlike her male counterpart, she has no intentions of conquering anything external. Instead, her journey is within. She travels into the spiraling depths of her own unknowns, constantly discovering and changing in the process. Her intention is to become self-defined. The female hero reaches full individual potential, taking enormous personal risks . . . nurturing the emergence of a new, more integrated self . . . living a creative lifestyle . . . the unfolding of the self-defined, creative woman who lives within each of us.
C. DIANE EALY, PH.D.,
THE WOMAN'S BOOK OF CREATIVITY

Those people with the Edison gene are not always high-energy; sometimes they seem off to be drifting in space or disconnected. This particular manifestation of the gene seems to appear more often in girls than in boys. But why—and what does this difference mean with regard to diagnosis?

The Edison gene isn't associated with the X or Y chromosome involved in gender selection and so occurs with equal frequency in both boys and girls. Among men and women, for example, the rate of ADHD diagnosis is about 1:1, and the gene involved is something that is with us at birth and at death. So why would it be that boys are five to seven times more likely to be identified as ADHD than girls during the school years?

BE A GOOD GIRL

In our culture, boys are rewarded when they *do* things—build businesses or buildings, fight wars, track down criminals, make money. Boys are defined more by what they *do* than by anything else. In fact, men often introduce each other by job description: "This is Bill. He's a stockbroker." In our society a man's status is a function of how the nouns defining what he does stack up or compare with the those of other men.

Girls in our culture, on the other hand, are rewarded for who they are or are perceived to be. Adjectives describing characteristics, such as *sexy, beautiful,* or *intelligent,* are more often applied to them than are nouns defining what they do, and their status and worthiness is most often defined by how desirable those characteristics are.

Culturally defined gender differences are absolutely pervasive in our world. They fill our media, particularly our advertising images in which women's bodies are used to sell everything from cars to beer to clothing. They fill our movies and television shows. They fill our literature and fairy tales. No matter how egalitarian or enlightened we try to be as parents, it's impossible to shield our children from these cultural stereotypes, norms, and expectations.

The result is that in our schools—where teachers are also not immune to these messages—our boys are noticed for what they do, for better or worse. And an Edison-gene boy's *doing* can be very conspicuous in that he externalizes his internal need for stimulation and meets this need doing: moving, interrupting, playing, wriggling.

The majority of Edison-gene girls, on the other hand, have learned by the first few years of school that there are punishments associated with such doing, that it's not ladylike or acceptable. From early glances of disapproval by family members (studies show that a single negative glance from a parent can cause a child's cortisol levels to increase) to outright punishment for misbehaving, most little girls learn early on that their safety is threatened if they externalize their need for stimulation, adventure, and excitement.

But the need doesn't go away. They still have the brain wiring, turned on by this extraordinary genetic background, that demands novelty and arousal. Unable to get that necessary stimulation, unable to satisfy their need for novelty by acting up or acting out, many girls instead turn within, to their own minds.

Thought can be stimulating—so much so that it can alter physiology. While a book it really just printed squiggles on paper, reading a good novel can get our heart racing, keep us up all night, and alter the neurochemicals in our brain. Similarly, when an Edison-gene girl engages her mind with fantasy and traveling thought, her body can be altered physiologically, meeting her genetic need for stimulation.

The problem is that from the outside it looks like nothing is going on. The girl is so absorbed in her "daydreams" that she's not paying attention to the outer world. Instead of interrupting people around her, as an externally hyperactive person would, she's interrupting herself in her own mind—often she can't remember what she was thinking just two minutes earlier. This behavior, known as *inattentive ADHD*, ensures that she remains a "good girl"—who may also be cast as a "space cadet" or as "ditzy." These terrible sexist stereotypes are most often applied to Edison-gene girls and women.

CINDERELLA IN A HOSTILE WORLD

Modern women with ADHD face many of the challenges confronted by men with ADHD, but to all these they have two added layers of difficulty. Subtle yet pervasive and powerful, these two layers are composed of *cultural barriers* and *cultural programming/expectations,* which can work together to wound all girls and women, but are particularly hurtful to those who were born as neurological Edisons, frustrating to a greater degree their attempts to find success and emotional balance.

CULTURAL BARRIERS

Franklin Delano Roosevelt pointed out that "those who forget history are doomed to repeat it." Yet many of us have never learned the history of the role of women in our culture. Lest we repeat that history (and there are those, like Jerry Falwell, who strongly suggest we should), it's important to quickly review it. In order to understand the unique challenges of girls and women with the Edison gene, it's important to first understand the cultural basis from which those unique challenges arise.

While we find equality between women and men in most indigenous cultures (their *roles* may be very different, but their relative *power* within the family and community is in balance), this has not at all been the case since the eruption of our modern civilization in Sumeria around seven thousand years ago. Even though logic indicates that a creator of new life would have a womb, monotheism brought with it the notion that if there was to be only one god, this god must have a penis. According to his priests and scribes, this male god explicitly directed the quarantine or slaughter of all peoples who worshiped goddesses, a process that continues to this day in some parts of the world.

As time passed, the men of these early agricultural and pastoral younger cultures came to vilify women as the source of first sin, ban worship in the natural world, and list only males (with very few exceptions) in their historical and religious literature. They produced histories, myths, and fables that taught women their (inferior) role, and instituted laws (often punishable by death) that insured their new view of women was adopted. They tortured and murdered millions of women in Europe and the Middle East over several centuries and brutally crushed all traces of Europe's older, natured-based, female-centered religions, including their healing medicines and rituals (and continue to do so in much of the world today).

Midwifery and herbalism were renamed witchcraft, women who respected and interacted with nature were called consorts of the devil, and girls were officially banned from formal education. The echoes of

this cultural departure from millennia of matriarchy or gender coopera-
tion were again heard in the opinions and beliefs of the male-dominated
European psychology profession as it was birthed in 1690 by England's
John Locke (in "An Essay Concerning Human Understanding") and in
1692 by Germany's Christian Thomasius (in "Further Elucidation by
Different Examples of the Recent Proposals for a New Science for
Discerning the Nature of Other Men's Mind").

When Paul created the Pauline Church to compete with (and eventually replace) Peter's Jerusalem Church, he directed the Ephesians that
wives must submit to the authority of their husbands. This single phrase
was enshrined in British law about a thousand years ago, and became
a cornerstone of American colonial law in the 1700s.

Among the earliest laws the Colonies passed were those putting
power over women into the hands of men: A married woman was not
allowed to make out a will because she was not allowed to own land or
legally control anything else worthy of willing to another person. Any
property she brought into the marriage became her husband's at the
moment of marriage and would only revert to her if he died and she did
not remarry. Even then, she'd get only one-third of her husband's property, and what third that was and how she could use it were determined
by a court-appointed male executor, who would supervise for the rest
of her life (or until she remarried) how she used this inheritance. When
a widow died, the executor would either take the property for himself
or else decide to whom it would pass. The woman had no say in the
matter because she had no right to sign a will.

Women could not sue in a court of law, except by the weak proce-
dures allowed to the mentally ill and children, supervised by men. If the
man of a family household died, the executor would decide who would
raise the wife's children and in what religion. The mother had no right
to make those decisions and had no say in such matters. If the woman
was poor, it was a virtual certainty that her children would be taken
from her. It was impossible in the new United States of America for a
married woman to have legal responsibility for her children and control
of her own property, to own slaves, to buy or sell land, or even to
obtain an ordinary license.

While women were given the right to own property in the mid-

1800s and the right to vote in 1920, and laws against discrimination were passed in 1962 and 1964, it was only in 1973 that the U.S. Supreme Court (in *Roe v. Wade*) overturned the 1873 *Bradwell v. State of Illinois* Supreme Court decision that "the Law of the Creator" defined the "paramount destiny and mission" of women as limited to "the noble and benign offices of wife and mother."

Today, in this twenty-first century, we still live in a world where "women's work" is very much a defined reality (nurses, waitresses, teachers, secretaries, child-care workers, and maids). From hospitals to hotels, from big business to our nation's schools, the patriarchal idea of women's roles is still very much with us. The archetypal spectrum runs from deified to cursed, from Madonna to prostitute, but at almost every level the role is still very much one subordinate to and in service of men (and the rare few powerful women). And the nature and quality of this male-dominated culture's definition of woman's service to men demands, in almost all cases, a more farmerlike brain wiring very different from the hunter wiring carried by Edison-gene women.

"You've come a long way, baby," and other slogans of our time promulgate the myth that men and women are operating on a level playing field. It's a useful myth for those who want to keep their secretaries and avoid further rebellion by women, and it's particularly useful for corporate marketers who want to sink their hooks deep into women's psyches, but it's false. (While this may come as a revelation to some men, I imagine most women reading this are well aware of this fact.)

Born in 1951, I spent a bit more than the first decade of my life in an America where women and minorities were routinely and legally oppressed without most people questioning this treatment. It shaped my worldview, as well as that of my contemporaries of both genders. None of us escaped unaffected; neither have our children. The consequence of the reality that women have only recently achieved some of the legal protections and prerogatives that men have enjoyed for six thousand years but are still not truly equal to men is substantial and far-reaching, and we see it clearly on at least three different levels.

First, many women say that they experience a deep sense of disempowerment in modern culture. My wife, Louise, tells how, when she was CEO of a multi-million-dollar advertising agency in Atlanta in the 1990s, men would often call her "honey" or "sweetie" and use an adult-talking-to-child tone to establish who was in charge of the discussion.

"I learned to ignore it," she said, "because if I confronted it I'd be labeled a 'bitch.' When men take power, they're called 'alpha dogs' or 'leaders'; when women take power they're called 'bitches.'"

In April 2001 I was in a meeting with author and social activist Marianne Williamson when word came of the Supreme Court ruling that police could now arrest, strip search, and imprison people for "crimes" for which there were no jail penalties (such as jaywalking, littering, or not wearing seatbelts). Commenting that the ruling effectively eviscerated the Fourth Amendment's protections against unreasonable search and seizure, Marianne said, "Now white men could get a taste of what black people and women have been experiencing for centuries in this country."

Second, many women share the sense of being "outsiders" that comes from a long heritage of exclusion and male domination and control. While for some this sense creates solidarity with other women (witness women's groups and the various feminist movements), it's the solidarity of the oppressed. Women, who are and always have been an absolute majority in our culture, are still treated as a minority by both the males in charge and, to a large extent, by each other.

Third, when women come into contact with the largely male-dominated medical, educational, and pharmaceutical industries, they are often treated with condescension or categorization, or—even worse—as though they are invisible. My editor and friend Dave deBronkart tells this poignant story: "Around 1990 I attended a Fourth of July parade in Keene, New Hampshire, in support of a charity for handicapped kids, of which my wife was a board member. The entire board of the organization is women; I was standing behind them and off to the side. After our float went by, U.S. Senator Judd Gregg came along in the parade, campaigning. He walked right past the board of directors, and shook my hand instead, exactly as if they were invisible. I was so shocked that I didn't have the presence of mind to take him over and introduce him to the ladies."

Being patted on the head and told to go home and take your pills is bad enough; being ignored or referred to as a "bitch" or as "ditzy" is wounding. Compounding this for women with the Edison gene is, in my opinion, the fact that "daydreaming" or turning inward is an expression of the fundamental and visceral human need to experience their own aliveness. Just like with men, when Edison-gene women are confined in highly structured schools or workplaces, their need to feel alive is unmet. While men are encouraged to meet this need by reaching out and interacting with the world around them, women are encouraged to be quiet, to be ladylike. Hence, their search for "aliveness" in their internal world, the hallmark of inattentive ADHD, often takes the form of daydreaming.

CULTURAL PROGRAMMING AND EXPECTATIONS

To a large extent the wounding of Edison-gene girls begins in school. Adding to the hurt are our cultural expectations that wound all girls and that started long before women were allowed to attend school: Women, according to the patriarchs of our culture, were created to serve men and can find their fulfillment only in that role.

I remember well the shock I experienced the first time I read the story of Cinderella to one of our daughters: I later told Louise that I felt as though I'd just participated in a cultural experiment or brainwashing session. Cinderella was the good girl, the pretty young woman. She was compliant, uncomplaining, hard-working (as a maid!) in the service of authority, and, like many Edison-gene girls and women who find themselves in similar circumstances, she spent a lot of time in a dream world. Her stepsisters were women who knew what they wanted and were on a mission to get it. They were characterized as ugly and undesirable.

The object of all this competition was the assumed goal of every woman: a man—but not just any man. This was a man of wealth and power, which allowed everybody to overlook the fact that he was so self-obsessed that after dancing with Cinderella for several hours, he couldn't remember what her face looked like.

The messages of the story are frighteningly clear, and to find out if these messages have been picked up by the females of our culture just spend ten minutes in a shopping mall and watch the teenage girls as they primp and preen and compete for the attention of the boys.

Add to this the fact that modern girls and women are more often the targets of market-directed advertising than boys and men and that corporate messages most often destroy girls' self-esteem by focusing on body image and appearance, and it's easy to see why women are more likely to take to heart the message of modern advertisers. Whether it's bleached teeth or hairless legs, breast size or hair color or wrinkle-free skin, girls and women are explicitly told that they're unfeminine, unworthy, and undesirable (by males) if they don't modify their bodies with corporate products.

In this regard, our culture is now organized as a self-fulfilling feedback loop. Women were defined in the distant past as powerless beauty objects for the pleasure of men, and so fairy tales communicate this to little girls, who then grow up to carry the story that their role is to be powerless beauty objects for the pleasure of men. When women try to break out of this loop, they are referred to as "feminazis" or "bitches" in environments ranging from national talk shows to the work place.

In the morning-after of the twenty-first century, Cinderella is still present and accounted for, but midnight is now past and she's in a world of pain, especially if she's been born with Edison-gene neurology, which drives her need for constant mental stimulation and, in the absence of such stimulation in many of our schools and workplaces, causes her to "daydream," thus making it even more difficult for her to assume the "traditional" feminine roles.

HEALING THE WOUNDS

It's axiomatic that healing begins with recognition of the wound and what has caused it. Both men and women heal as they're exposed to the raw realities of the history of women's rights in America, realize the dangers in the growing political movement to roll back women's recently won gains, and recognize the institutions and beliefs that fuel the entire process.

But in order to truly heal, people must place the past behind them and see in front of them a shining, powerful future with a clear picture of themselves and a world in which they can be a dynamic force for change and success. For Edison-gene girls and women, this is particularly critical because, while they so often face the same difficulties and challenges in school and the workplace as do Edison-gene boys and men, they have the added burden of cultural myths and expectations that don't match their neurology.

The Iroquois were very clear that we don't inherit the earth from our ancestors but instead borrow it from our grandchildren. Therefore, they built an absolute injunction into their system of governance stipulating that every decision be made in the context of its impact on the seventh generation from that time. Can you imagine how a similar policy would transform our political, corporate, and educational processes? Even more significant, the Iroquois knew women were the ones among them who were most concerned with the seventh generation. Therefore, in four of the five nations of the original Iroquois Confederacy, only women could vote on matters of long-range importance.

When Ben Franklin invited forty-two members of the Iroquois Confederacy to attend the Albany Plan of Union in 1754 (an early attempt to write a U.S. constitution), he said in a speech to the Albany Congress: "It would be a strange thing . . . if six nations of ignorant savages should be capable of forming such a union and be able to execute it in such a manner that it has subsisted for ages and appears indissoluble, and yet that a like union should be impractical for ten or a dozen English colonies." (Franklin later agreed with Jefferson and Madison that the Iroquois way of voting was backwards and should be changed so that only men could vote in the new United States.)

But the evidence of archaeology and anthropology indicates that egalitarian cultures are humans' greatest and most long-lasting societal models. There have been (and continue to be around the world, largely among indigenous peoples) thousands of cultures based on egalitarian principles, where women play a real and important role in the politics and structure of the community, and where individual women can rise as far as they can dream. Since this is more the absolute norm for tribal peoples, such people make up the majority of your and my ancestors, regardless of our race or national origin. Egalitarianism is encoded in us, at the core of our humanness, built into our genetic code. We are most directly wired for cooperation rather than domination.

We can work together to create a world where men and women

exist in balance, neither one dominating the other, a world in which we can safely raise all our girls—those with and without the Edison gene—with pride and respect, so that each of them is free from damaging stereotypes, so that each sees herself as a powerful force for the future. Let's transform our schools into places of stimulation, interest, and a passion for learning. Let's work to create opportunity and cooperation, a bright future for our children, and a world that works for all.

There may still be time.

16

Spirituality and the Edison-Gene Child

Relation is the essence of everything that exists.
MEISTER ECKHART

It's been my observation that people with non-mainstream brains seem to be drawn to non-mainstream religions, ranging from fundamentalist movements to meditative practices to a fervent commitment to the belief system of atheism. This seems to be particularly true of Edison-gene people.

Perhaps it's because they've felt like outsiders their entire lives, and many of the people who attend the "middle of the road" churches, synagogues, mosques, and temples are the stable and steady "farmers" who've excluded or outperformed them in other venues such as school (the farmers, after all, represent more than three quarters of all humans). Or maybe they crave the stimulation to be found in intense worship or meditative activities or have a stronger need for the unique sense of tribe or community that exists in such places. Or perhaps, because Edison-gene people tend to focus more strongly on what interests them, they tend to seek spirituality where their interest lies. Or perhaps religions have always ended up representing the cultures that have given rise to them, so that hierarchical, male-dominated agricultural cultures have produced hierarchical religions with a male god, whereas egalitarian hunter cultures have produced religions that emphasize more an individual's personal spiritual experience and diminish the role of priests and institutional structures—a religious context more comfortable for Edison-gene people. (Most well-known commentators on this, from Maria Gimbutas and Riane Eisler to Daniel Quinn, have suggested that agricultural cultures will always end up being both hierarchical and male-dominated; for further information on why, I recommend their books to you.)

Whatever the reason, being aware that Edison-gene children are spiritually drawn in this way can be useful. Such children are more likely to find great solace in religion. For the Edison-gene people I've known over the years, spirituality tends to be intensely personal and experience-based, often including a wide variety of religious institutions and philosophies and even the use of ethnogens. For Edison-gene teenagers and children, however, this can present difficulties. Because they're more likely to experiment and seek their religious experiences in unconventional venues, they're more at risk for coming under the influence of destructive cults (those organizations demanding complete compliance with doctrine, practices, and authority) or for abusing drugs. Even within conventional religions, they tend to be drawn to the intense, experience-based fundamentalist or fringe sects and denominations.

On the other hand, because of their rich connection to the present, young people with the Edison gene often report an intensity of emotion and spiritual experience that's startling or even alien to their more sedate peers. They're more likely to be drawn to the mystical aspects of spirituality, and, indeed, among the ranks of the world's best-known mystics—such as St. John of the Cross and St. Theresa of Avila—there undoubtedly have been many restless hunters.

EDISON-GENE MYSTICS

The arena of religion known as mysticism is one to which I've found many Edison-gene people are drawn. Mystics, who may come from any religious denomination, are those who have experienced a direct and profound connection with the divine or spiritual, often quite separate from any formal religious institution. St. Francis of Assisi, St. John of the Cross, and the German monk Meister Eckhart are three mystics from the Christian tradition. The most famous Muslim mystic is Rumi;

in Judaism it's arguably the Baal Shem Tov. The most famous Hindu mystic known to Americans is probably Paramahansa Yogananda, author of *Autobiography of a Yogi,* the swami who first brought Hinduism to the United States in the 1930s.

Mystics are different from the mainstream religious in that they speak of *personal spiritual experience* as being of the greatest consequence. They speak of their personal transformation as coming from a direct connection to Jesus, God, Allah, Krishna, Hashem, or, in Buddhism, from stepping beyond the beyond into the real of pure knowing.

Among tribal peoples—particularly hunter tribes—mysticism is part of life. Many tribes use ethnogens—plants that open doors into other worlds—to achieve their connection to the beyond. For example, peyote is used by some Native American tribes of the southwest and Mexico, and hallucinogenic mushrooms that are detoxified through reindeer kidneys are have been used by the tribal people of Norway, who cultivated the mushrooms in reindeer grazing areas. More commonly, rituals involving dance, chanting, prayer, meditation, or sweating are used to alter states of awareness and lead to higher levels of spiritual consciousness.

I have traveled among and spent time with indigenous peoples on four continents. Some were hunter cultures, and others were agricultural societies, and some were the pastoral herders whose cultures lie somewhere between these two. One of the things I found most interesting was the difference between how hunter cultures and farmer cultures define their religious rituals and practices. Indeed, many anthropologists and observers over the centuries have remarked on these differences. A study on indigenous religions undertaken for the United Church of Canada, for example, notes, "The forms of Native Spirituality tend to vary according to whether the people were farmers or hunters and gatherers."

The farming and herding peoples I've met are quite connected to the soil and their crops, and their deities reflect this. Their gods tend to come from the sky or inside the earth, and are either a bit abstract or carry the form of their crops in human disguise such as the Hopi religious figures that incorporate corn. These people know that their survival is tied to their crops or herds, which are tied to their land.

The buildings that they live in are also tied to their land; they are usually permanent structures. Many of these cultures attach a sacred function and sacred powers to one particular building in their community, even to the extent of bringing their gods indoors to dwell in the building. These are the antecedents of our modern mosques, churches, and synagogues.

The spirituality of agricultural peoples tends to be more oriented toward past and future than present. A divine system of actions, rewards, and punishments is defined, with the emphasis on how well the crops will do when harvest season comes. Some ancient agricultural peoples, such as the Inca, even practiced elaborate ceremonies of human sacrifice and the spilling of human blood on croplands, or in ceremonial places considered surrogates for croplands, in order to please the gods who controlled the weather and how well the crops grew.

Hunting peoples (and to a smaller extent, herders) more often seem to find divinity within the whole of the natural world. Everything in the world has its own spirit, and individuals or families in such cultures often take on animal totems as personal guides or as part of their identity. Australian Aboriginal elder Geoff Guest explained to me that because the totem of his tribe or clan was a large Australian lizard, it was an animal he could neither offend nor eat, and in honor of it he had to perform particular rituals and actions when in the bush.

Unlike the spirituality of farming peoples, which is focused on past or future, that of hunter/gatherers tends to be more grounded in personal experience and the present. And while both groups use psychoactive plants to heighten spiritual experience, agricultural peoples are more likely to emphasize group activities in their ritual and hunter/gatherer peoples are more likely to incorporate elements of solitary vision quest or mentorship.

One of the things I've found most common in the spiritual understanding of all the indigenous hunter peoples I've studied is the concept of the interconnectedness of all things, a belief in a web of *knowing* in which humans and the natural world are equal strands.

THE HUNTER'S REALITY

Psychologist Robert Wolff grew up in Malaysia and often visited and stayed among the Sng'oi, an ancient indigenous tribe that over the years have been the subject of several books, including *Original Wisdom,*[1] written by Robert himself. The Sng'oi are a hunter people, and so every few months they move their settlements, which are mostly made up of simple lean-tos, to new areas in search of plants and game.

In my two extensive interviews with Robert, held at his home in Hawaii, he suggested that the Sng'oi were excellent representatives of the Edison-gene part of the spectrum of human behavior (Robert calls them "wild people" as compared to us "tame people") and show what humans with the Edison gene can be like if they grow up in a culture that is appropriate to their neurology and nurtures them. In that regard, the following text about Robert's experiences with these extraordinary hunter people gives us insights on many different levels into how our Edison-gene ancestors may have lived, how Edison-gene children and adults today experience spirituality, and how we can best respond to their concerns and spiritual yearnings.

To reach the Sng'oi, Wolff had to walk several miles along an obscure jungle trail leading from a main road. He was never sure they'd be where he last found them (and they usually weren't). The trail eventually petered out and vanished; many people who wanted to visit or photograph the Sng'oi would become lost at that point. Every time Wolff visited, however, there was always a member of the tribe sitting at that place where the trail ended. As Wolff approached, the person would wordlessly stand up and start walking into the jungle, leading Wolff to the village.

At first, Wolff thought that perhaps there was always a member of the tribe there as a sentry or gatekeeper of sorts who could hide in the treetops if the person coming wasn't somebody the Sng'oi wanted to welcome into their community. That theory evaporated, however, once he lived among the Sng'oi and learned that none of them ever went to that part of the jungle . . . except when he was coming to visit.

Could they have heard him park his car by the roadside, many miles away? Not only was that a physical impossibility, but many of the villages he visited were much farther from the meeting spot than his car was, meaning the Sng'oi who met him would have had to leave the village before he had even parked his car in order to be at the meeting spot when he arrived.

How did the Sng'oi know he was coming to visit when he himself hadn't made the decision to go to them? In a 1999 interview, Wolff told me:

> The first time when it really dawned on me . . . was that every time I went there, there was no way for them to know when I was coming. I never said, "I'll be back in a week or ten days" or whatever, because I didn't know when I'd be coming back. So, very often early in the morning, I'd discover I could take a day or two days off and I'd just hop in the car and go. They would usually in one settlement say, "Oh, we have some friends you should go visit." And then they would tell me, "You take that road and you stop at the store and then you walk through the jungle and it's an hour." They always said, "It's an hour," but I discovered quickly that that didn't mean anything at all, it could take four hours. But there was absolutely no way that I could let them know that I was coming. And the paths, by the way, were just really paths. Not a marked road or anything like that. Often I was worried that I'd lose my way or not find my way back, so often I did little tricks like marking trees . . . so I could find my way back.
>
> And every time, I mean without fail, when I was coming, about a half an hour before I got to their settlement, or to the [visible] end of the path, there would be somebody sitting on the path, a man or a woman and sometimes a child, and they would get up and just walk in front of me [through the unmarked jungle to the settlement].
>
> There was absolutely no [way they could have known], and I kept asking them, "How did you know we were coming?" and they'd say, "Oh, we didn't know you were coming." "Then why were you sitting here?" "Oh, I was just sitting there."
>
> And I had a hard time understanding that and accepting that. That was where my Western mind just absolutely couldn't go

along with that whole concept. Later on I understood—because I've done it myself now—that they'd had a dream. And in the dream, the thought had come into their head, "You're going to have visitors today." Or something like that—I'm putting it in Western terms. So somebody would say, "Oh, I think I'm going to go and sit over there."

Once I was there when they felt that somebody else was coming—even the words are misleading. Somebody just left . . . you know, there was a group of people and one young man just kind of wandered off, and I asked, "Where are you going?" And he said, "Oh, I'm just going away," and a few hours later he came back with another young man he had picked up in the jungle. And so I asked him, "Did you know this man was coming?" And he said, "No, but I had a feeling I should go over there."

You know, it's hard to describe, but when you listen to your inner voice, these things happen. I've learned since that time to listen to my inner voice. I [now] do the same thing. I'll go somewhere because I feel I should be there at a certain time or a certain date. And then usually it's for a reason. For example, I was living in Volcano [Hawaii], which was a little village a mile from the crater of Kilauea . . . which is in a national park, so the whole area is a national park, many square miles, and I had a pass and I'd go to the park often. Usually I went in the morning, because I'm a real morning person. But once, in the afternoon, I just had this kind of itchy feeling, an antsy feeling, and I thought I should go to the park. And so I went . . . to the administration building, which I never went to. I mean, literally, my car went that way. . . . And when I was there, one of the rangers who was working there at the visitor's center, who knew me, she said, "Oh, hey, come on—somebody's looking for you." And she introduced me to this man from somewhere in Europe, who had just walked in and asked about me.

It's that kind of stuff. And that happens a lot.

In his learning of a different way of *knowing,* Wolff confronted a reality that most people have experienced at one time or another in their lives but attributed to coincidence. While it's fashionable now to attribute this knowing or intuition to some coming evolutionary leap in human consciousness, the fact is that the oldest stories of humanity, from the Vedas to the epic *Gilgamesh* to the Bible, are filled with similar stories, and they echo the regular lives and experiences of hunter peoples around the world.

THE WORLD OF THE HUNTER'S DREAMS

The great psychiatrist Carl Jung was fascinated with dreams; his autobiography, *Dreams, Memories and Reflections,* gives extraordinary insight into their role in his own life and discoveries about psychology. Wolff had a similar insight, shared with him by the tribal people of Malaysia.

I asked him how he had first discovered the Sng'oi had a different way of knowing. He said that it was years after World War II, after he'd finished his university studies and earned two Ph.D.s (anthropology and psychology) and had been assigned by the Malaysian government to the job of trying to figure out why the Sng'oi were so "lazy"—why they didn't want to leave the jungle and work on rubber plantations for money. Trying to understand them, he visited them often and sometimes slept overnight in their various settlements. And he shared dreams with them. "Your own dreams are not stories," Robert said, as he explained his experience.

> Usually they're not stories. They're like flashes of this and that, and impressions. And what I found that was fascinating, once I found out what was going on, was how you weave all these things together into a story. There were some people among the Sng'oi who where really good at that, and if you happened to be sleeping in the same house with one of those people, it was amazing how you could draw out and make a story from very disparate elements.
>
> It was very common for several people to have the same dream. Very common. The children were usually the first ones to speak up. The children's dreams were simple. I remember one little girl (laughter). She slept in my arms and when we woke up she said she dreamed "warm."

And somebody spoke up and said, "What do you mean, 'warm'? Do you mean you were hot, sweating?" She said, "No, not hot or sweating." And then somebody else said that they felt there was a light in the room—this was a young man, a boy, who said that. He couldn't sleep because he felt there was a light in the space.

And there was an old woman who was the dream weaver at that particular occasion, and she said, "What do you mean, there was a light in the place?" And he pointed at me and he said that he felt that I was a light in the space. And the old woman nodded her head and she said, "Yes, he is a light, he is a light." And then she said to the little girl, "That's why you feel warm."

It's how you weave the story . . . in another place or time, if that woman hadn't been there, that girl could have said she felt warm and they would have left it at that. But she followed up, saying, "What do you mean by that?"

DREAMING WITH THE NATIVES

I asked Robert to elaborate on the experience of sleeping with these hunter people of the Malaysian jungle.

"I don't know what you call their huts," he said:

It's like a really rickety little simple dwelling. A roof and a floor and walls. But the wall is like woven bamboo.

The first night I slept with them I was very uncomfortable because I wasn't used to sleeping with other people in such close contact. People touch each other all the time. While they're sleeping, they're touching all the time. When you're communicating with somebody you always have your hand on somebody's side or their knee or something. But the Malays and the Thais do that, too.

Of one of his early visits, he said:

The feeling I had very strongly was that their day was sort of determined by the dreams they have, or by the dreams as they're discussed in the very early morning. It's not really a ritual, but as people sit around in the early morning, you know, you wake up and you sit around and there's usually five or six people at the most in one house, one shelter. And you sit around and everybody's still sleepy and you rub your eyes and stretch and yawn, you know, and then somebody says, "Ah, I dreamed of a bird," and somebody else will say, "What kind of a bird was it?" And then they ask where the bird was going, and what direction, and all. But sometimes it comes out as a story. It doesn't always come out as a story, but sometimes one thing will just lead to another and somebody else will say, "Oh, yeah, I dreamed about a bird also, and it was going in so-and-so direction." And then they say, "Oh, the bird reminds me of so-and-so." And sometimes when it's a story, they'll follow through on that.

[Here's the story of] the first time it really came together to me. It always seemed very casual to me in the beginning because you sit around and people say, "I dreamed of this and that," and when it doesn't make a story, what remains is the feeling of it. I remember when somebody was worried about something she had dreamed about, she was a little girl, and the whole day was kind of like, you know, people were kind of apprehensive, like they were waiting for something to happen.

[On this one morning,] I was in this house, this shelter, and there were a few of us sitting around, and the story was that there was a very unusual plant, and they described where it was in their dream. Sort of like, "Wow, really did you see that?" "Yeah and it was really very, very big."

And so when we came out of the house in the morning and people started their day, I realized that some of the people from my dwelling were talking to people from the other house. And I didn't think about it much at the time. I mean, you see a flower or a plant, and so what. But about late morning this little girl came to me and she said, "Come on, we've got to go look at the flower," and I said, "What flower?" and she said, "You know, from the dream." I had forgotten about the whole thing, but apparently it was a part of their whole day.

And she took my hand and we went onto a path and followed this path, and I remember particularly that she sort of chatted along and said, "You know, sometime later, when you are more accustomed to our ways, then you will also see the animals that flit around us and that we walk through, on both sides of the path." And I hadn't noticed anything at all, and then I realized later that when I paid attention, I could *see* and the jungle was full of animals that were watching us. Anyway we came to this clearing in the jungle and in the middle was this huge, enormous plant. Very smelly. What I remember most was the smell—it smelled like rotten meat, you know, to attract flies.

And the whole village was sitting around, when this girl and I sat down, and when I looked around I realized that everybody else was sitting around there, too. They didn't say anything, they were just sitting there. Not exactly like a religious experience, but like, "I have to study this." Really paying attention to the experience, to being there. And so we stayed for nearly an hour. It was a long time. As a Westerner I was impatient. I was ready to go home or do something else. But they stayed there, and then we all wandered back and nobody said anything about it. So in the evening I asked them about it, what is this flower, and they told me that it was very rare, and that only a few people had ever seen it before, but they'd heard about it. The flower was three feet high and there was no other visible plant part of it.

I said, "Did the psychologist in you think that somebody had earlier noticed that the flower was about to blossom, or had caught the smell during their dream?"

"No," Robert said. "I'm completely convinced that the dream of the flower had nothing to do with the physical environment. I'm quite convinced that the dreams that they call 'important dreams' are from another world, from another reality. I don't think there were any . . . subconscious cues that they picked up. It was quite a far distance away, a half hour walking."

I asked, "Did anybody ever come right out and discuss with you this issue of how they know things, how they dream things?"

Wolff answered:

There was one man who was my "informant"*—I hate that
word—anyhow, this man, Amit, became my friend . . . And I asked
him one time about dreams, and he told me there were different
kinds of dreams. Some dreams happen when you eat too much
before you go to bed, and there are other dreams that tell you of
something that might happen in the future. And so he told me
those dreams are important dreams and you have to pay attention
to them. The kind of dreams that are vague and don't mean anything or just give you a kind of feeling, you don't have to remember. But the important dreams, you have to remember. He always
used the word "important" dreams.

"What does 'important' mean?" I asked.
Wolff said:

I asked him to give me an example of an important dream, and he
wouldn't do that. He said, "I can't tell you that because my dreams
are not your dreams." And he said that I will know when a dream
is important. And of course I've had important dreams and I
always knew when they were important dreams, and they always
came true, also. I've had, all my life, had dreams that, waking
dreams, you know, I don't know what to call them, there's no
word for it. Not exactly dreams, but information came to me.

I asked him, "Did people know you were coming to visit the communities because they dreamed it or 'knew' it during the day?"
Wolff replied:

I remember one instance when I went to one place and they were
just in the process of getting settled [into a new location in the jun-
gle]. And they said, "How did you know we were here?" And I

---

* *Informant* is the term anthropologists use for an individual from within a particular culture who is willing to explain the meaning of cultural events, and/or translate for them.

said that other people [in another Sng'oi community] had told me where they were. And they said, "Oh, they must have dreamed it." That was very peculiar because the people who had told me where to find them had told me two months earlier. And two months earlier those people weren't there yet.

"So they had to have dreamed it," I said.
Robert said, "Yes."

LEARNING TO KNOW

I asked Robert, "How did you come to learn that you could 'know' in the way of Sng'oi?"

He then told me a story that started with his having to visit an Indonesian town on the ocean. He invited his "informant," Amit, to go along with him. Amit had never been outside of his own community, had never left the jungle, and certainly had never seen the ocean, which was hundreds of miles from where the Sng'oi traditionally lived. None of the Sng'oi, in fact, had ever seen the ocean, as far as Robert could determine.

When, late in the afternoon, as the sun was setting, the two of them arrived at the oceanside home of the man with whom they were to stay, Amit walked outside and stood for an hour or two, just staring out at the ocean, as if he were in a trance. The next morning, before sunup, they left to return to the interior, and Robert and Amit returned late the next day to the Sng'oi settlement where Amit lived.

At the settlement, the people asked Amit about his experience, and he described the ocean in detail, the types of life in it, the topography of the sea bed, the history of the ocean in that region. This was all new information to the Sng'oi, and Robert had not told Amit any of it. He asked Amit how he'd learned these things, and Amit told him the Lord of the Great Ocean had told him while he stood beside the water the night before.

Robert was shocked:

When Amit started to tell his story about the Lord of the Great Ocean, it just boggled my mind that he knew these things because all he had done was stood on the beach and he hadn't even put his foot into the water. We were only there overnight; we got there around five in the afternoon and it was awful dark and we left the next morning. So he couldn't have learned anything about oceans. The man had never seen that much water in his entire life. And he came back and he told a story about the oceans that cover the earth, that the land floats on the earth, that in the oceans there is a whole landscape like on the top of the earth, that there are rivers in the ocean and mountains in the ocean. It was staggering. How did he know that?

UNDERSTANDING THE *REAL* WORLD

I asked Robert, "And the Sng'oi differentiated between knowing the *real* world of nature, with all its energies and dreams, and knowing the man-made, workaday world we all seem to think is reality?"

He said:

Oh, yes. They don't work. They don't. They refuse to work for somebody. In Malaysia at that time they [the government] had this land scheme and they would clear cut the jungle, many thousands of acres a year, and plant it in rubber. And they often came across aborigines [like and including the Sng'oi] and they would say to them, "We'll plant the rubber trees and if you wait two years then you can scar the tree and rubber will flow into little cups and you just collect the cups and bring them to us and we'll pay you." And the people said no.

And the Malaysian government just couldn't understand. We're offering them an easy way to make money, but they just said no. So I was in the government and they knew I was having contact with these people and they said, "Can you find out why they're so stubborn?" And so the next time I went to a settlement I asked them, "How come, when people tell you that they want to plant rubber and all you have to do is stab the tree and get rich, you say no?"

And there was this long silence . . . every time I asked a question, there was always a silence. It was like people were communicating with each other. I mean, I had the strong impression that they were consulting with each other. And then one person would give the answer. And I never knew which one would answer it. It wasn't the oldest one or a man or a woman; sometimes it was a young man or a child, even.

But this time it was a young man, and he said, "You know, when you plant one thing, it grows for the life of that one plant, that one species, and afterwards the soil is dead." And that's all they wanted to say about it. And at that moment I didn't even capture how profound that was. Because rubber trees will live for about forty years, and so what he said was that we're not willing to get rich for forty years and then have to live with dead soil.

So when I came back to town later on, I reported to this department of forestry, and I remember in this office I started my story about these aborigines who said that you could grow one generation of this rubber tree and then the soil is dead. And there was an Englishman sitting in the corner, and he jumped up, very excited, and said, "Come on with me and I'll show you something."

So we went in his Land Rover and drove to this little one-hectare plot of land outside of the city, one hundred meters by one hundred meters, and they had it all marked off with ropes and string, and they were counting what was in this piece of virgin forest. They had counted all the trees, and they were beginning to count all the bushes, and they were going to count the ground cover and the bushes, and then the animals. . . . But they had only gotten so far as counting the trees at that point.

They showed me this piece of paper with all the trees on it, and I forget the exact number but I think they'd said there were seven hundred different species of trees in that hectare, and there were only two trees of the same species. And he gave me this whole lecture. He said, "You know, it's absolutely true, because people think of the jungle as something very rich and very fertile, but actually it's not fertile. It's a very thin ground, the soil is so thin. It's not the ground, but it's the air and the moisture in the air that makes it so lush, because what one plant takes out of the soil, another plant puts back in." Those were his words. He said, "It's absolutely true. If you grow one species, a hundred acres of corn, it takes out of the soil certain nutrients and you want to plant something else after that corn is harvested, you have to put lots and lots of stuff back in." And that's one of the reasons why monoculture doesn't work, but we [still] haven't learned that in the fifty years since he said that.

WILD PEOPLE AND TAME PEOPLE

I asked, "How did we become so disconnected from natural wisdom?"

"We were domesticated," Robert said. "Wild people *know* these things. Tame people have forgotten them."

"Wild people and tame people?"

Robert said:

Tame people, to me, are people who live by man-made laws. In America, particularly, we have a government that tries to control our morals. Wild people are controlled only by the laws of nature. There are lots of things you can't do, but you can't do them because *nature* tells you so.

Taboos [and laws] are from hierarchical societies. . . . To me, fixed, categorical types of laws are obviously man-made, and they're just stupid. They don't work. They don't take account of individual differences or circumstances or weather or whatever.

I said, "But don't 'wild people' have rules about rape and murder? Or is their 'knowing' such that they just know what to do?"

"I don't think they have rules. No. I think very strongly that wild people generally have experience that cooperation works a lot better than competition."

I asked, "And cooperation would preclude rape and murder?"

Yes, of course. [For example,] the children that I remember, they don't have games exactly. Their play is real life. How to get across a river, or how to get a boat into the water. The natural thing to do is to help each other, and the unnatural thing to do is to compete with each other. I see in my own grandchildren, when they play together without toys, they collaborate. As soon as you bring in toys or a game with rules, then they compete. If you ask kids to pick fruit, they will help each other to climb this tree. But when you say, "Let me see who can pick the most of this fruit," then you introduce a whole different element into it.

The lifestyle Robert describes is similar to that found by Europeans when they first discovered the Americas and Australia. When Columbus first met the Tiano Indians on the island of Hispaniola (now Haiti and the Dominican Republic), they greeted him on the beach with gifts of food and sacred objects. Native Americans showed early European settlers how to survive in the wilds, and Americans commemorate this early show of cooperation with the holiday we call Thanksgiving.

Instead of working all day to make a small segment of their society "rich," indigenous people—which is what your ancestors and mine were for most of human history—spend their time awash in a sea of *knowing*. They know their world, they know their relations, they know the deep and rich spirituality that is part of all life. They talk to their world, and it answers them. They're so finely tuned to each other and the life around them that they sense when somebody may come to visit or somebody needs help. Their lives are a natural sort of harmony.

THE LOSS OF TRUE WISDOM

They would have clearly understood Jesus when he said, "Split a piece of wood; I am there. Lift up the stone, and you will find me there."[2] And his statement in the Sermon on the Mount, which has confounded agriculturalists for millennia, makes perfect sense to hunters: "Therefore I say unto you, Be not over anxious for your life what ye shall eat, or what ye shall drink; nor yet for your body, what ye shall put on," as he pointed out that none of the other animals in creation "gather into barns."[3]

I asked Robert what has happened to the Sng'oi in the years since he knew them.

"They've died out," he said with sadness in his voice. "Essentially, they no longer exist because their environment has been taken away from them. Most of Malaysia now is under cultivation and there's virtually no jungle left, and the few [surviving] people have merged into the Malay society." After a pause, he added, "In my dreams I visit them."

In the single century between the years 1901 and 2001, over half of the two thousand known human languages on Earth became extinct. Groups like Cultural Survival[4] are working to preserve and protect the habitats of indigenous peoples, because they realize that in all natural systems diversity brings strength. We destroy the diversity of the human race at our own peril, and in destroying it, we lose our contact with much ancient wisdom, including the ability to *know*.

While the Sng'oi were a heart-based culture, we live in a thinking-based culture, focusing on our heads instead of our hearts. We honor science as the highest form of knowing. Increasingly, the hard sciences are demonstrating that our five senses are only the narrowest of cracks through which we see the full spectrum of reality, and that the nature of the real, physical world is much more mysterious and awesome than we'd ever guessed was possible.

WHEN ACCESS TO PERSONAL SPIRITUALITY IS LOST

Our Edison-gene children don't have the luxury of growing up in a culture like that of the Sng'oi and instead are bashed and bruised by the lack of fit between their neurology and the demands of our culture—particularly in school. The National Institute on Drug Abuse points out that this lack of fit, in part, is why nearly three quarters of all American teenagers have tried illegal drugs by the time they graduate from high school, and in any given month, at least one fifth of all teenagers have taken an illegal drug. Additionally, numerous studies indicate that those children diagnosed with ADHD or other neurological differences are more likely than others to be among those who regularly use drugs.

What are these children trying to achieve?

Back in the 1950s, in an early version of the theory of multiple intelligences, Harvard psychology professor and researcher Dr. Timothy Leary developed an the concept of the "eight-circuit" brain: Each part of the brain, he suggested, has its own unique intelligence, and as each intelligence is exercised or grows, it influences all the others in synergistic ways. Leary's definitions were rather lengthy and academic, but Antero Alli, author of *Angel Tech*, redefined these "eight interactive functions of intelligence" as: "physical, emotional, conceptual, social, sensory, psychic, mythic/imaginative, and spiritual intelligences."5

While hunter cultures train their young in each of these areas, our television- and school-driven culture focuses almost exclusively on conceptual and social intelligences. This seems to have caused us to lose some essential part of our connection to the web of humanness, a connection that perhaps our teenagers are trying to find through experimenting with drugs.

In his book *Heart of the Hunter*, the famous South African writer Laurens van der Post tells a fascinating story. Because it reminded him of his time among the Sng'oi, Wolff summarized it very elegantly for me: "Van der Post and his hunting party are staying deep in the Kalahari with a small group of Bushmen," Wolff wrote. He continued:

> One day they take a few hunters with them to find some meat. They drive 12 miles or so and shoot an eland, which is a very special animal for the Bushmen. They load the eland on their Land Rover . . . and van der Post says to Dabé [one of the Bushmen] that the women will be surprised when they come home with so much meat.
>
> Dabé looks at him with astonishment. "But they already know," he says. And sure enough, when they get back to the women and old people, they have the fires ready and are dancing and singing because they are eating eland.6

After summarizing the story, Wolff wrote that this was very much like his experience with the Sng'oi, adding: "Thom, we lost so much when we chose machines!"

Its those losses, the cultural and spiritual disconnection from the hunter roots of our culture and our once-daily interactions with the natural world, that have led so many of our Edison-gene children into the world of drug abuse.

One way many Edison-gene children and adults find their way back to "tribe" and respect for all of creation is through the intense experience of personal mysticism or fundamentalist religions that emphasize a personal connection to spirit. When these are found in the context of a religion familiar to the family, the possiblity of the need for intense expression leading to involvement with a cult or another dangerous outlet is minimized. Every religion has mystical roots and most have mystical components that are still very much alive.

Part 3

The Future

*Nobody wishes more than I do that ingenuity
should receive liberal encouragement.*
THOMAS JEFFERSON

The environmental and cultural conditions for survival in the modern developed world of the twenty-first century are far different from what they were a hundred years ago and significantly different from what they were just fifty years ago. Yet most of our institutions are still based on models that were developed in the eighteenth, nineteenth, and early twentieth centuries.

The result is paradoxical: Just as we most need innovators, entrepreneurs, inventors, creators, and revolutionaries, our social and educational systems are becoming rigidified and less tolerant of difference and variation. But the very children who would have otherwise become many of our inventors, innovators, and change agents of this century are instead often medicated into docility and indoctrinated with the notion that they have "disordered" brains with neurochemical imbalances.

If the human race is have a bright and positive future through the twenty-first century and beyond, we need fully enabled, fully competent Edison-gene children, undamaged by stories of mental disorder, derogatory labels, or the influences of powerful—and unnecessary—psychoactive drugs. We need to empower such children not medicate them.

We can do this by changing our approach to public education, changing the stories we tell ourselves about what it means to be a hunter in a farmer's world, protecting our children from the mind control of consumerism and television, and encouraging exploration of educational alternatives such as Montessori schooling and homeschooling.

A new generation of enlightened, empowered children may yet save our world. But only if we, as the adults who care for them, allow them to grow up undamaged and unencumbered.

17

How Edison-Gene Children
May Change the World

The world owes all of its onward impulses
to men ill at ease. The happy man inevitably
confines himself within ancient limits.

NATHANIEL HAWTHORNE

A culture that lacks the ability or willingness to innovate and change is a culture that's headed for trouble. Societies like that of Japan during the Meiji era or Europe during the feudal Dark Ages used violence and fear to prevent change as long as possible but eventually disintegrated under the weight of their own inability to adapt. On the other hand, when cultures do change it's often because extraordinary individuals step forward and show the way to a new life. Among the five Native American nations that formed the original Iroquois League of Nations, it was a young man named Deganwidah who stepped forward as a Christ-like figure, showing his people a new and peaceful way to live. Deganwidah spoke with a stutter, so his articulate companion, Hiawatha (not the Hiawatha of Longfellow's famous poem), communicated many of his insights about cooperative government to his people. Out of these men's words came a constitution that the Founders of the United States used, in part, as a model for our own.

Similarly, Europe lurched into the Renaissance with the stepping forth of empowered radical thinkers like Galileo and Michelangelo, and, as we've seen, the ever-changing Ben Franklin helped give birth to the United States of America.

But society's nurturing of such individuals is often not that simple. Cultures select for certain types of behaviors and against others (and different cultures select in different ways) by a system of rewards and punishments that has aspects both subtle and coarse. Understanding how cultures work, and the delicate interplay between culture, neurology, and the beliefs we all hold is critical to helping raise a generation of children who can successfully bring humanity through the twenty-first century without disaster.

GLIMMERS OF HOW CULTURE WORKS

In 1934, Ruth Benedict wrote a book titled *Patterns of Culture*, which electrified the worlds of both anthropology and popular understanding. In a preface to a 1958 reprint of the book, Margaret Mead wrote: "That today the modern world is on such easy terms with the concept of culture, that the words 'in our culture' slip from the lips of educated men and women almost as effortlessly as do the phrases that refer to period and to place, is in very great part due to this book."[1]

Patterns of Culture examined in detail the histories, stories, lives, and cultures of three groups of indigenous peoples: The Zuni Indians of New Mexico, the Dobu people of eastern New Guinea, and the Kwakiutal tribe of the Vancouver area. Benedict contrasted the way of life of the agricultural Zuni with their hunter cousins, the Plains Indians; she looked at the war-based culture of the Dobu farmers and compared it with the potlatch-based culture of the Kwakiutal fishermen; and she placed all in the broader context of questions about what creates and drives culture in the first place.

WHAT CAUSES CULTURE?

Toward the end of this brilliant and seminal book, Benedict ruminated on the question first raised by Darwin a century earlier: Is culture a product of biology, or a learned tradition, or both?

"This brings us to one of the most hotly debated of all the controversies which impinge upon configurational anthropology," she wrote nearly seventy-five years ago. Benedict continued:

> It has been vigorously contended that traits are not culturally selected but biologically transmitted. According to this interpretation the distinction is racial, and the Plains Indians seek visions because this necessity is transmitted in the chromosomes of the race. Similarly, the Pueblo cultures pursue sobriety and moderation because such conduct is determined by their racial heredity. If the biological interpretation is true, it is not to history that we need to go to understand the behavior of groups, but to physiology.[2]

The problem with this possibility, however, was that in 1934 nobody had any competent means to measure minute neurological or genetic differences between tribal people, or even among people within a tribe: "In order to prove their point it would be necessary for those who hold this view to show physiological facts that account for even a small part of the social phenomena it is necessary to understand," Benedict wrote. This, she added, means, "It is not an anthropological problem, but when the physiologists and the geneticists have provided the material it may be of value to the students of cultural history."

This was an era when American and British eugenics programs were attempting to purify humanity by genetic means: The countries' governments were forcing sterilization of Native Americans, cultural misfits, and the mentally ill, and their programs were growing and being cited by Hitler as a great idea upon which to build a racially pure nation. Benedict was justifiably concerned about any biological explanation for behavior or culture.

Her observations, however, clearly indicated a possibility of that reality. In *Patterns of Culture* she wrote: "Cultural interpretations of behavior need never deny that a physiological element is involved." But it shouldn't be considered the most pertinent variable, she believed. History was far more important than genes—all behaviors are molded in the crucible of the culture in which the individual matures. Nonetheless, she said, "To point out, therefore, that the biological bases of cultural behavior [are mostly] irrelevant is not to deny that they are present."[3]

In the years since Benedict's observation, the correlation between genetics and behavior was used by Hitler to try to exterminate the Jews and Roma (Gypsies) from Europe and is used today by many in the fields of psychiatry to justify giving psychoactive drugs to children to control their "genetically-mediated behaviors" such as ADHD. This could rightly be called "the dark side of the force," the result of a substantial simplification of the highly complex interactions between genetics, culture, and individual upbringing.

THE BIOLOGY OF CULTURE

We now know far more about genetics than did anthropologists in Benedict's day. We know, for example, that some of our children and adults still carry the gene that apparently evolved forty thousand years ago and conferred an adaptive to its carriers for surviving a time of crisis.

We know that those children born with this advantageous gene have variously been called "disordered" (ADHD) and evolved or mutant or brilliant (Indigo Children). They certainly have a history of transforming the world—people with this gene are well-represented among our most successful inventors, entrepreneurs, and politicians.

As a society, we're entering new and extraordinary times, facing dangers and opportunities rarely even imagined by our ancestors. Our environment has become so toxic that one in three humans will develop cancer, and our culture so stressed by overpopulation that during the twentieth century more people died in war alone than populated the entire civilized world at the time of Columbus.

Like all living things, humans are biologically adaptive. During the five million years of the *Homo*'s hunter time, we developed a brain highly adapted to the hunt, bodies capable of long runs and sustained effort, and communication systems adapted to hunting and gathering in teams.

We passed through several evolutionary leaps on the way from *Homo erectus* to *Homo sapiens,* each in response to a dramatic change in our environment.

PRIMAL HUMAN CULTURES

Human cultures have traditionally taken one of three forms: the nomadic hunters, the agricultural farmers, or the pastoral herders, which lie somewhere between the two. While farmer-based cultures have emerged only in the past six to ten thousand years, pastoral (domesticating and herding) cultures go back at least twenty thousand years. Hunting-based cultures have dominated human history for over two hundred thousand years, and pre-human history for at least five million years. The most successful such cultures have emerged in the past forty thousand years, with the !Kung Bushmen of the Kalahari Desert in Africa being their most direct cultural descendants.

Life in a hunter culture was vastly different from life in an agricultural culture. Hunters faced constant change and continual, unknown dangers, while farmers usually lived in protected enclaves or settlements. Hunters were called on to make rapid choices from moment to moment and split-second decisions; farmers had to learn to enjoy (or at least tolerate) the routine of plowing, planting, tending, and harvesting.

Hunter peoples, unencumbered by crops, were (and are) almost always nomadic, (as were and are some herding peoples) ranging over a large territory in small groups. Farmers are anchored to a single place, and have large families to participate in the work or to form "armies" to defend their crop land from other farmers.

The very different environments of hunters and farmers produce very different skill sets, although humanity is sprinkled with people carrying the genetic template for success in both. This is a good thing, because every human society needs both—competent and empowered— to function with optimal success. We need hunters with their rapid-action brains that constantly scan the environment and are ever ready for change and challenge, and farmers who, with their patient, methodical ways, are rooted to the land that is their sustenance or can function well in schools, factories, and offices.

During the past ten thousand years, humans split up into two very different types of cultures memorialized in the biblical story of Cain (the first farmer) and Abel (the first hunter-herder). Only in the past three hundred years (since about 1700) have farmers (including aboriginal agricultural peoples, such as the Bantus who have taken over most of Africa) come to numerically dominate the world, wiping out or assimilating the vast majority of the world's hunter cultures.

CULTURAL AND GENETIC SELECTION

That the form a culture takes is in part a function of the world within which its people live is undeniable. Culture—and all its components, from language to ritual—adapts to environment. From that adaptation, within different cultures, different types of human characteristics will become more or less valuable. Time and natural selection tend to subtly modify individuals and thus whole peoples who live in isolation for long periods of time.

For example, as explained earlier in this book, only in the past 250 generations, or five thousand years, has lactase persistence (that is, after a child is weaned, the stomach continues to produce the enzyme necessary to digest milk) appeared in the human genome, and predominantly only in those people whose ancestors are European herders. While about 80 to 85 percent of those with European ancestry can easily digest milk as adults, the number drops to only 10 to 30 percent among Asian, African, and Native American populations, depending on the local tribal subgroup.

Five millennia ago, in the frozen reaches of northern Europe, people discovered that milking their cows, goats, and sheep was a useful way to have fresh and ongoing food supplies through the long winters. A few people had a variation (or mutation) in the gene for lactase production—there are always genetic variations appearing in millions of genes all the time in all species. Those people thrived on a milk and cheese diet during the winters, while those without this genetic mutation suffered cramps, bloating, diarrhea, and only partial absorption of nutrients and thus were less healthy.

Those people with the lactase gene who were more fit were more desirable as mates and more capable of producing and nurturing offspring, so their gene came to be increasingly represented in the human populations of northern Europe, while those lacking the gene were more susceptible to disease or failed to find mates or didn't survive pregnancy.

As mentioned earlier, a similar genetic pattern can be found in the ability to digest the protein gluten found in wheat, rye, and barley. The first evidence of humans eating grains comes from archeological digs at Catal Huyuk in Turkey, where eleven thousand years ago, people used oxidian blades formed into sickles to cut grain, most likely barley.

The practice spread through the Middle East over the following four thousand years, into southern Europe about five thousand years ago. From their the cultivation of grain moved into northern Europe with the Celtic and then Roman invasions three thousand and two thousand years ago respectively, finally reaching Scandinavia a mere one thousand years ago. As a consequence, the farther north you go in Europe, the more people there are who have gluten intolerance or celiac disease.

Genetic variations are widespread and account in some part for the diversity of human characteristics, abilities, and tendencies. The lesson of this is that genetic variations that drive behavior cannot be thought of in terms of *good* or *bad,* in either an abstract or a practical context. As Ruth Benedict pointed out:

> The cultural pattern of any civilization makes use of a certain segment of the great arc of potential human purposes and motivations . . . The great arc along which all the possible human behaviors are distributed is far too immense and too full of contradictions for any one culture to utilize even any considerable portion. Selection is the first requirement.[4]

Every culture will select—that is, reward the behaviors that sustain that society and discourage those that don't. This may occur overtly and explicitly, as in the modern trend toward calling genetically-caused ADHD a "disorder," or it may happen simply through the relatively automatic mechanism of natural selection, as in the proliferation of gluten and lactose tolerance among the agricultural peoples of southern Europe and the Middle East.

And as pollution, population, and war increasingly challenge our world, we may face the beginning of a new form of natural selection.

18

Is Human Evolution Finally Over?

Nothing is eternal on the earth below;
And fortune delights in constant change,
So she may more plainly show her power.
MACHIAVELLI, *THE PRINCE*

The second week of February, 2002, saw an interesting debate at Edinburgh, Scotland's Royal Society. Titled "Is Evolution Over?" the Society brought together some of the world's top scientists to debate the question of whether or not we humans have reached the pinnacle of our evolutionary potential.

AS GOOD AS IT GETS

On one side were scientists such as University College London's Professor Steve Jones, who said, "If you want to know what Utopia is like, just look around—this is it. . . . Things have stopped getting better—or worse—for our species."

Others, such as University of California at San Diego's Christopher Wills, suggest that in our trickle-down world, those with the greatest ability to accumulate cash will eventually evolutionarily crowd out the rest of us. "There is a premium on sharpness of mind and the ability to accumulate money," he said in an article published in London's *Guardian* newspaper, which also quoted Jones: "Such people tend to have more children and have a better chance of survival."[1]

Please send us this card to receive our latest catalog.

❏ Check here if you would like to receive our catalog via e-mail.

E-mail address _____

Name _____ Company _____

Address _____ Phone _____

City _____ State _____ Zip _____ Country _____

Please check the following area(s) of interest to you:

❏ Health   ❏ Self-help   ❏ Science/Nature   ❏ Shamanism
❏ Ancient Mysteries   ❏ New Age/Spirituality   ❏ Ethnobotany   ❏ Martial Arts
❏ Spanish Language   ❏ Sexuality/Tantra   ❏ Children   ❏ Teen

Order at 1-800-246-8648 • Fax (802) 767-3726
E-mail: orders@InnerTraditions.com • Web site: www.InnerTraditions.com

INNER TRADITIONS

BEAR & CO.

BEAR CUB BOOKS

HEALING ARTS PRESS

DESTINY BOOKS

Park Street Press

BINDU BOOKS

Inner Traditions • Bear & Company

P.O. Box 388

Rochester, VT 05767-0388

U.S.A.

WE'RE GOING DOWNHILL

Others have historically disputed Wills's and Jones's notion. In *The Descent of Man,* Charles Darwin wrote in 1871 that, "Man scans with scrupulous care the character and pedigree of his horses, cattle, and dogs before he matches them; but when he comes to his own marriage he rarely, or never, takes any such care. . . . Both sexes ought to refrain from marriage if they are in any marked degree inferior in body or mind."

Like those today who echo the Calvinist notion that wealth and power are indications of either superior genes or blessings from above, Darwin also fell prey to the worries of his cousin, Sir Francis Galton, that if the "underclass" wasn't somehow prevented from reproducing, they may one day crowd out all the wealthy and worthy people, thus reversing the natural process of evolution. "All ought to refrain from marriage who cannot avoid abject poverty for their children," Darwin wrote in *Descent of Man,* "for poverty is not only a great evil, but tends to its own increase by leading to recklessness in marriage. On the other hand, as Mr. Galton has remarked, if the prudent avoid marriage, whilst the reckless marry, the inferior members tend to supplant the better members of society."

Although sentiments like Darwin's were often cited by American and British eugenicists in the 1920s and then picked up with great enthusiasm by National Socialists in Germany in the 1930s (who often reproduced American eugenics posters), Darwin also strongly believed that compassion, love, and what he called "the moral qualities" were even more important than any inherited physical or mental fitness, as he stated in *Descent of Man:*

> Important as the struggle for existence has been and even still is, yet as far as the highest part of man's nature is concerned there are other agencies more important. For the moral qualities are advanced, either directly or indirectly, much more through the effects of habit, the reasoning powers, instruction, religion, &c., [*sic*] than through natural selection; though to this latter agency may be safely attributed the social instincts, which afforded the basis for the development of the moral sense.

That Darwin himself would have been (and was) horrified by political, social, and economic systems that created oppression and perpetuated poverty is something the advocates of economic trickle-down-theory conveniently overlook.

For whatever reason, it may be that we've slowly evolved over the past ten thousand years. In the same *Guardian* article quoting Jones and Wills, Professor Chris Stinger of the Natural History Museum of London notes that "brain size has decreased over the past 10,000 years. A similar reduction has also affected our physiques. We are punier and smaller-brained compared with our ancestors only a few millennia ago."

While many people think we're larger and stronger than our ancestors, this is a common misconception in our culture. We modern people *are* physically larger and stronger than our agricultural city-state ancestors, particularly those who lived during the last five centuries, mostly because of better nutrition, modern medicine, and the introduction into our food supply of animal growth-hormones and plastics that imitate human hormones. But when we compare ourselves with our hunter ancestors from ten thousand years ago, the fact is that they were as large as we are, lost fewer teeth over the course of their lives, and were substantially stronger.

IT'S THE FAULT OF THOSE PEOPLE WITH ADHD!

There are even those who suggest that people with the Edison-gene are driving the deterioration of the human genome and, thus, the survival quality of the human race (at least in the developed world). Hope Press, which published Dr. David Comings's book *The Gene Bomb,* offers this cautionary warning on its Web site:

> Have you often wondered why in recent years there seems to be an increase in the number of children and adults with attention deficit disorder, learning disabilities, anxiety, anger and rage? Why the frequency of depression, suicide, crime, and related behaviors is increasing? Why our youth are so frequently dropping out of school and turning to drugs and alcohol?[2]

The reason, according to Comings's book, is that people with ADHD are more impulsive and thus more likely to impulsively have sex and produce babies. Like Sir Francis Galton, it seems he's intimidated by the reproduction of those who can't make it through college. "These trends are usually attributed purely to environmental factors and to the stress of our increasingly complex and technological society," the Hope Press Web site notes. But society isn't the problem, according to Comings: It's genetics. "In *The Gene Bomb,* Dr. Comings proposes a revolutionary new theory that just the opposite is occurring—that our increasingly complex society, with its requirement for more and more years of education, is selecting for the genes associated with these behavioral disorders, and that these genes are increasing and will continue to increase in frequency."[3] Comings, by the way, does not see this as a good thing.

ARE WE STANDING STILL?

Other geneticists such as the University of Washington in Seattle's Peter Ward suggest that human evolution is neither advancing nor retreating. In his book *Future Evolution*[4] Ward writes, "I don't think we are going to see any changes—apart from ones we deliberately introduce ourselves."

Similarly, outside of fringe groups like the Raelians (who claimed, in 2003, to have cloned a human), most scientists don't believe the human genome has changed much in either direction during the relatively climate-stable era of the past ten thousand years to the present. Nor do most see any rapid changes on the horizon, other than the possible impact of the third-world AIDS epidemic that may leave alive only those with the genetic mutation that enables them to withstand the disease.

The startling changes in the age at which young girls are reaching puberty in the developed world (as young as five years in some communities, particularly those in poor areas) are largely attributed to environmental rather than genetic factors. Estrogen-mimicking chemicals such as plasticizers found in the packaging of much of our food, or hormone-interrupting pesticide chemicals designed to render insects sterile are considered the main culprits, as put forth in the 1997 book *Our Stolen*

Future: Are We Threatening Our Fertility, Intelligence, and Survival?: A Scientific Detective Story by Theo Colborn, Dianne Dumanoski, and John Peterson Myers. Others suggest that growth-regulating hormones regularly injected into or fed to cattle and other feed animals are driving the explosion of early menarche—and the correlated explosion in breast, uterine, testicular, prostate, and ovarian cancers. No scientists or researchers, though, suggest it's a function of evolution.

DISTANT BOTTLENECK EVENTS

Most serious scientists looking into human evolution agree with Stephen Jay Gould's hypothesis that significant die-offs or bottleneck events are necessary for small mutations or variations to emerge as substantial and visible changes in the human genome and in the appearance, abilities, and behavior of humans. Outside of local genocides, wars, and plagues, the entire human race apparently hasn't faced a planet-wide disaster in about forty thousand years.

But, as British science writer David Keys notes in his book *Catastrophe,* based on current increased activity, there is the potential for several huge volcanic events in the future, all of which are on schedule to occur in a time frame ranging from a few dozen to a few hundred years. He notes, for example, that the world's largest explosion could take place in North America:

> Brooding an estimated six miles beneath the scenic wonderland of America's Yellowstone National Park is a vast liquid time bomb the size of Lake Michigan or the Irish Sea. Made of molten rock, this ultra-hot subterranean reservoir of volcanic magma will almost certainly one day burst forth upon the world, changing our planet's history just as proto-Krakatoa did fifteen centuries ago. For Yellowstone is host to the world's largest dormant volcano— a huge caldera covering around fifteen hundred square miles.[5]

Keys notes that it could go any time: "It appears to erupt roughly once every 600,000 to 700,000 years—and the last eruption was 630,000 years ago. What's more, the last decade or so of the twentieth century has seen a substantial increase in potential pre-eruption activity there."

While volcanic activity will no doubt one day create a worldwide disaster and punctuate the evolutionary process of humans and other species (as it has in the past), there's a more present and probable danger that's going to require the most of our human ingenuity and Edison-like abilities. Whether we face and conquer this terrible danger of our own creation, or we allow it to wipe out as many as 90 percent of all living humans, this threat may well drive human evolution to a new plateau.

19

One Generation
to Save the World

You shall be treated to the ironical smiles and
mockings of those who remain behind you.
WALT WHITMAN, *SONG OF THE OPEN ROAD*

The good citizens of England awoke on January 9, 2003, to see the title of this chapter as a headline in one of their newspapers (the *Guardian*). The lead sentence of the article by Paul Brown said, "The human race has only one or perhaps two generations to rescue itself, according to the 2003 *State of the World* report by the Washington-based Worldwatch Institute."

The report went on to document that more than 20 percent of the world's people live on less than a dollar a day (a percentage that will triple within twenty years) and that a quarter of the planet's crop land has been lost in the past century. In addition, a quarter of the world's mammal species and 12 percent of the planet's birds are on the edge of extinction, in part because: "Toxic chemicals are being released in everincreasing quantities, and global production of hazardous waste has reached more than 300 million tons a year." The report adds that, "There is only a vague idea of what damage this does to humans and natural systems."

Wetlands—the world's filtering kidneys—have decreased by more than 50 percent in the past century, while forests—the world's lungs—are "being cut down at the rate of 50,000 square miles a year."

Not only is this all unsustainable, but an even larger threat looms on the horizon.

CLIMATE FLIP-FLOPS TO THE NEXT ICE AGE

Dr. William H. Calvin, the author of nearly a dozen books and a professor at the University of Washington, has written one of the most important and extraordinary books published in 2002, and the best of a small (but growing) handful of books about the relationship between global climate fluctuations and human evolution. Titled *A Brain For All Seasons: Human Evolution and Abrupt Climate Change,* Calvin's book lays out in exhaustive detail the history of this planet's climatological flip-flops. He notes:

> Even a decade ago, we didn't know much about the climate flips; we simply thought that climate creep was starting to occur and that we needed to prevent greenhouse gasses from slowly ramping up the heat. That too is still true, but we now know that the biggest threat from global warming is that it could trigger a far worse abrupt cooling, something akin to accidentally shifting into low gear when cruising at high speed.[1]

He adds, "I hope never to see a failure of the northernmost loop of the North Atlantic Current, because the result would be a population crash that would take much of civilization with it, all within a decade." And, as he documents in his book, the flushing of the Gulf Stream waters in the North Atlantic (the mechanism creating those giant whirlpools) may already be tottering on the edge of a collapse like the one that caused the last ice age: "In the Labrador Sea, flushing failed during the 1970s, was strong again in the 1980s, and then declined. In the Greenland Sea over the 1980s salt sinking [which drives the Great Conveyor Belt] declined by 80 percent."

The mechanism that's driving this possible crash of the Great Conveyor Belt and the Gulf Stream is a sudden and unprecedented (in ten thousand years) flow of fresh water into the North Atlantic from melting glaciers in Greenland and a melting of the Arctic ice cap.

On April 6, 1909, Admiral Peary was the first person to stand on the North Pole. Along with Matthew Hansen and four Inuit (once called Eskimo) trackers, they crossed hundreds of miles of ice on foot and by dogsled to finally plant a U.S. flag at "the place where compasses act oddly."

The North Pole has been solid ice for thousands of years, maintaining the delicate balance between cold salt water and colder fresh water, that keeps the Great Conveyor Belt and the Gulf Stream running so that Europe is livable and North America experiences summers. Russian icebreakers were amazed to find the North Pole open in the summer of 2000, for the first time in human history, and, as Calvin notes, though Peary could stand and plant a flag at 90 degrees North, today there is "no place to stand at the North Pole—unless you stood up in a boat."

The reason is found in the report that made top-of-page-one headlines all across Europe in January of 2003. As the United Kingdom's *Guardian* bluntly noted: "Global warming is accelerating, and [the greenhouse gas] carbon dioxide in the atmosphere has reached 370.9 parts per million, the highest level for at least 420,000 years and probably for 20 million years." The world's scientists report that globally the rate of melting of polar and glacial ice has *doubled* between 1988 and 2002.

The ancient and massive glaciers forming Mt. Kilimanjaro's famous snow-capped peak, immortalized in Hemmingway's short story *The Snows of Kilimanjaro,* will be entirely gone within the next few decades, according to scientists from the University of Massachusetts.[2] The same is true of glaciers all around the world: Montana's Glacier National Park, which sported 150 glaciers in 1850, is now down to thirty-seven, and those may be gone within twenty-five years.[3] People around the world who rely on glacier melt for their fresh water supplies—from the Andes of South America to the mountains of central Asia—are facing drought as one-hundred-year-old glaciers melt away entirely, leaving only dry land.

The United States, with about 6 percent of the world's population, produces more than a quarter of all the planet's carbon dioxide and other greenhouse gases, mostly through our inefficient use of oil and gasoline. The average European consumes one half the energy of the typical American. Indeed, the Europeans are leading the world in the production of electricity using wind and solar power, their trains and mass transit are comfortable and efficient, and their cars—some of the best in the world—consume on average about half the fuel of the vehicles Americans drive.

A GLOBAL-WARMING BOTTLENECK

The world faces the possibility of another human bottleneck, the death of hundreds of millions to billions of people over a period as short as a few years, and this time caused by our own actions (or inaction). Scientific opinions vary, but there's broad agreement that the current trend of global warming may be enough to flip the world into the next great ice age within our lifetimes, and that it will almost certainly happen within our grandchildren's lifetimes. The disaster will be so vast and worldwide as to be unimaginable.

What might be done to stem the devastation is minimal. Calvin suggests it may be possible to keep the Great Conveyor Belt in the North Atlantic from shutting down by strategically damming the melting fjords of Greenland. Other scientists have suggested the ambitious project of opening the isthmus of Panama to allow the Pacific to flow freely into the Atlantic, as it did three million years ago. Such engineering projects are dubious, expensive, or, in the case of the Greenland project, only temporary fixes.

If, as the Iroquois say, we've borrowed the world from our children, then we're repaying the loan in a way for which they may never forgive us—assuming they survive the consequences of our profligate petroleum consumption.

To find a way out of the mess we've created is going to take ingenuity, creativity, and a type of thinking-outside-the-box that hasn't been necessary since the warming of the last ice age .

If ever the world needed its Edison-gene children, now is the time.

Afterword
Yesterday's Child

The following text, "Yesterday's Child" by Janie Bowman, was originally published in *The Missing Piece* (Winter 1993), the newsletter of the Learning Disabilities Association of Washington State.[1]

Yesterday's child was born in the 1800s. As a young boy, he was considered medically fragile. Every respiratory illness known to mankind in that age seemed to seize him. Even though Yesterday's child spent many of his early years ill, this did not stop his insatiable curiosity and boyish escapades. Today's child would be described as "just being a boy."

Yesterday's child often found himself in risky life-and-death situations. One time, around the age of five, this boy nearly drowned in a canal; and later he almost smothered as he sank into the depths of a grain elevator. Today's child would be described as "having no common sense."

Yesterday's child was found asleep in the barn in a nest he had constructed, lying on top of the chicken and goose eggs he was trying to hatch. Today's child would be called "weird, eccentric." "Get off those eggs, you'll crack them!"

Yesterday's child drove his parents to exhaustion by his persistent questioning of the world around him, determined to know the "whys," "what fors," and "what abouts" of his world. Today's child is searching for someone to ask the questions to.

Yesterday's child, with no malice aforethought but only out of the intense curiosity of an inquisitive mind, set his father's barn on fire. For this he was publicly thrashed by his father, who tried to instill in him the serious consequences of his actions. Today's child would be called a "juvenile delinquent."

After only three months of formal education, Yesterday's child walked out of his school in a fit of rage. Running home, he could hear the thoughts of the schoolmaster echoing in his head: "stupid . . . stubborn . . . difficult." Thus, at the tender age of eight, Yesterday's child refused to return to school. The next day, Yesterday's mother gave the schoolmaster a piece of her mind and withdrew the boy from school. From that day onward, she became Yesterday's teacher. Today's child would be called "a problem child, a bad boy, oppositional." And Today's mother would be told she was "highly excitable, and coddling her child." She would be encouraged by all the experts to force her child to return to school because "He'll outgrow it. He's got to learn to adjust."

Yesterday's child went swimming with a friend in a nearby creek. When the friend didn't surface for air, Yesterday's child waited for what seemed like forever. As darkness fell, he—in his own unique five-year-old logic—concluded that it was time to go home. As the town was trying to piece together the disappearance and drowning of his friend, Yesterday's child tried to explain how he waited for what seemed like forever. . . . Today's child would be treated for "Conduct Disorder" and undoubtedly find himself one step away from the juvenile justice system.

Yesterday's child just couldn't comprehend consequences; that much seems true. One day he attached wires to the tails of two cats and energetically rubbed their fur. This experiment in static electricity went astray when he was brutally clawed. In another instance, one unsuspecting childhood friend suffered an upset stomach after Yesterday's child gave him some sort of powder just to see if the resulting gas it produced would send him flying. Today's child would be in long-term therapy for Attention Deficit Hyperactivity Disorder, Pervasive Development Disorder, or some other behavioral disorder.

Yesterday's mother complained constantly about the life-threatening condition of his bedroom. Fearing for the safety of her family and any others who ventured into the family home, Yesterday's mother moved his experiments into the cellar. Yesterday's child called it his laboratory and immersed himself in science, to the exclusion of what other "normal" kids were doing at his age. Today's child would be called "Schizoid," and Today's family would be labeled "dysfunctional." Today's child would be spending time in a court-ordered alternative school program, meeting with a psychiatrist twice a week for therapy, and be attending a class to learn social skills.

At age twelve Yesterday's child insisted on going to work and began successfully earning his own wage. Today's child, at that age, would face a closed door to the world of mentorship in the workplace. Today's child would have to search beyond home and work for other avenues to have his abilities accepted and appreciated.

As you read about Yesterday's child, you are probably wondering how he could have survived and how he could have contributed to society in a positive way. Clearly, Yesterday's child had somebody who accepted his uniqueness, changed his environment to meet his needs, was not intimidated by his gifts, and tried sincerely to see the world through his eyes.

Yesterday's child's name is Thomas Alva Edison.

What is your child's name?

Notes

Introduction

1. "Hail The Hyperactive Hunter," *Time,* June 14, 1994.

2. Wilson Harrell, *For Entrepreneurs Only: Success Strategies for Anyone Starting or Growing a Business* (Hawthorne, N.J.: Career Press, 1994).

3. Wilson Harrell, "Born or Made: Do Entrepreneurs Have the Genes of Hunters?" *Success,* June 1994, 14.

4. John F. Shelley-Tremblay and Lee A. Rosen, "Attention Deficit Disorder: An Evolutionary Perspective," *Journal of Genetic Psychology* 157, no. 4 (1996): 443–53.

5. Jensen, Mrazek, Knapp, Steinberg, Pfeffer, Schowalter, and Shapiro, "Evolution and Revolution in Child Psychiatry: ADHD as a Disorder of Adaptation," *Journal of the American Academy of Child and Adolescent Psychiatry* (December 1997).

6. Ibid.

7. Swanson, Flodman, Kennedy, Spence, Moyzis, et al., "Dopamine Genes and ADHD," *Neuroscience and Biobehavioral Reviews* 24 (2000): 21–25.

8. Ding, Chi, Grady, et al., "Evidence of Positive Selection Acting at the Human Dopamine Receptor D4 Gene Locus," *Proceedings of the National Academy of Science* 99, no. 1 (January 2002).

Chapter 2: The Dawn of Civilization

1. S. J. Gould, and N. Eldredge. "Punctuated Equilibria: The Tempo and Mode of Evolution Reconsidered," *Paleobiology* 3 (1977): 115–51.

2. www.cdc.gov/ncidod/dbmd/diseaseinfo/escherichiacoli_g.htm.

3. The Krakatoa eruption in 535 C.E. and its consequences are brilliantly chronicled in David Keys, *Catastrophe* (New York: Ballentine Books, 1999).

4. O. Semino, et al., "The Genetic Legacy of Paleolithic *Homo sapiens sapiens* in Extant Europeans: A Y chromosome Perspective," *Science* 290 (2000), 1155–59

5. Ibid.

Chapter 3: Three Ways Humans Were Killed Off by Weather

1. www.phivoles.dost.gov.ph/vmepd/qrn/bulusan.htm.

2. http://kavkaz.virtualave.net/kmv_env.html.

3. www.lonelyplanet.com/destinations/europe/dodecanese_islands/print-able.htm.

4. www.biketravel.net/english/sicily/estrombo.shtml.

5. www.nps.gov/mora/ncrd/hazards.htm.

6. "Ancient 'Volcanic Winter' Tied to Rapid Genetic Divergence in Humans" at www.sciencedaily.com/releases/1998/09/980908074159.htm.

7. Shaw and Brown, "Laterality, Implicit Memory and Attention Disorder Educational Studies," *Educational Studies* 17, no. 1 (1991).

8. Bonnie Cramond, "Attention Deficit Hyperactivity Disorder and Creativity: What is the Connection?" *Journal of Creative Behavior* 8, no. 3 (Third Quarter, 1994).

9. Stephen J. Ceci and Jayne Tishman, "Hyperactivity and Incidental Memory: Evidence for Attentional Diffusion," *Child Development* 55 (1984): 2192–203.

10. Ibid.

11. Ibid.

12. Ibid.

13. Ibid.

14. Ibid.

15. Ibid.

16. Richard Klein with Blake Edgar, *The Dawn of Human Culture* (New York: John Wiley and Sons, 2002).

Chapter 4: Anatomy of a Diagnosis

1. Stephen J. Ceci, *On Intelligence: A Bioecological Treatise on Intellectual Development* (Cambridge, Mass.: Harvard University Press, 1996).

Chapter 5: The Mystery of Novelty-Seeking Behavior

1. There's a detailed discussion of the mechanism of this in my book *Thom Hartmann's Complete Guide to ADHD* (Novato, Calif.: Underwood Books, 2001).

2. R. P. Ebstein et al., *Nature Genetics* 12, no. 1 (1996): 78–80.

3. *The Scientist* 10, no. 2 (January 22, 1996): 31.

4. D. H. Hamer, et al., *Nature Genetics* 12, no. 1 (1996): 81–84.

5. *The Scientist* 10, no. 2 (January 22, 1996): 31.

6. R. P. Ebstein, et al., "Dopamine D4 Receptor and Serotonin

Transporter Promoter in the Determination of Neonatal Temperament," *Molecular Psychiatry* 3 (1998): 183–85.

7.   www.sciencedaily.com/releases/1999/01/990126081714.htm.

8.   www.ucihealth.com/News/Releases/ADHD-advantageousGene.htm

9.   G. J. LaHoste, J. M. Swanson, S. B. Wigal, et al., "Dopamine Genes and ADHD," *Molecular Psychiatry* 1 (1996): 121–24.

10.   D. C. Rowe, C. Stever, L. N. Giedinghagen, et al., "Dopamine D4 Receptor Gene Polymorphism Is Associated with Attention Deficit Hyperactivity Disorder," *Molecular Psychiatry* 3 (1998): 419–26.

11.   S. L. Smalley, J. N. Bailey, C. G. Palmer, et al., "Evidence that the Dopamine D4 Receptor Is a Susceptibility Gene in Attention Deficit Hyperactivity Disorder," *Molecular Psychiatry* 3 (1998):427–30.

12.   J. M. Swanson, G. A. Sunohara, J. L. Kennedy, et al., "Association of the Dopamine Receptor D4 (DRD4) Gene with a Refined Phenotype of Attention Deficit Hyperactivity Disorder (ADHD): A Family-Based Approach," *Molecular Psychiatry* 3 (1998): 38–41.

13.   V. Jovanovic, H. C. Guan, H. H. Van Tol, "Comparative Pharmacological and Functional Analysis of the Human Dopamine D4.2 and D4.10 Receptor Variants," *Pharmacogenetics* 9 (1999): 561–68.

14.   A. D. Paterson, G. A. Sunohara, J. L. Kennedy, "Dopamine D4 Receptor Gene: Novelty or Nonsense?" *Neuropsychopharmacology* 21 (1999): 3–16.

15.   D. Pauls, "Genetics of Childhood Disorders IV: Linkage Analysis," *Journal of the American Academy of Childhood and Adolescent Psychiatry* 38 (1999): 932–34.

16.   Cathy L. Barr, "Genetics of Childhood Disorders: The Dopamine D4 Receptor Gene," *Journal of the American Academy of Childhood and Adolescent Psychiatry* 40 (January 2001): 1, 118–22.

17.   H. H. Van Tol, C. M. Wu, H. C. Guan, et al., "Multiple Dopamine D4 Receptor Variants in the Human Population," *Nature* 358 (1992): 149–52; and J. B. Lichter, C. L. Barr, J. L. Kennedy, et. al., "A Hypervariable Segment in the Human Dopamine Receptor D4 (DRD4) Gene," *Human Molecular Genetics* 2 (1993): 767–73.

Chapter 6: Genes Move Around and Turn On and Off

1.   Andrew Bridges, the Associated Press, "Intestines Give Cholera a Boost," in the *Burlington Free Press,* 6 June 2002, 10A.

Chapter 7: Other Genes and Influences

1.   *Proceedings of the National Academy of Sciences of the United States* 99, no. 1 (January 2002).

2. Ibid.

3. Edward M. Hallowell and John J. Ratey, *Driven To Distraction* (New York: Simon and Schuster, 1994).

4. John J. Ratey, *A User's Guide To The Brain* (New York: Vintage Books, 2002).

Chapter 8: Scientists Find the "Adaptive" Edison Gene

1. Moyzis's colleagues include Yuan-Chun Ding, Han-Chang Chi, Deborah Grady, Pam Flodman, M. Anne Spence, Sabrina Schuck, and James Swanson of UCI; Ya-Ping Zhang of the Chinese Academy of Sciences, Kunming, China; and Atsuyuki Morishima, Judith Kidd, and Kenneth Kidd of Yale University.

2. Ding, Chi, Grady, et al., "Evidence of Positive Selection Acting at the Human Dopamine Receptor D4 Gene Locus," *Proceedings of the National Academy of Sciences of the United States* 99, no. 1 (January 2002).

3. H. Harpending and G. Cochran, "In Our Genes," *Proceedings of the National Academy of the Sciences of the United States* 99, no. 1 (January 2002).

Chapter 9: The ADHD Gene and the Dawn of Human Civilization

1. University of California Irvine news release, January 8, 2002.

2. Ding, Chi, Grady, et al., "Evidence of Positive Selection Acting at the Human Dopamine Receptor D4 Gene Locus," *Proceedings of the National Academy of Sciences of the United States* 99, no. 1 (January 2002).

3. Norwich Free Academy, *Ben Franklin: The Man and the Printer* (Northfield, Vt.: Norwich Free Academy, 1925).

4. Ibid.

5. Ibid.

6. Ibid.

Chapter 10: Brain Development and the Edison-Gene Child

1. National Clearinghouse on Child Abuse and Neglect Information, "In Focus: Understanding the Effects of Maltreatment on Early Brain Development," www.calib.com/nccanch/pubs/focus/earlybrain.cfm.

2. Joseph Chilton Pearce, *The Biology of Transcendence*, (Rochester, Vt.: Park Street Press, 2002).

3. B. D. Perry, R. Pollard, T. Blakely, W. Baker, and D. Vigilante, "Childhood Trauma, the Neurobiology of Adaptation and 'Use-Dependent' Development of the Brain: How 'States' Become 'Traits'" (1995): www.childtrauma.org/states_traits.htm.

4. This research is in numerous books and sources, although one of the most complete is Allan Schore's book, cited in chapter 7, note 5.

5. Allan N. Schore, *Affect Regulation and the Origin of the Self: The Neurobiology of Emotional Development* (Hillsdale, N.J.: Lawrence Erlbaum, 1994); Paul MacLean, *The Triune Brain in Evolution: Role in Paleocerebral Functions* (New York: Plenum Press, 1990); Paul MacLean, "The Brain and Subjective Experience: Question of Multilevel Role of Resonance," *The Journal of Mind and Behavior* 18, nos. 2 and 3 (Spring and Summer 1997): 247–68.

6. B. D. Perry, "Traumatized Children: How Childhood Trauma Influences Brain Development," *Journal of the California Alliance for the Mentally Ill* 11 (2000):1, 48–51.

7. Allan N. Schore, "The Experience-Dependent Maturation of a Regulatory System in the Orbital Prefrontal Cortex and the Origin of Developmental Psychopathology" in *Development and Psychopathology* 8 (1996): 59–87.

8. M. D. DeBellis, M. S. Keshavan, D. B. Clark, et al., "Developmental Traumatology, Part 2: Brain Development," *Society of Biological Psychiatry* 45 (1999): 1271–84.

9. B. D. Perry, "Traumatized Children: How Childhood Trauma Influences Brain Development," *Journal of the California Alliance for the Mentally Ill* 11 (2000): 1, 48–51.

10. A good book documenting this is Marie Winn, *The Plug-In Drug* (New York: Penguin, 2002).

11. National Clearinghouse on Child Abuse and Neglect Information, "In Focus: Understanding the Effects of Maltreatment on Early Brain Development," www.calib.com/nccanch/pubs/focus/earlybrain.cfm.

12. J. Hart, M. Gunnar, and D. Cicchetti, "Salivary Cortisol in Maltreated Children: Evidence of Relations between Neuroendocrine Activity and Social Competence," *Development and Psychophathology* 7 (1995): 11–26.

13. Allan N. Schore, "The Experience-Dependent Maturation of a Regulatory System in the Orbital Prefrontal Cortex and the Origin of Developmental Psychopathology" in *Development and Psychopathology* 8 (1996): 59–87.

14. See Joseph Chilton Pearce, *Magical Child* (New York: Plume, 1992) and *The Biology of Transcendence* (Rochester, Vt.: Park Street Press, 2002).

15. C. N. Alexander and E. J. Langer, *Higher Stages of Human Development: Adult Growth Beyond Formal Operations* (Oxford: Oxford University Press, 1990).

16. Joseph Chilton Pearce, *The Biology of Transcendence* (Rochester, Vt.: Park Street Press, 2002).

17. Allan N. Schore, *Affect Regulation and the Development of the Self* (Hillsdale, N.J.: Lawrence Erlbaum, 1999).

18. Walter J. Ong, *Orality and Literacy: The Technologizing of the Word* (London: Methuen, 1982).

19. Robert K. Logan, *The Alphabet Effect: The Impact of the Phonetic Alphabet on the Development of Western Civilization* (New York: St. Martin's Press, 1986).

20. Leonard Shlain, *The Alphabet Versus the Goddess: The Conflict Between Word and Image* (New York: Viking, 1998).

21. Erik Erikson, *The Erik Erikson Reader,* ed. Robert Coles (New York: W. W. Norton, 2000).

22. Allan N. Schore, *Affect Regulation and the Development of the Self* (Hillsdale, N.J.: Lawrence Erlbaum, 1999).

Chapter 11: The Edison Gene, Drugs, Exercise, and Nutrition

1. Interview with the author, August 2002.

2. A. M. Meyer, "Historical Changes in the Mineral Content of Fruits and Vegetables: A Cause for Concern?" *British Food Journal* 99 (1997): 207–11.

3. Judy McBride, "Nutritional Deficiencies Affect Behavior" (January 29, 1997) at www.ars.usda.gov/is/pr/1997/970129.htm.

4. "Deficiency in Omega-3 Fatty Acids Tied to ADHD in Boys," www.purdue.edu/UNS/html4ever/9606.Burgess.html.

5. *British Journal of Psychiatry* 191 (2002): 23–28.

6. One of the best books on this is Richard J. DeGrandpre, *Ritalin Nation: Rapid-Fire Culture and the Transformation of Human Consciousness* (New York: W.W. Norton, 2000).

7. Shankar Vedantam, "Placebo Outperforms Top Antidepressants, Study Says," *Washington Post*, 8 May 2002.

8. http://my.webmd.com/content/article/52/50229.htm.

9. Rep. Bernie Sanders (I-VT), constituent newsletter, Autumn 2002.

10. Ibid.

11. Rep. Bernie Sanders (I-VT), "Is Congress Capable of Taking on the Drug Companies?" in *Roll Call,* a newsletter covering Capitol Hill since 1955, February 14, 2002.

12. H. A. Nasrallah, J. Loney, S. C. Olson, et al., "Cortical Atrophy in Young Adults with a History of Hyperactivity in Childhood," *Psychiatry Res* 17, no. 3 (March 1986): 241–46.

13. C. Saunders, J. V. Ferrer, J. Shi L, Chen, et al., "Amphetamine-Induced Loss of Human Dopamine Transporter Activity: An Internalization-

Dependent and Cocaine-Sensitive Mechanism," *Proceedings of the National Academy of Sciences* 97 (2000): 6850–55.

14. L. J. Vanderschuren, M. J. Donné, E. Schmidt, T. J. De Vries, et al., "A Single Exposure to Amphetamine Is Sufficient to Induce Long-Term Behavioral, Neuroendocrine, and Neurochemical Sensitization in Rats," *Journal of Neuroscience* 19 (1999): 9579–86.

15. N. Ginovart, L. Farde, C. Halldin, C. G. Swahn, "Changes in Striatal D2-Receptor Density Following Chronic Treatment with Amphetamine as Assessed with PET in Nonhuman Primates," *Synapse* 31, no. 2 (February 1999): 154–62.

16. www.nih.gov/news/stemcell/achieve.htm.

17. Ibid.

18. Howard M. Schachter, et al., "Long-term Effectiveness of Ritalin Questioned," *Canadian Medical Association Journal* 165, no. 11 (November 27, 2001): 1475–88.

19. Sachar, Asnis, Halbreich, et al., "Recent Studies in the Neuroendocrinology of Major Depressive Disorders," *Psych Clin North Am* 3, no. 2 (1980).

20. Plato, *Timeaus and Cortias*

21. Griest, Klein, Eischens, et al., "Running as Treatment for Depression," *Comprehensive Psychiatry* 20, no. 1 (January/February 1979).

22. Folkins, Lynch, and Gardner, "Psychological Fitness as a Function of Physical Fitness," *Archives of Physical Medicine and Rehabilitation* 53 (1972): 503–08.

23. *The Importance of Not Being Earnest,* http://news.bbc.co.uk/hi/English/health/newsid_208000/208729.stm.

24. See *Newspaper of Education Rights,* no. 189, October 2001, at www.eaglforum.org/educate/2001/oct 01/recess.shtml.

Chapter 12: Providing Discipline and Structure for the Edison-Gene Child

1. www.hrw.org/children/labor.htm.

2. Bruce Bower, "Raising Trust: Some Forager Groups May Nurture a Sharing Sense in Their Offspring," *Science News*, July 1, 2000.

3. Elizabeth Marshall Thomas, *The Harmless People* (New York: Vintage Books, 1989).

4. Colin M. Turnbull, *The Forest People* (New York: Simon and Schuster, 1968).

5. Marshall David Sahlins, *Stone Age Economics* (London: Tavistock Publications, 1972).

6. Robert Wolff, *Original Wisdom* (Rochester, Vt.: Inner Traditions, 2001).

7. From correspondence with the author, April 8, 2002.

8. Claude Levi-Strauss, *The Savage Mind* (Chicago: University of Chicago Press, 1969).

9. Robert Lawlor, *Voices of the First Day* (Rochester, Vt.: Inner Traditions, 1991).

10. Ibid.

11. http://news.bbc.co.uk/hi/english/health/newsid_2018000/2018900.stm

12. Jay Haley, *Uncommon Therapy: The Psychiatric Techniques of Milton H. Erickson, M.D.* (New York: W. W. Norton, 1993).

13. Martin Seligman, *Learned Optimism* (New York: Pocket Books, 1998).

14. From correspondence with the author, April 8, 2002.

15. John D. McPeake, B. P. Kennedy, and S. M. Gordon, "Altered States of Consciousness Therapy: A Missing Component in Alcohol and Drug Rehabilitation Treatment," *Journal of Substance Abuse Treatment* 8 (1991): 75–82.

16. There are a series of links to various studies on this at www.thomhartmann.com/newsletter-2.shtml.

17. Marie Winn, *The Plug-In Drug* (New York: Penguin, 2002).

18. www.research.fsu.edu/researchr/springsummer98/features/fear.html

19. American Psychological Association, "Violence on Television: What do Children Learn? What Can Parents Do?" (Washington D.C.: American Psychological Association, 1992).

20. Marie Winn, *The Plug-In Drug* (New York: Penguin Books, 1977).

21. Robert Kubey and Mihaly Csikszentmihalyi, "Television Addiction is No Mere Metaphor" at www.sciam.com/2002/0202issue/0202kubey.html.

22. Richard J. DeGrandpre, *Ritalin Nation* (New York: W. W Norton, 2000).

23. Jerry Mander, *In the Absence of the Sacred: The Failure of Technology and the Survival of the Indian Nations* (San Francisco: Sierra Club Books, 1992).

24. Jerry Mander, *Four Arguments for the Elimination of Television*, (New York: William Morrow, 1978).

Chapter 13: Alfred Adler's Principles for Raising Children

1. Rudopf Dreikurs, *Children: The Challenge* (New York: Plume, 1991).

2. www.activeparenting.com

3. http://ourworld.compuserve.com/homepages/hstein/guid.htm.

4. J. Bowlby, *Attachment and Loss,* vol. 1, *Attachment,* 2nd ed. (New

York: Basic Books, 1982); J. Bowlby, *Attachment and Loss,* vol. 2,
Separation: Anxiety and Anger (New York: Basic Books, 1973); J.
Bowlby, "The Making and Breaking of Affectional Bonds, Part 1:
Aetiology and Psychopathology in the Light of Attachment Theory,"
British Journal of Psychiatry 130 (1977): 201–10; J. Bowlby, "The
Making and Breaking of Affectional Bonds, Part 2: Some Principles of
Psychotherapy," *British Journal of Psychiatry* 130 (1977): 421–31; J.
Bowlby, *Attachment and Loss,* vol. 3, *Loss: Sadness and Depression*
(New York: Basic Books, 1980); J. Bowlby, *A Secure Base: Parent-Child
Attachment and Healthy Human Development* (New York: Basic
Books, 1988).

Chapter 14: Educating the Edison-Gene Child

1. Peter S. Jensen, David Mrazek, Penelope K. Knapp, et al., "Evolution
   and Revolution in Child Psychiatry: ADHD as a Disorder of
   Adaptation," *Journal of the American Academy of Childhood and
   Adolescent Psychiatry* 36, (1997).

2. Ibid.

3. Ding, Chi, Grady, et al., "Evidence of Positive Selection Acting at the
   Human Dopamine Receptor D4 Gene Locus," *Proceedings of the
   National Academy of Sciences* 99, no. 1309–314 (January 8, 2002).

4. www.nimh.nih.gov/events/prmta.cfm.

5. Ibid.

6. Howard M. Schacter, et al., "Long-term Effectiveness of Ritalin
   Questioned," *Canadian Medical Association Journal* 165, no. 11
   (November 27, 2001): 1457–88.

7. www.rexsikes.com.

8. www.cnn.com/2002/ALLPOLITICS/01/09/education.bush.

9. From a great Web site on reinventing education:
   www.polyarchy.org/education.html.

10. See www.preciouschild.net.

11. From "Unschooling With ADD" at
    www.geocities.com/Heartland/Hollow/1093/unschoolingadd.html.

12. Rebecca Winters, "From Home to Harvard: Homeschooled Kids Have
    Earned a College of Their Own—and Admission to Elite, Traditional
    Campuses, *Time,* September 11, 2000.

13. Ibid.

Chapter 16: Spirituality and the Edison-Gene Child

1. One of the best is Wolff's own book, *Original Wisdom* (Rochester, Vt.:
   Inner Traditions, 2001). Another is *In Search of The Dream People* by

Richard Noone (New York: Morrow, 1972). The novel *The Kin of Ata Are Waiting For You* seems to be loosely based on them.

2. Gospel of Thomas, verse 77.

3. Matthew 6:25–26.

4. www.cs.org

5. Antero Alli, *Angel Tech* (Tempe, Ariz.: New Falcon, 1991).

6. From correspondence with the author, April 10, 2002.

Chapter 17: How Edison-Gene Children May Change the World

1. Ruth Benedict, *Patterns of Culture*, first published by Pelican Books (New York, 1934).

2. Ibid.

3. Ibid.

4. Ibid.

Chapter 18: Is Human Evolution Finally Over?

1. Robin McKie, "Is Human Evolution Finally Over?" *Guardian,* 3 February 2002.

2. www.hopepress.com/html/the_gene_bomb.html.

3. Ibid.

4. Peter Ward, *Future Evolution* (New York: Times Books, 2001).

5. David Keys, *Catastrophe,* (New York: Ballantine Books, 1999).

Chapter 19: One Generation To Save The World

1. William H. Calvin, *A Brain For All Seasons: Human Evolution and Abrupt Climate Change* (Chicago: University of Chicago Press, 2002).

2. www.umass.edu/newsoffice/archive/2001/022301snows.html.

3. http://greennature.com/article979.html.

Index